DEVOTIONS FROM THE HEARTLAND

Compiled by
Dave & Dot Mulder

Atlas of Sioux Center, 315 1st Avenue NE, Sioux Center, IA 51250

ATLAS is a 501(3)(c) non-profit organization. All contributions are tax deductible.

Printed in the United States of America

Dedication

Dot and I want to dedicate this book to the life of our nephew Steve Scholten. As this book is being published Steve is 50 years old and battling the terrible disease A.L.S. ("Lou Gehrig's disease") Steve, his wife Nancy Anne, daughters Nicole and Allison, their husbands Mark and Dustin, and grandchildren Caleb and Bella have been great care givers and an inspiration to us all. It's the salvation Steve has achieved, and the one we all aspire to, that can bring joy to the human heart.

Foreword

I have known Dave and his family since he was a very little boy. His dad was one of my best friends. Dave played high school basketball and baseball for me in Alton, Iowa.

His work ethic is outstanding and he is a person who lives out his Faith in God in his daily life.

I am sure his writings will both entertain and inspire all who use this book.

Orval J. Madden
Teacher and Coach

After serving nearly 3½ years in the Navy during WWII, I made my home in Alton, Iowa. Eventually I bought the Floyd Hatchery, got married to Esther, and we raised our family.

In the summer of 1951, a youngster came and asked to come to work for me. He said he liked chickens and would work hard. That's how I got to know Dave Mulder. He worked for me until he graduated from high school and it was a good experience for both of us.

I do remember his mischievous nature as at times he would clean the old wooden floor in the hatchery. It was necessary to use lots of water, a squeegee, and a rather strong disinfectant. Of course this mixture would conveniently seep through the floor into the basement. He seemed to take a particular glee in the screams coming up the staircase from the young ladies candling eggs below. But he was a good worker and developed into a strong Christian leader. He was dedicated then and still is today. I have always appreciated his sense of humor and friendship.

This is a fine collection of daily devotionals, filled with inspiration and motivation toward the Christian walk we all pursue. Meditate, Pray, and Reach Out.

Rev. Bob Vander Schaaf, Sr.

I first met Dave and Dot when I became Superintendent of the Sioux Center Schools in the spring of 1963. Dave was in his second year of high school business teaching and coaching. I could tell he loved kids and teaching. He is blessed with a wonderful wife, two children, and two grandchildren. He also possesses a great sense of humor, which is so important in our lives.

He always had a big heart for the students. He was one that they could go to if they had a problem of any kind. His disposition always stays the same—never gets angry at anyone. He never had a bad remark against anyone. For this, he is truly a great Christian, husband, father, and friend. He stays active in his church and community. He was involved with the Fellowship of Christian Athletes organization for many years and continues to give great speeches and sermons when called upon.

We are excited about this book of devotionals and know that the ones Dave and Dot have written and collected will be inspiring for you and so many others. But this isn't all about Dave, he will be the first to tell you that Dot has been and is the greatest asset he has. She was a tremendous school nurse for over 25 years and all her students loved her and appreciated her care. Where he is weak, she is strong, and that makes a great combination.

Angie and I are so happy that they are our friends. We still have lots of fun together.

Chuck Irwin

Acknowledgments

We were amazed at what it takes to get a book published. Even one that had the main goal of honoring our Lord and Savior. So obviously we have heartfelt thanks for all of the writers of these 365 devotionals. You have greatly affected our lives and spiritual growth.

Amy Keahi and the great staff (especially Ashley Egdorf and volunteer, Mary Du Mez) at ATLAS of Sioux Center have been amazing. Please continue to support their great work. Tina Jansen at Northwestern College did some yeoman service as she edited, provided great technical computer expertise, and an amazingly pleasant attitude in dealing with this highly incapable "technocrat." Thank you.

And of course we thank the ATLAS of Sioux Center Board for taking on the risk of this venture. We hope it becomes a financial success of course. In that regard, Dave Hulsart at the Dove Christian Book Store in Orange City is not only a good friend but very helpful.

The publisher, Alpha Omega Publications, is thanked and applauded for taking on this project and being patient.

We certainly hope you enjoy this devotional for many years to come. Buy lots of them and give them to all of your friends and relatives. Remember, all the money goes to ATLAS.

In Christ's Love, Dave and Dot

We at ATLAS of Sioux Center want to give a special thanks to Dave and Dot for putting this devotional together and for generously choosing us to receive any proceeds from this project. Dave and Dot have been important members of this community and have given back to the community and to the kingdom throughout their lives. I knew Dave in college when he was the director of FCA at Northwestern College. He was well known for his love for young people and for his character, so when he told me about his idea to publish and sell a devotional, it was thrilling to be a part of this project.

I am also grateful to Alpha Omega Publications for their support of ATLAS of Sioux Center! It is fun when ministries have opportunities to work together to expand the kingdom. May God expand your kingdom-business!

Although I have not yet had the opportunity to read each devotional in this book, I have read many of them and I'm encouraged by the spiritual depth of the writers. Although I haven't come across anything I disagree with, I should mention that ATLAS of Sioux Center does not necessarily endorse every thought and belief stated in this book.

Thank you to everyone who contributed to this book. Dave and I were both astounded at the willingness of people to seek the Lord and then write what He said. It is so much fun to see the perspectives of people on what God is "up to."

Most of all I want to thank God for what you have done through ATLAS of Sioux Center. Speaking for the board, the staff, the mentors, the volunteers, the singers and musicians, You have touched our lives deeply with Your love as we have sought to touch the lives of those in our community.

ATLAS, which stands for Attaining Truth, Love, and Self-control, is a ministry in Sioux Center that seeks to: (1) Help hurting people, (2) Equip followers of Jesus to do the work of the kingdom, and (3) Unite the community under the authority of Jesus. We pray that we will have the opportunity to do this work for many years to come!

Amy Keahi

Contents

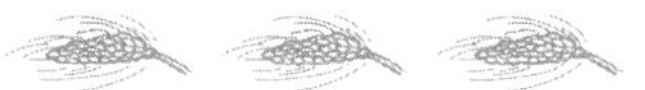

Introduction

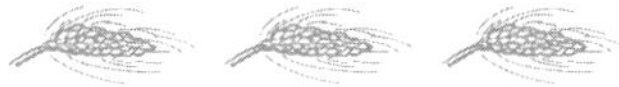

I'm not a very original thinking person. Most coaches/teachers are "copycats"; we see something that works and then incorporate it into our own "repertoire." Who was it that said "There's nothing new under the sun"? (Actually, it was King Solomon in Ecc. 1:9b.) So when this idea came to me it was quite a surprise – but Dot and I did get excited. Not only was it good for us to pour over our old notes, but also to really get into the Word of God to find answers and ideas.

The most exciting part has been the involvement of so many friends and family members. What great people and great inspiration. What I also found interesting is that so many of you said some variation of, "You probably won't want to use this, I'm not much good at this kind of thing." (Or something else equally self-deprecating). I can honestly say that I got something worthwhile out of every one of your entries. Thanks so much to all of you and I hope you enjoy your copy.

Here are some suggestions for the use of this devotional. When you look up the verses each day, underline them and place the name of that day's author near the verse. Then every time you run across that verse again, say a prayer for them and their family. You might also let them know verbally or by a note of some kind. Read about the author's relationship and remember how this person impacted us and how you can and do impact people – many times when you don't even realize it. Reestablish some relationships that have slipped away over the years.

Many times you will see the names of the husbands and wives listed (unless they each did one or more). The first name was the main writer, but I want you to know the spouse as well.

Another great positive to this venture is that any and all proceeds will go to the great work of ATLAS of Sioux Center. It was never a goal of Dot or me to "make anything" with this project. We wanted to get a good product finished and published, be able to give a copy to each writer, and then find a charity that can benefit.

Working with Amy Keahi has been great. May our Lord continue to bless her and all of the fine people at ATLAS of Sioux Center.

Finally, never forget the one commandment Jesus gave us (John 13:34-35), "**Love one another**." Please pray for the daily writers and for us. May you always feel our Lord's blessings.

Dave and Dot Mulder

January 1

2 Timothy 1:7

Timidity & Power

The verse of scripture that comes to mind today is the verse above from 2 Timothy. "For God has not given us the spirit of timidity but of power and love and self-discipline."

Strangely enough, I read this verse of scripture to our football team before we played Florida for the National Championship in the Fiesta Bowl in January, 1996. Both teams were undefeated and we were ranked number 1 and number 2. It may seem strange to quote a verse of scripture to a football team; however, I felt that this verse of scripture was particularly appropriate to that team on that particular night.

We had gone through a great deal of adversity that year, in that we had received quite a bit of criticism nationally for the behavior of one of our players, yet the players were bound together very closely. They obviously were not timid. They were very powerful, they loved each other, and they respected their opponents, and they certainly were very disciplined.

We played very well that night, as we had all season long, and I think the attributes of power, love, and self-discipline served that team very well.

Prayer: Dear Lord, thank you for the opportunity to work as a team in so many situations. Teach us to love, forgive, and respect all with whom we work. Amen.

Tom Osborne
Former Head Football Coach and member of the House of Representatives, and presently the Athletic Director at Nebraska

In my humble opinion Coach Tom is the best ever at the NCAA Division 1 level. I can't take the space to enumerate all of his accomplishments, but suffice it to say he won 3 National Titles, never won less than 9 games in a season, and has been elected to the Hall of Fame. He was an outstanding college athlete at Hastings and played pro football for the Washington Redskins. ("Google" him if you want to be really amazed). I met him through the FCA and we have been friends since 1982. He has come to NWC twice and also delivered the address at the annual Easter Prayer Breakfast in Des Moines. He and Nancy have been married longer than Dot and I and his family is doing well as one might expect. Tom Osborne is a real-life example that "good guys do finish first" and they do it many times, and they can remain humble.

January 2

Psalm 37:3-5

The 10 Most Influential

As a teacher I had to go to a lot of meetings designed to motivate and advise us. One speaker gave an assignment to write down the "10 Most Influential" people in our life. Our parents, grandparents, and other immediate family members were to be excluded. So I did it. It was a great assignment and I would encourage you to do it as well. Let me add a little to it. The speaker who challenged us said that probably half of the people would be teachers. This made me realize how important it was for me to be the best teacher possible, and how important it was for me to work at being a positive role model.

May I also encourage you to let the people on your list know they are there, and why you put them there. Can you think of a better list on which to be mentioned?

On the first days of the month in Feb.-Nov. you will read about my 10. All of those still living have made a contribution to this book. There is no way I could list them in ascending or descending order.

Prayer: I thank you for each of these people as I have done many times before. Please continue to bless them and their families. Lord, we all need your blessing today! Amen.

Dave

January 3

Revelation 3:15-16

Attitudes

Do people say/think you have a good attitude? – Or a bad one? Does it depend on the subject? Can anyone always have a good attitude? Can you change your attitude? Have you ever tried?

Sorry about all the questions, but it's nearly impossible to reach positive goals with poor attitudes, don't you think?

Each of us must evaluate our self. We also have to teach those around us the importance of having a good attitude.

Optimism vs. pessimism, and being positive as opposed to negative play important roles. Think about those you like to work with and why. I'll bet their attitude has a lot to do with it. I firmly believe we can change our individual attitudes for the better. But, it's not easy, and it takes lots of work and concentration – it's worth it. Give it a shot!

Prayer: Dear Lord, we ask you to help us get rid of negativity and poor attitudes. Thank you for always having a good attitude about us. Amen.

Dave

January 4

Job 32:10; 1 Kings 18:21

Opinions

Are first opinions really lasting? Opinions/impressions can be formed very quickly and on very little basis. One can form an opinion about someone based entirely on appearance for example. Can you really tell what a person is like by the length of his hair, or if he wears an earring? How about a woman that wears "too much" make-up or tight-fitting clothes?

I know I've been too quick to judge at times. Give the person, the statement, or the situation a chance with an open mind.

Opinions are easier to change than attitudes. This is true whether you are trying to change your opinion about something, or you are trying to get others to change an opinion about you. Isn't it great to know that God's first opinion about us is love and understanding? That's a pretty good goal for all of us to follow.

Prayer: Dear God, once again we thank you for loving us before we ever started loving you. Amen.

Dave

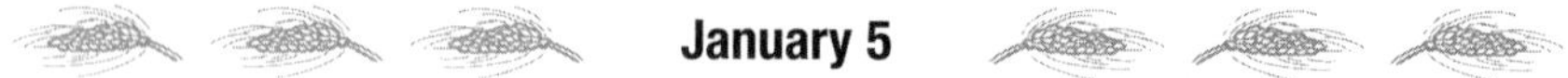

January 5

Romans 14:23b

Values

Now we're talking about what you really believe. These feelings are deep-seated. Your conscience really gets involved with your values. Guilt feelings can really make one uncomfortable. These guilt feelings present themselves when we go against our values.

What is really important to you? These things that you value have been formed within you since birth. It's very difficult to change or go against one's values. But you have to know what they are.

Human life, basic honesty, trust, kindness, reverence for God are typical values. What do you add to this list? If you go against what you truly believe, or what your beliefs in God tells you is right or wrong, it is sin for you. Stick to your values and joy will be yours.

Prayer: Thank you Lord for understanding us and giving us the great values of life. Help us each day to be aware of what you value. Amen.

Dave

January 6

1 John 2:6; 1 John 3:16; Mark 10:43

Who's Your Role Model?

Charles Barkley, the Hall of Fame NBA basketball star, once said, "I am not your child's role model!" Sorry Charlie – but you are! We all are or should strive to be. Barkley later explained (because he took a lot of heat on this), that he meant to say that athletes "shouldn't have to be kid's role models – their parents should." That's true too.

Being a role model is a great responsibility that all of us must accept and hopefully relish. What can be better than to be a positive influence on another person's life? Particularly a young person. As a young person, and throughout the rest of my life, I've been blessed with great examples of how to live in, and with, a variety of situations. I've written about 10 of these as part of this book of daily devotionals. Read about each of them (they are described on the first day of the months Feb. thru Nov.), and do some reflecting.

Of course, the perfect role model is Jesus, and the more we can learn about Him, the better examples we can be.

Prayer: Thank you Jesus for showing us how to live. Please help us do a better job and to always remember people are watching us. Amen.

Dave

January 7

Jeremiah 17:14; Jeremiah 30:17

A Little Family History

The male Mulders from a generation or two ago didn't live long lives. My Grandpa died at 62, my Dad at 56, and his three brothers died at 57, 49, and 38 – all from heart attacks. This knowledge greatly influenced my life and thinking. Since all of them smoked, I never let that become a factor. Weight was also a problem for three of them. So, I've done a fair job of controlling that. Good medical help and vitamins have also been important.

In spite of this I never thought I'd live past 62. Praise the Lord I'm now well past 70. These "extra" years have helped me define purpose. There's a God-given reason why all of us are still living. Having a purpose, regardless of age, is exciting. He's not done with us yet!

Today is the day my Dad was born back in 1904. If you still have your Dad, let him know you love him. Oh, how I wish I could.

Prayer: Thank you Lord for our parents and families. There are so many reasons to love them, and so many times we haven't told them. Help us share that love today. Amen.

Dave

January 8

1 Timothy1:14

It Just Keeps On Coming

December of 2009 and the first days of 2010 were days that those of us who live in NW Iowa will not soon forget. These were days of record snow, snow. – And more snow!

Our home has a rather steep driveway. In the forty plus years we've lived here we learned quickly to get the snow off before it gets ridden down and gets slippery. As a result, my husband cleared out the driveway a couple of times during each storm. A sentence that was repeated a few times was, "It just keeps on coming," as the snow continued to pile up.

Wow! That's just like God's grace! God gives us His grace so freely and abundantly. If we believe in Him, God gives His grace without having to ask for it. Ephesians 1:8 tells us God lavishes His grace on us. As the hymn writer puts it, "Marvelous, infinite, matchless grace, freely bestowed on all who believe!"

Prayer: Father, thank you for your gift of grace – grace greater than all our sins. Amen.

Noreen and Ted DeHoogh
Retired Teachers and members of the Hy Vee Saturday Morning Breakfast Group

Noreen was my first student-teacher. She did an excellent job and was hired into the dept. Ted taught Art for his entire career at SCHS. They are very mission-minded and continue doing the Lord's work. It's great to have friends like these.

January 9

Revelation 21:1-5; 10-27

Heaven

What do we know about Heaven? God is present; Streets of gold; Perfected bodies; No sleeping or eating; Never ends; No marriages; "You will know as you were known"; Lots of praising and singing; Angels are present; And there is no illness or death.

Does this raise some questions?

Will we miss anyone that doesn't make it?

Will there be animals?

What age will everyone be?

Will we have questions about things that happened on earth?

When we get there, will we be able to see what's happening on earth?

Will there be meetings, concerts, speakers, games, and what will we do with all that time?

News about Heaven is pretty vague isn't it? It's interesting to talk and think about though. Some feel they will go fishing, play ball, and have pets.

When you realize what an awesome God we have, that He created this earth, knows every person, and is omniscient, our feelings may change. Only He can conjure up a place that is perfect in every way. A God that can "save a wretch like me" can certainly make a place that is heavenly. Everything about God requires our faith in Him.

I know I want to go there especially when I consider the alternative!

Prayer: Thank you for promising us Heaven. Thank you too for always keeping Your promises. Help us to do a better job of believing, preparing, and keeping promises ourselves. Amen.

Dave

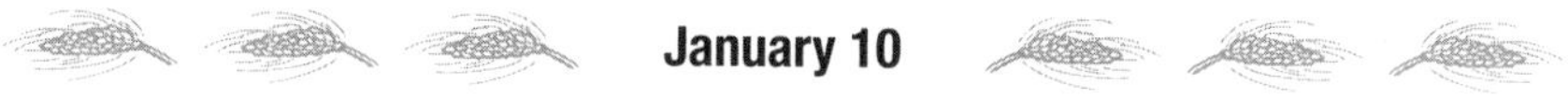

January 10

Colossians 1:15-17

The "Glue" That Holds Us Together

God's mark is on every cell of our bodies. God knitted our human bodies together with amazing detail and wonder. How can ANYONE deny that a Creator did all of this?? We can trust the God who created all this, also has the power to hold it all together when things seem to be falling apart -how our loving Creator is also our sustainer.

Ever heard about laminins? Here is how Wikipedia describes them: "Laminins are a family of proteins that are an integral part of the structural scaffolding of basement membranes in almost every animal tissue." You see, laminins are what hold us together – LITERALLY. They are cell adhesion molecules. They are what hold one cell of our bodies to the next cell. Without them, we would literally fall apart.

And I sort of knew this: But what I didn't know is what laminin LOOKED LIKE. But now I do! And I have thought about it many, many times since. Here is what the structure of laminin looks like – AND THIS IS NOT a "Christian portrayal" of it – if you look up laminin in any scientific medical piece of literature, this is what you will see:

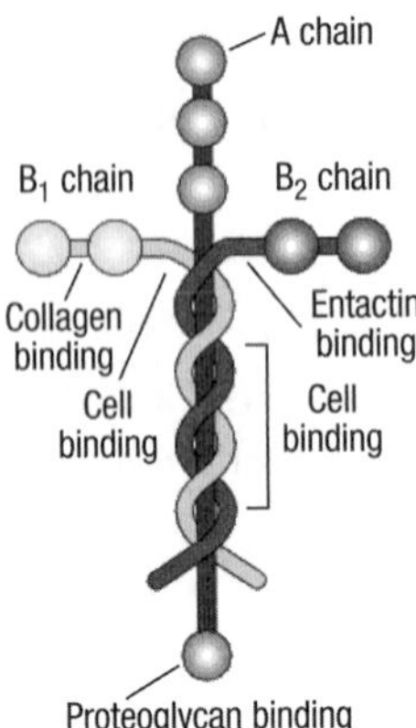

Now tell me that our God is not amazing. The glue that holds us together ALL of us is in the shape of the cross. Immediately, the passage in Colossians comes to mind. Be sure to study it as it is "in Him that all things HOLD TOGETHER."

Thousands of years before the world knew anything about laminin, Paul penned those words. And now we see that from a very LITERAL standpoint, we are held together, one cell to another, by the cross.

You can never convince me that is anything other than the mark of the Creator who knew EXACTLY what laminin "glue" would look like long before Adam even breathed his first breath!

"Faith is not knowing what the future holds, but knowing who holds the future."

Do you truly understand and believe that YOU are being held together by the cross of Jesus Christ? Believe personally His love, His forgiveness, His marvelous power, His mercies, and His unending grace today and then for all of eternity.

Prayer: Truly You are an awesome God. Thank you for including us in Your magnificent plan. Enable us to live for You. Amen.

Harold Hoftyzer

Harold is the Women's Golf Coach at NWC and a good friend.

January 11

Psalm 118:24

Celebrate Each Day

This verse is one that I can reflect on every day and know that it speaks directly to me. It's simple and straightforward. It's a gentle reminder that we need to find something to celebrate in every day.

No matter how I feel when I wake up, no matter what the weather might be like or the challenges I face in my daily life, each day is an amazing gift. Each new day brings so much to celebrate. Even if there are disappointments and challenges, there are always moments that are worth celebrating. The rejoicing might come during a spectacular sunrise, seeing a robin in my yard or sharing a cup of coffee with a friend. It's easy to forget and take those special moments for granted.

What I do each day is a reflection of how YOUR love has influenced my life. I know that I don't always live each day to the fullest which makes me realize how much I take for granted. Help me rejoice and celebrate the gifts I receive from each of you.

Prayer: Dear Lord, You have given so much to me and I am so thankful that you continue to surround me with Your love. Each day you give me a blessing and I thank You for it. I thank You for the people that I come into contact with each day; the sunshine and the changing seasons, flowers, friendships and family, You give me the ability to enjoy all these wonders of Your world. With each day that I am given, I am reminded that waking up and being able to rejoice in a new day isn't enough. Good health isn't to be taken for granted, loved ones may face challenges and times might not be easy. But no matter what the moment, I rejoice in the wonders of another new day and believe and trust in the plan You have for me. Amen.

Char and Dave Krahling
School Librarian and Interstates Electric employee

Char and Dave are very special people in our lives. Char is one of Dot's best friends. Dave is a former Ag. Teacher at SCHS and we worked together there. These are two great people that make our lives better and do lots for kids. Dave also serves on the ATLAS of Sioux Center board.

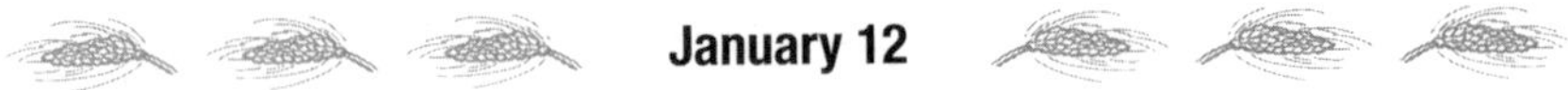

January 12

I Corinthians 1:9; Philippians 1:9-10

God Is Faithful

What an awesome statement. And I discovered His faithfulness for blessing my life when I really didn't include Him in my decisions. It started with my choice of nursing as a career. It has been a span of 40 years nursing and loving it. My marriage – Dave did propose on our first date! I said, "You have to be joking!" (Our marriage has been blessed since 1962, including some ups and downs.)We moved to Sioux Center and decided to attend a church right across the street. No hassle to walk, and besides some of the other teachers went there. We have two healthy children, a boy (Dick) and a girl (Amy).

It was a gradual awakening. It started with daily devotions, an adult Sunday School class, some adult mentors, and being very honest with God when I had and have doubts. I'm taking the mask off for Him. He knows anyway.

I am so humbled that He didn't give up on me. Another mentor friend gave me this family prayer.

Prayer: This is my prayer that your love may abound more and more in knowledge and depth of insight, so that you may be able to discern what is best and may be pure and blameless until the day of Christ, filled with the fruit of righteousness that comes through Jesus Christ to the glory and praise of God. Amen.

Dot

January 13

Romans 8:19

God's Revelation

In all of the hustle and bustle of our day, as well as our minds, concerning the war on terror, the economic downturn/recession, and our personal interests – how evident is this verse for today? The world is turbulent and seems to be rushing toward the end times. Current events appear to be centered on the Middle East and Israel, where the Bible says Jesus will return and stand on the Mount of Olives.

As Christians, we should be praying that all creation will display that eagerness for Jesus return. Are we ready for the day when Jesus returns to fully reveal His Kingdom and His followers?

Prayer: Dear God, thank you for the promise of Your return. We look forward to it but understand Your reason for delay. Use us this day to reach others for You. Amen.

Dwayne Alons
Iowa State Representative, District 4

Dwayne was our leader on Thursday morning Bible Study at the Capitol. I appreciate his leadership, not only at the Bible Study, but in the House and as a friend.

January 14

Matthew 18:18-19

On What Can We Agree?

The enemy is working overtime to destroy the family structure. A Christian husband and wife *(two)* who bind the enemy and together pray in agreement with God's Word, present a powerful weapon against the enemy.

There is about a 50% divorce rate in our country (even higher for second and third marriages), but Christian couples *who pray together* have a divorce rate of less than 1 %!

My husband Dwayne and I daily join hands and pray together at bedtime. This simple time together with our God richly blesses our lives. God has given His people the weapons to win the victory through the authority in His name.

Let's join hands and pray in agreement with God's Word!

Prayer: Dear God, thank you for our extended families. Help us to agree to always share our love with others and seek Your love for all of us. Amen.

Clarice Alons

Clarice serves as the Clerk for her husband in the House. She is also a faithful member of the Thursday morning Bible Study group.

January 15

Colossians 3:16-17; James 3:2

What Are You Talking About?

Do you talk about important things? Think about the conversations you were involved in yesterday or today. Did the weather come up? How about those big games last night? Did a word of gossip slip off your tongue? Just because something is true doesn't mean you have to repeat it.

What things are important to talk about? Building each other up; The importance of forgiveness; Help for those not as blessed as we; Being thankful; Saying something positive and uplifting; I'm sure you can think of others.

Weather and sports may be good icebreakers, but then let's get down to the important stuff, especially with our families and close friends.

Prayer: Thank you Lord for helping us control our tongues. Help us always to be positive and uplifting in our conversations with and about others. Amen.

Dave

January 16

Luke 15:4-7

Let's Not Fit In…

I have never felt like I really fit into any place or group. That used to bother me a lot. I felt rejected or unloved by people because I didn't seem to fit in. Since coming to Jesus, I have started to learn that being a part of a group may not be as exciting or good as I thought it was. Instead, I tend to notice others who also seem to be on the outside as well. I try to talk to them and it has led me to some truly amazing people. It has also led me to an independence.

When I start to feel like a part of the group, I find myself needing to walk away. For me, being a part of a group is a dangerous place because I have seen what it does to those who do not feel included. I have also seen the arrogance it brings to some of those who do fit in. Why am I a part of this particular group? Is it to get the "leaders" to like and accept me? Who do I look to for value in this group? Is it the elite? What about the ones who are not fitting in? Do I look to them?

Again this leads me to Jesus. When He was here on earth, He looked for those who were on the fringes. He did not focus only on those who lead or held prestigious positions. He noticed people that no one else did. Jesus looked for the lost sheep, the one out of the ninety-nine. I wonder if that lost sheep strayed away because he was actually lost or felt excluded by the others. Maybe he just "didn't fit." Jesus reached out to that sheep and showed His love to him. I can't describe how many times I have felt that way. We have many people around us today who have strayed because they did not feel a part of the group, and felt no love.

I believe that we are too often seeking the acceptance of others and not the acceptance of Christ. We want to fit in. We try to put on our Christian clothes and be what others want us to be so we can fit in. We crave popularity and the esteem of others. So we say what others want us to say – we look as others would have us look – we impose this on our children and on our communities. If you don't look like us or think like us, you do not belong with us. I really do not believe this was how Jesus treated the ones he hung out with.

We often want others to be just like us. If not, then we don't want them in our life. We will not be friends with someone because of their conduct. Is this love? So many people around us today do not fit in and certainly do not live a perfect live. Myself included. What I think Jesus is teaching us in this passage is to love the ones outside the inner circle. We need to get to know them and their needs, and listen to their heart. We all have stories that make us who we are. Many stand outside the group not fitting in because we don't give them a chance to tell their stories. How do I give them this chance?

I need to pray for them and with them. Talking to God about them and asking Him to intercede for them is vital. The power of prayer is not getting what I want from God. It is the relationship that builds between the people involved in prayer and God. If I pray for the lost, I must know of their needs. It means that I am learning more about how God views them – having His eyes and being able to put myself in their shoes. It allows me to hear their heart and God's heart for them.

Let's not take so much of our time trying to fit in, as much as trying to understand those who do not seem to fit. Let's do what God called us to do and love those around us, as well as our heavenly Father. Let's get past trying to be all things to all people, and be the person He has called us to be. Let's stop focusing on how to have everyone like us, and focus on having Jesus love us.

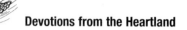

Prayer: Heavenly Father, thank you for including us even when we don't deserve to be included. Help us to reach out to those whom we know You love but we might not notice. Amen.

Jerry Kieft
Director of ATLAS Group

Jerry was a high school classmate of my son. He had tremendous athletic ability but didn't reach all of his potential because of outside influences. Jesus changes lives! Jerry's testimony is a great inspiration to me and everyone who hears it. Contact him and listen just as soon as you can.

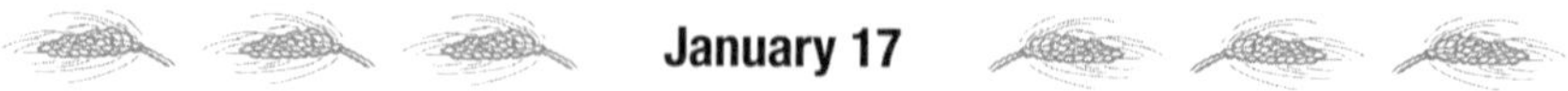

January 17

Psalm 54:6

A Truly Meaningful "Thank You"

How many times in our lives do we all prayerfully ask our Lord for help in times of need; strength in times of sickness; courage to say the right words; help in making a positive out of a negative. Every day we lean on God to produce. Most of the time, we faithfully and prayerfully expect God to come through for us.

When I was a child growing up, my Christian folks taught me to say "please" and "thank you." It was, and still is, a respectful thing to do. Do we all say enough "Thank You's" in our daily lives?

Twenty years ago, my wonderful Mom passed away from a sudden heart attack. To this day, I still want to say to her –Thank You – for who she was and all she did for me and others. I'm sure she knew, but did she? Three years later, my Dad passed away from cancer. I had some quality months to say my "Thank You's", and show appreciation for what he did as a husband, father, and grandfather.

Fellow Believers – don't wait to say "Thank You" to someone. Seize the moment when it's presented. Besides making you feel better, you will definitely make the person you thank feel better too.

We all know what a simple "Thank You" can do in our lives. Just think how God, our Heavenly Father, feels. Can we ever thank Him enough? To God Be the Glory!

Prayer: Thank you Lord. We never can say that too often to You and to the people we love. Thanks for loving us even when we don't show proper gratitude, and aren't so loveable. Amen.

Dave Aalbers
NWC Hall of Famer and Owner of his own digging service with his son

Dave and Rhonda live in Alton. Dave was a great baseball and basketball player for the Red Raiders. The 1973 team went on to the National Tournament. He is in the NWC Hall of Fame. He is a regular at the DutchMart Coffee Group, a proud father and grandfather, and just a fine friend! Say a prayer for him and his family.

January 18

2 Corinthians 9:6-8

God First

Reading the book, Treasures of the Transformed Life, by John Ed Mathison, it has a chapter on tithing the 10%. I will be using quotes from his inspiring book for you to consider.

Barry Sanders, the now-retired celebrated running back of the Detroit Lions, is said to have given a tenth of his more than $2 M. signing bonus to his church in Kansas. When asked why he did this, he simply replied, "Because the Bible says you should tithe." Now how can you argue with that?

All we have belongs to the Lord. May we not only tithe, but freely give our offerings to Him who paid the debt for our many sins. When we tithe there will be plenty left for ourselves. Remember, returned blessings are more than just financial. God changes something on the inside as well. The treasures we have; God is the OWNER, you are the OWER.

If you haven't been in the habit of tithing, why not start now, and offerings will follow. Be a generous giver, the Lord will reward you greatly, because you CAN'T out give Him.

Prayer: Lord, You love a cheerful giver. May we not steal from You Father; all we have belongs to You. Lord you gave Your only Son, may we out of love, give to You your portion. In Jesus name. Amen.

Pete Aberson
Retired High School Teacher, Alton, Iowa

Pete was my favorite teacher. It started in 7th & 8th grade and then we both moved on to Alton High School the same year. He taught science and here is what I learned about teaching. Don't ever try to fool the students, let them know what is expected, what is important, and that you want them to do well. Pete and Geri enjoy retirement in their hometown of Alton and I'm sure glad he's my friend. You'll be able to read a couple other of Pete's devotionals down the road a piece.

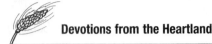

January 19

John 1:1

God's Holy Word

The Bible is undoubtedly the most amazing book ever published. Of course it had the most incredible author! How could words written thousands of years ago, still have such great relevance today? Just think about – Exciting stories that still bring joy and tears; Parables that have a variety of meanings and applications, and can explain decisions we make today; Songs, poems, wisdom, prophecy, and ways to treat others; It's all there.

What are your favorite verses and passages? I have eleven of them. Starting tomorrow, and each succeeding 20th of the month, you will read of them. Please place my name next to the verses in your Bible, and pray for me and my family each time you come across them. I need it.

Finally, select your favorites and pass them on to me and other friends. We will then pray for you. All of us will receive even more of God's blessings.

Prayer: There certainly is no other God but You! We are in awe, and give you all the praise. Thank you for knowing us and loving us anyway. Amen.

Dave

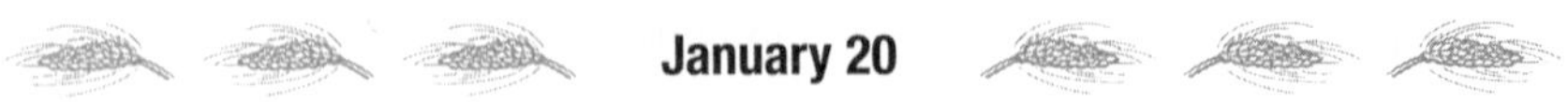

January 20

2 Timothy 3:15-17

God-Breathed Words

It is so important to REALLY believe in something. If you don't, it will be very difficult to improve, advance, or grow. Since I really believe these verses by Paul, the Bible does advise, critique, correct, and help me understand what God expects. Believing creates confidence.

As a former basketball and baseball player, I can tell you that it was a real rarity when a shot went in or a hit was made when I didn't have confidence in taking the shot or swinging the bat. One has to believe and be committed to what's being done or practiced, that it is the right thing. Can you find a place where the Bible is wrong? I've never found, or been presented with evidence showing it to be inaccurate, and it's centuries old. It has amazing relevance for today. Can you think of another book that is still 100% accurate after that many years?

I think we better believe it!

Prayer: Almighty God, we thank you for your precious Word. Bury it in our hearts and let us use this "two-edged sword" to bring about great changes in this world. Give us will power to improve our regimen of study in Your Word. Amen

Dave

January 21

Matthew 7:7-8; Proverbs 16:1-7

The Path to Great Adventure

Warning! Warning! If you truly seek out the Lord's direction for your life, it may become the path to great adventure, challenge, gratification and contentment. So be careful what you pray for. God is ever faithful to answer your longings.

As a mom and wife, faced with the prospects of my empty nest years, I turned to the scriptures to discern the guidance I needed to provide the new direction I was eagerly seeking. "Lord, how do I use the gifts and abilities you have given me at this special time in my life? Please show me the way so I can move forward with a commitment and enthusiasm to serve you." A seemingly simple prayer, none-the less, a powerful one; God was faithful to my plea. Our all-knowing God then answered me in a way I was totally unprepared for. "Anita, I call you to honor me by sharing a story of friendship, competition, family and faithfulness lived out by your son and his teammates. In doing so, I want you to become involved with a film production." Can you believe that was the answer God gave me? I had never dreamed of becoming a film originator and producer, but in faithfulness, I laid my insecurities on the Lord and followed the call.

We began production for the feature film "Winning Favor" in the late fall of 2007. The Lord challenged me to present the true story of a group of young men in our small Iowa town who achieved an almost impossible dream in the year 2005. The young men, friends yet sports competitors, attended two different, rival high schools in Orange City, Iowa, a community of about 6,000 people. Unbelievably, the two teams won not just the 2A but also the 3A State Basketball Championships, with respective sportsmanship trophies, in that same 2005 season. That journey, I knew, had been filled with unique obstacles that required much sacrifice on the part of parents, coaches, and friends. I was compelled to share how ultimately the young men come to discover what "winning" (Proverbs 3:3-4) is truly about.

Our small production team prayed our way through the entire process. We discovered that trusting the Lord meant turning everything over to Him. Our unlikely cast of local high school, professional TV and screen actors immediately jelled. Our production team of Christian artists gave us more creativity than we could have imagined. Our professional editing crew gifted us thousands of dollars of talent simply because they wanted the Lord's message to be heard. "Winning Favor" is still being presented for distribution and gaining momentum as I write this devotional. Already young parents and coaches are asking for DVD copies we haven't even produced. I can see that God is not finished answering my prayer!

My challenge to you is, "commit your works to the Lord, He will establish them" and know that "everyone who asks, receives; he who seeks, finds: and to him who knocks, the door will be opened." Walking through that open door may lead to discovering a surprising, new plan God has yet to unfold for your life.

Warning! Be ready! God will answer your prayers in a mighty way and true Christian adventure lies ahead!

Prayer: Lord, You are the all-wise God. Use me, a sinner, to further Your kingdom. Show me the path for my life. Help me to hear and respond to Your call. Through Christ, all things are possible. Amen.

Anita Plantage-Bomgaars
Producer, "Winning Favor," friend, and former student, babysitter, cheerleader, and baseball statistician for Coach Dave and Dot Mulder

As Nita mentioned, she was one of our special babysitters. She married Dave (see his devotional June 27) and have raised a great family. Be sure to check out "Winning Favor" at your earliest convenience and talk to Nita about a car/truck accident and the power of prayer that was another life-changing event in her life back during their college days at NWC.

January 22

Isaiah 41:10-13; Philippians 1:6

Challenge

As I write this devotional, it is cold and snowy outside; traffic is near a stand-still, and business has come to a halt. What a blessing we have; warm homes, food, and clothes, compared to those who live amongst us who have so little. God's word instructs us to give to those in need, not only physically, but also give instruction from His Word.

It is my hope that we would consider giving as a privilege. "It is more blessed to give than to receive" (Acts 20:35). It is not only the physical necessity of life must we give, but be willing to be ambassadors for Christ. God has called us to be heralds for our Heavenly Father.

As we go forward in this new year, may we be good stewards spiritually and physically, as the passage in Philippians speaks about. We can be confident that God keeps His promises and He will help us as we try to do good works.

Accept the challenge and the Lord will bless you richly.

Prayer: Again Father, we thank you for being so faithful to us. You have given us so much as we are compared worldwide. We know this gives us great responsibility to share. Help us to be willing. Amen.

Pete Aberson

January 23

Isaiah 43:1-4; Jeremiah 29:11-13

He Keeps His Promises

God has fulfilled so many of His promises as we live through our son's battle with ALS (Lou Gehrig's Disease). Strength, courage, and hope increase our faith. The passage in Jeremiah is our son's battle cry and our comfort.

We face many crises in our lives, but Christ's promise to walk with us every step of the way, has been a real help in our struggle to understand God's will. When I pray each day, I ask for God's peace and for God to go before me and show me the way.

Much of my acceptance has come from the book *Praying Through the Tough Times* by Lloyd Ogilvie. We also receive great strength from the love and support of our family and friends. Keep praying for us!

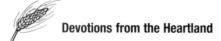

Prayer: Dear God, we can never get too much of You. We need You every day, all day. Please continue to help those that seek answers for this terrible disease. We thank you for caring and loving. Amen.

Colleen and Rod Scholten
Retired Educators, living in LeMars

Colleen is my only sister and I love her dearly. She and Rod are a great couple. She does yeoman work as a volunteer and Rod can absolutely fix or build anything! This battle with ALS is life-changing. It helps us all realize how much we need each other and how fragile life really is. Cherish your loved ones and frequently let them know how much they mean to you.

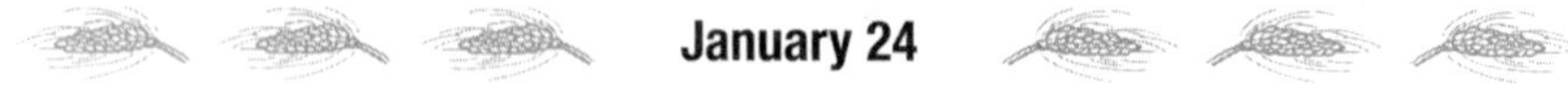

January 24

Ephesians 6:10-18

A Life of Mission

It was after WWII and the Korean Conflict in 1954 when I started out for Africa wearing the shoes of peace. I went in answer to God's call. My family and my church supported me financially and in prayer. When I entered the Sudan I discovered a kingdom of darkness that was REAL, where Satan was lord. The Kingdom of Light, where Jesus is Lord was beginning to penetrate as the Word of God was being translated into the heart language of the people. I was there while the books of John, Mark, and Luke were fully translated, and the book of Matthew was in process. A few of the people were learning to read the Bible, understand it and even believe it. But while the seed of the Gospel grew, the kingdom of darkness attacked it. This resulted in clashes and battles between the two kingdoms that intensified over the years I served there. The battle gear or armor of God became ESSENTIAL. The helmet, the breastplate, the belt, the shoes, the sword and the shield were all important. As the battle intensified and persecution came, the Light spread in spite of it.

Each time I returned home on furlough, I saw the same type of struggle in my home country. Life was changing. As materialism crept in, the worldly ways seemed to be seeping into the churches, while the church became more inwardly focused. The Kingdom of Light was growing dimmer and the kingdom of darkness was working hard to take over. The questions I asked then are questions I ask today: Do people even realize that there is a battle? Do they know that they needed the armor? Do they see that this battle, too, will only intensify?

Forerunners are needed! God is calling Prayer Warriors who focus on the principalities and powers and join with the prayer movement in the heavenlies! This battle between Light and darkness will continue until Jesus returns. I pray that as the battle intensifies and persecution comes, that the Kingdom of Light will spread in spite of it!

Prayer: Lord, help me to be one who spreads the Kingdom of Light in my lifetime. Amen.

Arlene Schuiteman
Retired Missionary Nurse

Arlene has retired here in her hometown of Sioux Center where she is a "Prayer Warrior" for ATLAS and a personal mentor for Director Amy Keahi. Arlene spent 35 years in the mission field of Sudan, Ethiopia, and Zambia, as a Nurse/Teacher. The Barkers, from the NWC Theatre Dept., have already written and performed one play about Arlene (Sioux Center Sudan) and are now working on a new one dealing with her life in Ethiopia. Now let's us say a prayer for Arlene and all of those missionaries working worldwide.

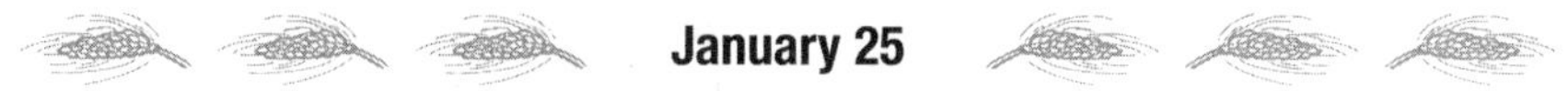

January 25

Jeremiah 8:17-27

Is There No Physician There?

When we saw the suffering of the people of Haiti in the days after their earthquake, we could ask along with Jeremiah, "Is there no balm in Gilead? Is there no physician there?" The women at the foot of the cross were also distressed at the mockery of those who passed by and the suffering of their Lord.

The New Testament women found their answer to ridicule and death on Easter morning.

We who grieve over the distress in Haiti can now appreciate the doctors who went as volunteers, especially those who set up hospital tents, fully equipped with medicines and surgical tools.

In the name of our Lord Jesus Christ, who suffered and died, we reach out in love and compassion to give water to the thirsty, food to the hungry, and healing to the wounded and sick.

Prayer: O Lord, enable us to be comforters in sorrow, listening to the cries of Your people, thirsty, hungry, and wounded. In the name of the Lord in Zion, our King, Amen.

Syl and Phyllis Scorza
Retired Prof. and Home Manager at NWC

These are two amazing people! They are both deep into their 80's and **very** active. Syl continues to take classes at NWC. He took all of mine, and did very well I might add. He has been paralyzed from his waist down since he was 20 and can only get around in a wheel chair. Many times Phyllis is pushing him, but many of his friends also get the chance. He is a regular member of the DutchMart Coffee Group. He misses very few activities that go on at the college, and I don't think he ever misses Chapel.

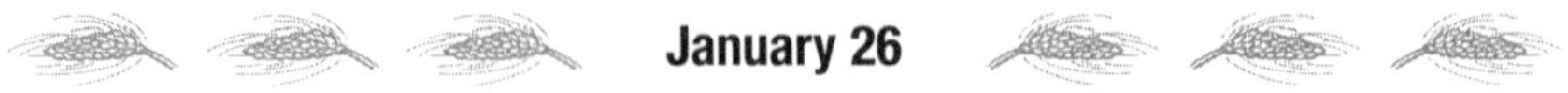

January 26

1 Peter 2:21; John 13:14-15

Do You Have A "Hero"?

Remember the old Simon and Garfunkel song that asked "Where have all the heroes gone?" The famous old Yankee Joe DiMaggio is mentioned as I recall. Well my hero was a baseball Hall of Famer too, Stan "The Man" Musial. Later, as an adult, I got the chance to meet "The Man" and tell him how important he was to me. Stan told me that it was important to him to try and set a positive example for kids and teammates. He did!

Now I know that none of us humans is perfect, or can be. But I do think it's important that we look for qualities in others that we can admire, and then try to emulate them.

Have you selected a hero? Have you let that person know? Do you want to, or try to be a hero to anyone? We definitely need more of them. This whole world can use more people that others admire for their good qualities. The media is certainly filled with enough "garbage" about the other kind.

In spite of the fact that I like the idea of having a "hero," so to speak, we have to remember that no one is, or can be, perfect but we can concentrate on doing our best. Let's strive for that goal.

Prayer: Thank you Jesus for placing many people in our lives that we can admire. Help us today to be that kind of person for someone else. Amen.

Dave

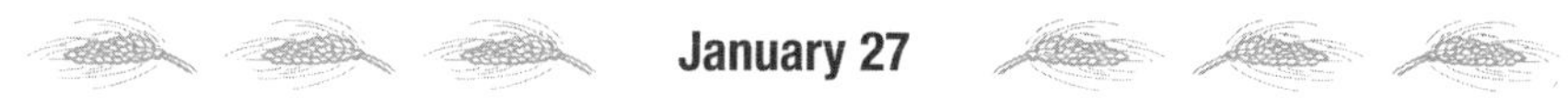

January 27

Proverbs 22:18

Credos To Live By

Throughout my life I've let other people influence me. That's not bad – if it's the right kind of people that are doing the influencing. I honestly don't know all of the authors of the 12 credos I've selected as goals to follow over the years. I have given credit wherever I could – but they certainly aren't original with me. Starting tomorrow, and then on the 28th, of each succeeding month, you can read about their significance in my life. I hope you will find them useful personally as well.

May I suggest that you make some selections (not necessarily from this list) that you try to follow? If you get the chance to share them with me – I'd like that! God Bless You.

Prayer: Dear Lord, You use many people to help accomplish Your goals for us. Please use us as well. Thank you for excitement, enthusiasm, and a willingness to learn and grow. Amen.

Dave

January 28

Proverbs 1:20

"Know Thyself" (Socrates)

Of course, old Socrates was one sharp cookie. I should study more about him, I guess. But these two words have been very meaningful to me for a long time. By studying myself, I have learned my gifts, my weaknesses, likes, dislikes, stress-causers, and motivators. These are important to know, not only for health reasons, but also to reach goals. Knowing myself has helped me deal with my allergies (wheat, rye, barley, malt), fears (heights) and being alone (I just don't like it!).

One can't build on strengths, or work on weaknesses, unless they are known. Give it a try.

Prayer: Thank you Lord for giving each of us at least one gift. Thank you, too, for enabling us to reach goals and help others do the same. Keep us humble and always striving to do good. Amen.

Dave

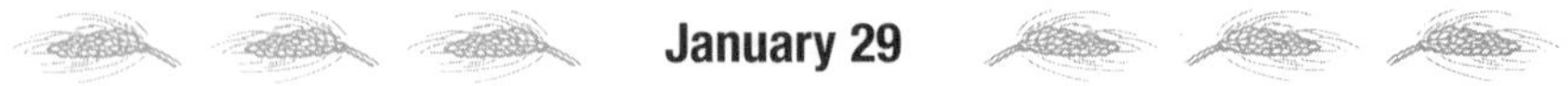

January 29

Psalm 78:3-7

God's Covenant

Even though she was peacefully asleep, it was an emotional moment. My granddaughter Ayda had just been baptized. She had fussed as the sacramental water was being applied but had not awakened. As she was lying in her Daddy's arms, Ayda was wearing the baptismal dress that her Mother had worn, and the ring that her grandmother wore when she was baptized. She was being surrounded by the love of two sets of great-grandparents and grandparents, her mom and dad, two brothers, and her entire church family. Ayda's mom and dad wanted her to know of the heritage that brought her to that altar and the legacy of those that came before. Therefore, they had asked me to share this verse as Ayda's baptismal scripture. It was because of that legacy she was entering into the promised covenant with Jesus through holy baptism. Ayda's parents and extended family were obeying God's command by entering her into God's covenant and starting the teaching of God's praiseworthy deeds, His power and His wonders.

I pray that Miss Ayda will one day remember who she is in God's covenant. I pray that one day by remembering her place in that covenant, she might claim "her inheritance" in Christ Jesus. I pray that somehow, even though I am sinful, I might in my daily living be able to remind Ayda of God's wonders and the promise of that inheritance. And I pray that we all may strive in this way to suffer the children to come to Jesus.

Prayer: Thank you Jesus for loving little children and allowing us to guide them toward You. It is such an awesome task to raise the little ones in this world. We can't do it without our families and we certainly can't do it without You. Amen.

Vern Den Herder

Vern was a member of the famous "No Name" defense that led the Miami Dolphins to 4 Super Bowls. He is a member of the National College Hall of Fame. He was a great 4-sport athlete at Sioux Center where I had the privilege of coaching him in baseball and basketball. As great an athlete as he was, he is an even greater gentleman and friend. He and his lovely wife Diane live in Sioux Center where Diane has just retired from an excellent teaching career.

January 30

Philippians 4:8-9

Listening – Learning – Watching

Recently a classmate of mine, a world-renowned scientist from California, lost his battle with cancer. One thing I will always remember him saying is "Can't we ever just sit and think?" That's a good question.

My life these past months has involved lots of listening, learning, and watching. I listened to a woman who is now a Prof. at Hope College speak about leaving the Mennonite Church. Another woman from Rwanda spoke of hiding 91 days in a bathroom with a few others, and thereby surviving the Rwanda holocaust. I studied Richard Stearn's, (President of World Vision) book entitled "A Hole in the Gospel." Richard, after living a very lucrative lifestyle, stopped to look at his life. He left his world of wealth, to help and reach out to those that have so little.

After watching the Hope/Calvin basketball game, I turned to a program that showed the tragic earthquake in Haiti. What a contrast! For me it was all listening, grieving, and in part – thinking. All of this makes a person think of one's own life. Even in old age, like me, to think about the Faith people needed to be able to live through all of these experiences. I am so thankful for my grandparents and parents who taught me about Christ's teachings. What a privilege. What a gift. It is all that really matters.

During this Lenten season, let us be thankful for all Christ has done for us and try to be an example in every way we can, even as old as we become.

Prayer: Dear Lord, thank you for each hour, day, and year You give us. Keep us mindful that our job is still to love each other. Amen.

Mildred Vanderbeek
Retired and living in Michigan

Mil is a dear friend that lived in Sioux Center back in the late '60's. We were part of a Bible Study Group and have been close friends ever since. Here is some frame of reference for you. Jim Kaat is her brother. Bob Boerigter is her son. Jan and Barb are her daughters. Jesus Christ is her Lord.

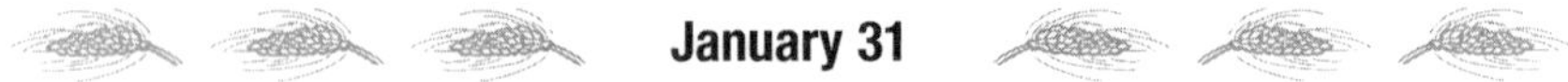

January 31

James 1:19

When To Be Quick, And When To Be Slow

As husbands and wives we think differently, we respond differently and different things touch our hearts. Unfortunately for our marriage relationship, we tend to ignore that fact and go through life with our own expectations of how our spouse should live and respond. The result can often be misunderstanding and resentment.

So how do we begin to understand each other? I believe we are called to be attentive to one another in marriage. I admit, and I'm sure Janet will agree, that I have not fully lived up to that calling, but I still believe it. Men – I encourage you to stop and listen to your wife. We must be willing to ask about their day, their life, even their feelings!!! We must also be willing to reveal what is going on in our lives – even those things deep inside us. This is very difficult and downright scary for us guys, because it makes us vulnerable and we don't necessarily like that. Ladies, if your husband shares a thought or a feeling and opens himself up, even if he fumbles through it, please love him for trying. Critical words will just cause him to hold back even more. Encouraging words will give life to your marriage. I believe you will learn a lot about one another and be drawn closer together by taking time to have regular, meaningful conversations.

Janet and I will be celebrating our 30th wedding anniversary in July, 2010. We have grown closer to one another, there is no question of that, but no matter how much you love one another, conflict is inevitable. What we must remember in these times of disagreement is that our spouse is not the enemy. Guard words and your actions. You are on the same marriage team. Janet has reminded me of this many times through our years together. I may have not always wanted to hear those words, but I can't think of a time when they weren't exactly right.

So, as we look at one another in marriage and we realize that our spouse is just the person we need to help us become who God has made us to be, our words and actions are more likely to respond in attentive tenderness.

Prayer: Thank you God for creating us to be able to learn to communicate effectively and in love. Instill that love deeply into our hearts. Help us to be better spouses, better team players at work and at play. Amen.

Doug and Janet Boone
Members of Central Reformed and both are very active in leadership

Doug and Janet were both high school students of mine and Doug was on the golf team. Janet is a real leader in the music dept. and a major contributor to the great "Kempers Quartet." These are two mighty fine people.

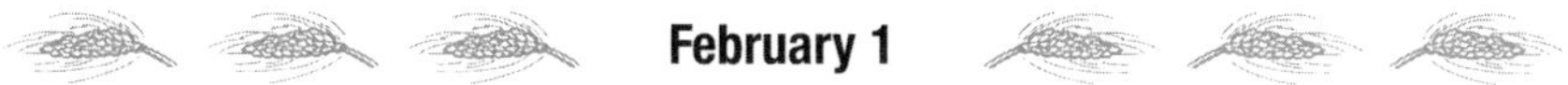

February 1

1 Corinthians 12:28

Coach

What a great thing to be called! That's all I've ever called him. Orval Madden was my coach. We only had two sports – baseball and basketball – and he coached 'em both. When one sport season ended, practice for the other one started, and vice versa. I loved 'em both (and still do). Coach also taught history, manual arts, mechanical drawing, physical education, and government. He was also the Principal and Athletic Director. I don't know what he did in his spare time, but he did find time to build the family house as well.

He was a great student of the games and he taught me a great deal. He actually was a legend in the State as a coach and athletic director. In fact he's been named to three Halls of Fame (Baseball Coaches, Basketball Coaches, and Athletic Directors).

Coach was a strong disciplinarian and his methods worked with and for me. Fundamentals were excellently taught and training rules strictly adhered to. Coach was great at pointing out deficiencies and keeping us from ever getting "the big head." I tried to copy many of the methods he used in coaching. He strongly influenced my personal life and continues to be a great friend today.

We can learn important things from a person by practicing what he/she does and doesn't do.

Prayer: Heavenly Father I thank you for the many positive role models you have placed in my life. Help me do a better job. Help all of us grow and express ways to help others and be a positive influence. Thank you especially for Coach. Amen

Dave

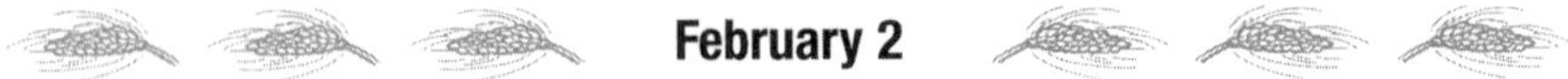

February 2

Acts 5:12-16

The Shadow Knows

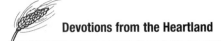

Today is Groundhog Day, a day when we think about shadows. In today's scripture, many people tried to be aligned with Peter's shadow. Even though shadows are mentioned in the Bible in both the Old and New Testaments, Peter's shadow is perhaps the most prestigious.

Think back on your life thus far. Whose shadow has passed over you that has truly affected you? Perhaps your parents, a teacher, a friend or a colleague? Today and all future February seconds should be a day for us to express our feelings and thanks to God for their presence in our lives.

Who will benefit from your shadow? What kind of influence can you have on others? When is your shadow the most effective? Where are you when that shadow is most productive? Take a minute to reflect upon the shadow you cast.

Prayer: Lord, let this be a day where we give thanks for shadows that have passed over us and to be aware of our example to others. Amen.

Doug Van Berkum
Former Alumni Director at NWC and presently a co-owner with his family at the Rainbow Trout Dude Ranch in Colorado. When he's home in Orange City he is also a regular member of the DutchMart Coffee Group.

Doug's a former high school math teacher and a great friend. I miss him when he's in Colorado. Our grandson Ethan chose the "Ranch" as his place to go with Grandma and Grandpa for a week. We all had a fabulous time. Doug and Linda are great hosts.

February 3

Matthew 7:1-5; Luke 6:37

Making Judgments

This passage in Matthew tells us not to judge others. Verses 3, 4 and 5 go on to tell us that we should not concern ourselves with the speck of sawdust in our brother's eye while ignoring the plank in our own eye. It suggests that we should first take the plank out of our own eye, so we can see clearly to remove the speck from our brother's eye. The verse in Luke reemphasizes this importance, and also speaks of forgiving and being forgiven.

This scripture is very important to me here at the Iowa Capitol as a state legislator. We are called upon to make many judgments on issues that come before the legislature. We, as Christians, need to constantly keep reminding ourselves that we are evaluating the measure of the law and not judging the individual or their beliefs if they differ from ours. God wishes for each and every one of His children to be included in His fold. We have no right to pass judgment as that is reserved for God alone. Our job is to show the measure of His love that will help draw all to Jesus.

Prayer: Heavenly Father, I pray for all politicians as they deliberate throughout this great nation. Please help them to make great judgments without being judgmental. In His name, Amen.

Cecil Dolecheck
State Representative from District 96 (Mount Ayr, IA)

Cecil is a regular at Bible Study, a respected Representative, and a valued friend.

February 4

Job 1:21

Lost Friends

I lost a friend today. He was one of our Saturday morning breakfast group. In fact, he was kind of the unofficial "head of the table" and I miss him already, even though Saturday is two days away. Cancer got him. We talked about "spiritual things" and I know "he was ready." But the separation pain is still there for those who remain.

All of our group has lost loved ones – but that doesn't make it easier. We're never quite ready to "give 'em up." Think about those cherished friends you have. It's painful to lose them to death – but it's even more painful to lose a living one. Don't let that happen.

Prayer: We will always thank you for Denny's life. Help us to make and keep many, many friends. Thank you too for Phil, Wally, Arnie, Herm, Phyllis ... Amen.

Dave

February 5

Hebrews 10:24

Love and Good Works

Love is definitely the key word for February. And what does love mean as one Christian to another Christian?

It's difficult to freeze stirred-up water because molecules in motion produce friction – heat. So water that is moving won't freeze easily. Now apply that principle to your spiritual life. The writer of Hebrews was a need for "peer pressure" in the household of faith: one Christian nudging another away from indifference ... toward Christ likeness.

The test of our spirituality comes when we encounter injustice and meanness and ingratitude, all of which have the tendency to make us spiritually drained. We want to use prayer and Bible reading as an excuse for seclusion. We utilize God for the sake of getting peace and joy; we do not want to follow Jesus Christ, but only enjoy Him.

It is a most disturbing thing to be poked in the ribs by some provoker of God, by someone who is full of spiritual activity. We do not wish to be stirred up; all we want to hear about is spiritual rest. Jesus Christ never encourages that.

Do you have someone who provides that vital function in your life? Someone who senses when you are coasting rather than "competing for the prize?" A "provoking partner." In the Christian life, there's only one thing better than having – and that's being one yourself!

Prayer: God, thank you for loving us first. Help us make certain of our relationship to You before it is eternally too late. Never do we want to forget what our redemption cost You. May we display an active love for you through our relationships with others. Amen.

Dot

February 6

1 John 3:11-24

The Promised Land

Recently, I had an opportunity to go to Israel – to walk where Jesus walked, to see what He saw, to hear what He heard, and to smell what He smelled – well, 2,000 years later. Of course before I went on this trip, I had to first learn everything I could about the history and the land. One interesting fact is that Israel did not have land from 70 until 1967. Now every time I read a verse like Jeremiah 30:3 where God promises to bring Israel back to her home land, it is clear to me that I can trust in God's plan, even if I can't see His promises come true today.

Another fact is that there has been a war over that little piece of land since the beginning of time. When you start to hear stories, you realize that there have been a lot of mistakes and a lot of bad decisions over the years by both Palestinians and Jews. People who live with generations of hate and conflict are living side by side. When I was in Israel, I talked to my Christian guide about this conflict. He wasn't quick to give an easy answer and pointed out the many wrongs that have been done on both sides. One thing that he taught me, not so much with his words but with his actions, is that the love of Jesus is the only answer. Our guide deeply and truly showed us how to love our Palestinian bus driver as well as the local Jewish shopkeeper. He humbly approached them as people who had something to teach him. And they loved him too. Wherever we went, everyone respected, admired and loved our guide.

I came home and I turned on the news and I saw another terrorist attack in Israel and I remembered that love is the only answer, the only way. This has impacted my work at ATLAS as well. Although I haven't met anyone with a battle as big as the Israeli-Palestinian war, people often come into our offices who have been hurt and they have hurt others. I learned something that Jesus taught my guide. The only thing I can do to help is to love.

Prayer: Jesus, give me a heart that loves like yours. Amen.

Amy Vanden Bosch - Keahi
Director/Staff Mentor for ATLAS of Sioux Center

Amy was a student of mine at NWC and also a fine ballplayer. What a joy it is to see the great work she does with not only the people that hurt, but also with her colleagues. Contact her at ATLAS 712-722-4900.

February 7

Psalm 145:2; 1 John 1:5

Help Us Each Day

Each day as the sun rises we realize God has given us innumerable opportunities. We live in a great land where we have freedom to decide our actions. Each new day we seek protection and guidance for our children and grandchildren. We are thankful for whatever measure of health we enjoy and try to do everything we can to become stronger. As the day goes on we seek more and more of God's grace.

As each day draws to a close we are thankful for answered prayers. We are thankful for work and accomplishment. We are grateful for any happiness we have experienced and for happiness we may have delivered to others.

What are you looking to accomplish this day? How can you help someone? When you say "Have a good day!" what are you willing to do to make it that way? Lord, help us.

Prayer: Lord, we thank you for restful nights, protection, our family's safety, and work. At the close of the day we thank you again for what we look forward to. Help us make tomorrow better. Be with us at this hour and the end of life on this earth. Amen.

Kay and Jack Kibbie
President of the Iowa State Senate

Jack has served for many years in the Senate and Kay is his clerk. They live in Emmetsburg and are valued friends to Dot and me. They often took part in the Bible Study and their faith is strong.

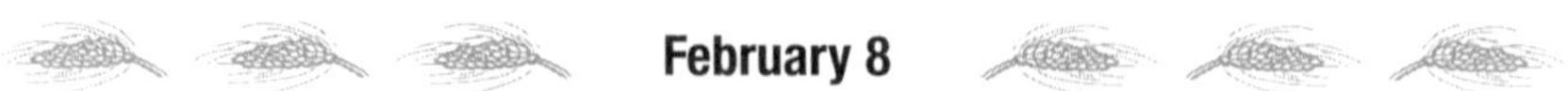

February 8

Luke 24:45

Understanding the News

When something painful happens it is so difficult to understand why. There is heartache, like when our daughter passed away, and yet our family still felt blessings. There seem to be so many poor, down-trodden, sick, and helpless people in the news all of the time. Yet we see avenues of hope. Little children seem so helpless and lacking of courage at certain times. In past history those fears and observations were there as well, yet these youngsters mature and become our leaders. Heartless criminals take advantage wherever they can. They try to destroy the weak, yet there seem to always be others strong enough and willing to help. We may not always understand what we read, see, and hear about. But we can pray, reach out, give, and be willing to serve. Let's watch for those opportunities today.

Prayer: God, grant me the serenity to accept the things I cannot change. Courage to change the things I can, and the wisdom to know the difference. Amen.

Gene and Faye Fraise
Iowa State Senator and Clerk

Gene and Faye became good friends as we served together. Gene was the Chairman of the Agriculture Committee on which I served. He and I also shared in leading devotions to open the Senate on many occasions. They are a great couple from the opposite corner of our state.

February 9

John17:3

The Prize of Eternal Life

Forgiveness

Power Over Sin

Peace With God

No More Pain, Suffering and Death (In Heaven)

No Hell

Heaven For All Eternity

I often wonder how many of us have trusted Jesus Christ for the gifts listed above and missed the true Prize of eternal life – **GOD**.

The apostle John makes clear that the prize of eternal life is the Christ-bought-faith-restored -personal-intimate-love **RELATIONSHIP** with the **GOD** of the Bible. God and not His stuff is the Prize of eternal life.

The Shorter Catechism sums this up with the answer to the ultimate question set before mankind. "*What is the chief end of man?*" Answer – "*Man's chief end is to glorify God and enjoy Him forever.*"

What is eternal life?

Do you have eternal life?

Prayer: Father God, I want us to know and love You more today than yesterday. Help us to know and act like we have your precious gift of eternal life. In Jesus Christ Name. Amen.

Bill and Kim Wegman
Former great pitcher for the Milwaukee Brewers (10 years in the majors)

Bill and Kim became our good friends when I heard of his Christian witness and his willingness to come to NWC and share. They have two beautiful daughters and live in Cincinnati. Both of them continue to share their faith and are very active in Christian Mission.

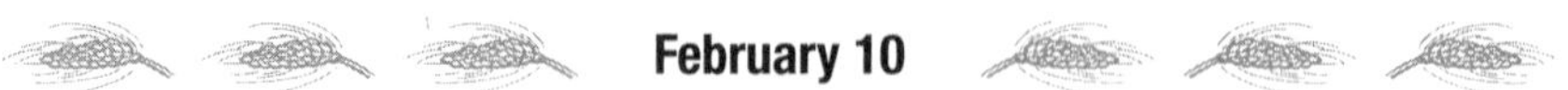

February 10

Ecclesiastes 3:1-8

Time Out

Time out!! Time out!! Have you ever felt like the world is moving way too fast, things are happening in your life that you think should be done differently, and that you just want to call a "time out" to catch your breath and try to change things? When life seems to be spinning out of control, I often lean on some words of wisdom someone once shared with me, "Everything in our lives has a purpose, it happens for a reason, and it will happen in God's timing!"

God has needed to remind me from time to time that He is in the driver's seat and that I just need to sit back and enjoy the journey! What peace that gives me when I listen to God "gently" remind me that He is in complete control of my life. If we are obedient, God does have a unique and special plan for each and every one of us.

Prayer: Lord, thank you for helping us recognize that we need "time outs" in our lives from time to time so that we may stop and listen to You. And thank you Lord, for helping us open our hearts and minds so that You may work in our lives. Lord, grant me the serenity to accept the things I cannot change, the courage to change the things I can, and the wisdom to know the difference. Amen.

Chuck Soderberg
Iowa State Representative, District 3

Chuck was elected to the House at the same time I went into the Senate (2004). We became great friends and I have great respect for him. He represents us very well.

February 11

Psalm 33:11-22

Rely On God

Have you ever bought an appliance which gave you a 90-day guarantee? What happened? On the 91st day it died. Man-made tools just don't last forever. But God's guarantees never run out, they are everlasting. Then what can we rely on from the Lord? God's Word gives us encouragement and it is absolute.

You can depend on God to forgive. (1 John 1:9)

You can rely on God to make your paths straight. (Proverbs 3:3-6)

You can trust God to be a fair judge. (Romans 12:19)

You can depend on God to be a giver of good gifts. (Luke 6:38)

You can trust God to take away our guilt. (1 Corinthians 1:8-9)

You can rely on God that He remembers our labor for Him. (Hebrews 6)

When things around you fail, when things are broken, look up to God and receive His precious promises, and you will find a guarantee that never fails. Isaiah 55:11 assures us that "My WORD shall not return unto me void." God's Word is Absolute.

Prayer: Lord, we stand amazed at what You have done for us. We want to pour ourselves out for You. Give us pure hearts to honor You with our thoughts and actions. May Your Name be praised. In that Precious Name we pray. Amen.

Pete Aberson

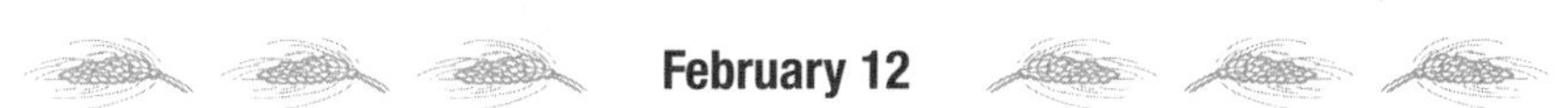

February 12

1 Peter 1:7

Abraham Lincoln: "The Dark Side of Greatness"

I just finished reading a thumbnail sketch of Lincoln's life. He experienced so many failures, depression, and humiliation, yet he persevered and became a great leader and President.

This brought back memories of my college days as a non-traditional, much older student. Dave was a faculty member and I received a big RED "F" on one of the first tests I ever took (not from him). I thought it might reflect on Dave so I definitely wanted to drop the class. I am an average student with not a great deal of confidence in my academic ability. Dave encouraged me and said I was no quitter. I argued that point but thought quitting would be a poor example for our kids. So I completed the course (I got a C), with lots of support from the younger students.

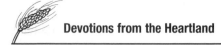

What did I learn? Be an encourager; accept my God-given average intelligence; and God provides light at the end of the tunnel. All are worthwhile lessons.

Prayer: Heavenly Father, thank you for Your faithfulness, even when ours is weak, and thanks too for Your constant and abiding love. Amen.

Dot

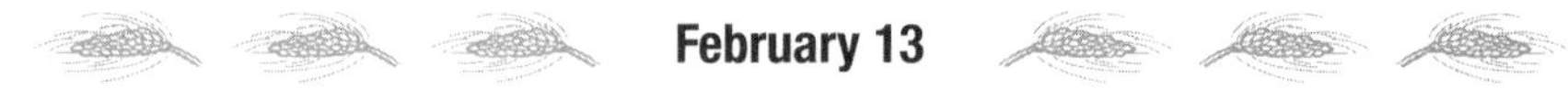

February 13

John 5:28-29; Revelation 20:11-15; Matthew 25:34, 41, 46

The Far Away Look – Destinations

Early in life, the earlier the better, the traveler here upon earth should ask himself or herself two tremendously important questions (really make two important decisions). The first is: "What destination do I hope to reach when my traveling days here upon earth are over?" The second question, equally important is: "What route must I travel to reach that destination?"

Just now we focus our attention on the first question. Try asking this question of people about you. Don't be surprised when you hear some startling replies. For example, here is a person who quickly responds something like this: "What do I expect, what do I hope for when I die and my body is laid in the grave? I expect and hope that it's the end, finished, I'll be blotted out, annihilated, obliterated, wiped out, erased, I won't exist anymore. I am no more."

What do we say to such a person? We remind him first that life is a gift of God. It is precious to Him. He too has instilled in the earnest human heart a sense of respect and love for life. With it has come also a sense of life's continuity.

One of the greatest joys and satisfactions life brings to the devout soul is the communion and fellowship he or she has with God who promises: "I will <u>never</u> leave nor forsake you." Is this to be cut off forever? That is incredible. The gift of life does indeed have continuity.

But something of even greater importance in this consideration must be said. Paging through the Bible, the Word of God, one finds absolutely no basis for the hope of ultimate obliteration. The Bible offers no such choice, no such option. Quite the contrary is true. The Bible teaches about the immortality of the soul.

Something more lies in the future. After the resurrection of Jesus, He returned to glory. However, he left the assurance that He is coming again and will raise us from the dead. His call to arise on the Day of Judgment will be obeyed by all. The passage in John states, "*All that are in the grave shall hear His voice and shall come forth.*"

Then follows judgment before the great white throne with the opening of the books. Then separation and division take place. (Rev. 20) In Jesus' parable of the Sheep and the Goats (Matt. 25), He pictures eternal separations – destinations.

To those on His right hand He will say: "Come ..."

To those on His left hand He will say: "Depart to ... eternal fire ..."

Prayer: Dear God, we know that life continues after death. We want to spend that with You. Thank you for making that possible. Amen.

Rev. Henry Eggink

Read about Rev. Eggink in the July 1 devotional. He was in my Top 10 of people that influenced me the most. This little man has passed on to spend eternity with his Lord, but he left me his book of devotionals. I have selected several to be included in this book and I hope you get as much from them as I received from this "man of the cloth."

February 14

1 Peter 3:8-10

Valentine's Day

These are the verses from our wedding. The original message was great, but it focused on our love and service to each other throughout our marriage. Ironically enough, our first date was on Valentine's Day, the one day of the year when you are to express your love and devotion to one individual. As we reread the verses, we thought it should be looked at from a little different perspective. The verses tell us to love and serve others, not just each other. Your spouse should be loved every day. Your challenge today is to "make your spouse's day," but there's a catch. Challenge your spouse to pass that gift to others. For God's gift to us is His grace and love, our gift to God is how we use it to help others.

Prayer: God, thank you for showing us how to love each other. Truly You are a God of love. As we go about our activities this day please guide us to places where we can share Your matchless love. Amen.

T.J. and Lisa Speer
A Banker and a Nurse

T.J. is Stan and Nancy's youngest son and he played football at NWC. This fine young couple lives and works in Sioux Falls. So the son of a niece is a grand-nephew – I guess I'm anxious for another great grand-nephew or niece!

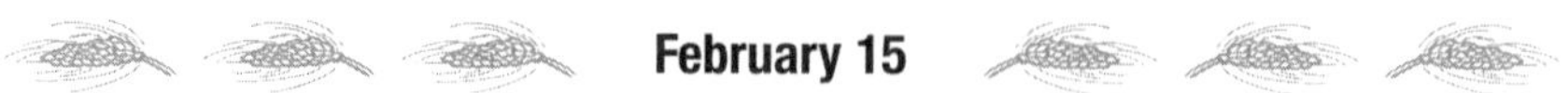

February 15

Revelation 7

A Slice of Heaven

"...from every nation, tribe, people and language, standing before the throne and in front of the Lamb..." (v 9) NIV

Worship is an international language. One of the benefits I have received in being an athlete, coach, and educator is that I have had the privilege to travel to several different countries. On many of these trips I have been able to participate in local worship services, often in a language I did not understand. Without exception, I experienced corporate worship. I discovered that joy, celebration, Christian devotion, passion for Christ – in short, worship – can be communicated in any language, be it English, Spanish, Czech, Ukrainian, or even sign-language. All these international worship experiences have given me a greater appreciation of the "holy catholic church" (that is, the universal Church of believers).

These worship experiences have given me a greater context for understanding Revelation 7:9. However, there is one worship experience in particular that provided me with a real life illustration of this verse. On a recent trip to Beijing, China, I had the opportunity to worship at one of the Beijing International Christian Fellowship worship services. At this service there were about 200-300 people from about 30 different countries, all worshiping the "Lamb." I was profoundly struck by the magnificent beauty of the diversity of God's people. I was deeply moved by the transcending experience of worshiping together with Christians from throughout the world.

Prayer: Lord God, thank you for the opportunities that You give us here on earth to declare together with people from "all nations and tribes, all races and languages. Salvation to our God on His Throne! Salvation to the Lamb! Amen.

Paul and Sharon Bartlett
Former Head Wrestling and Women's Golf Coach at NWC, NAIA Hall of Fame

February 16

Colossians 3:1-17

The Battle Within

Introduction:

I coach men's wrestling, a slightly combative sport that pits one person against another as well as against his own inner demons. It is not uncommon to see a young man fall prey to his earthly nature that says, "This is too hard" or "I can't do this anymore." Each day we seek out opportunities to stretch our wrestlers by putting them in situations where they wrestle with the spirit of pride or the spirit of mediocrity. We want them to learn to battle this defeatist nature because we know they will be faced with similar temptations later in life. I continue to learn that within me lays a battlefield where my flesh wages war with my "new self." In difficult situations, wrestlers, like many athletes, must draw on an inner strength to complete a task.

Paul reminds me in this Colossians passage that I am not my own. Outside of wrestling, I battle with my earthly nature. The voice inside that tells me I am not good enough to succeed, or that what I need can only be provided by the world. It is this earthly nature that fights for my attention each and every day. However, in verse 12 Paul discounts the world and challenges me to remember that I am one of God's chosen, and that I am holy and dearly loved by our Father in to Heaven. Being one of His chosen, I am motivated to live contrary to my earthly nature.

Verse 17 is ultimately what sets my mind on course during times of adversity. It keeps me humble, it motivates me, and in the end, it helps me put things in the right perspective. If I truly want to glorify God in my work, in my family, and on the wrestling mat, I need to commit all that t I do to God the Father, and verses 12-14 describe the standard by which I am to live.

Challenge:

1. What nature are you choosing to live by today?
2. How can you prepare yourself to live a life according to the six characteristics which we are to clothe ourselves? (Verses 12-14)
3. What is getting in your way from allowing Christ to rule in your heart today?

4. Can you find more references to the battle that wages within us? (Eph. 6:12; 1 Tim. 6:11-12, 12:2; 2 Tim. 1:6-7)

Prayer: God our Father, thank you for Your provisions. Thank you for directing us how we are to live. Even more, thank you for showing us how to live by sending us Christ our Lord as an example of compassion, kindness, humility, gentleness, and patience. May You grant me the strength to set my mind on things above and not on earthly things. For it is in Your name we pray. Amen.

Ric and Amy Dahl
Head Wrestling Coach at NWC

February 17

Ecclesiastes 3:2a

My Birthday

Whew! I've had quite a few of them since 1939. Isn't it interesting how people view them? At first we can't wait for each one, and there are some special milestones we're anxious to reach (#13, 16, 18, 21). Then there is a period where we aren't so anxious, and those that end with "O" may be kinda tough. Number 40 was the worst for me because I knew my baseball playing days were over. Finally there's that time where there seems to be some pride in each one we reach (80's, 90's, 100's).

Birthdays are important. I'm sure Michael Jordan is pleased he shares this one with me, don't you think? However, it is important to treasure each one the Good Lord gives us. Find out who has a birthday this week and let them know you appreciate him/her.

Prayer: I do thank you for this special day and the very special people around me. Please help us to find even more happiness. Amen.

Dave

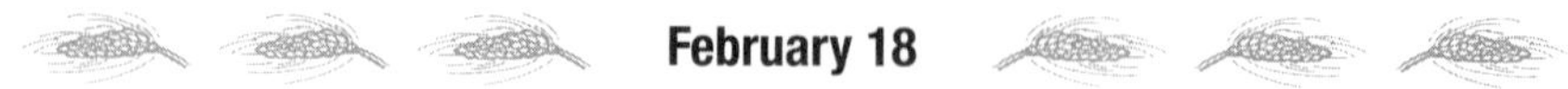

February 18

Song of Solomon 2:5; Genesis 2:24-25

Looking for Love in all the Right Places

"I'm about to faint with love" was the verse that attracted me to the card I gave my wife, Janeo, recently for Valentine's Day. Sound a little too hot or embarrassingly candid? Guess what, you can find it in Song of Solomon 2:5 (The Message)

And if you want to know what eros looks like, you don't have to read a racy book, watch a movie, or turn on the TV; just pick up your Bible and read aloud to each other the rest of the Song of Solomon. Warning: You might not get too far ...

As Christians, what grade would we give ourselves for acknowledging a biblical foundation of sexuality and for modeling that out? Have we forgotten that it was God who said that "a man should leave his father and mother and embrace his wife. They should become one flesh"? And that "The two of them, the man and his wife, were naked, but they felt no shame"? (Gen 2:24-25)

Few of us would admit to being transparent or articulate when it comes to this God-given gift of sexuality. We have a hard time talking to our children about it, and too often, even talking with our spouses. Let us remember that God gave us the precious gift to celebrate within the context of marriage – joyfully and richly.

Prayer: Thank you Lord for creating us the way You did. We have strengths, weaknesses, and a variety of other characteristics, but we also have the ability to love. For those of us who are, have been, or will be married, we thank you for great partnerships. Amen.

John and Janeo Greller
Retired Financial Administrator for NWC

This great couple gave a lot of very productive years to NWC – John in Finance and Janeo in the Theatre Dept. It was my privilege and pleasure to coach their son Michael in golf. Unfortunately for us, they have moved out west in their retirement to be closer to Michael and the rest of the family. We wish them all of God's best.

February 19

1 Corinthians 6:19-20

Smoking and Drinking

I guess I've been battling these two issues nearly all my life. My personal use of them was minimal. (Started and quit smoking when I was 12! I've had two beers in my life, and those were the result of a bet during my senior year in college, and I never have touched "hard liquor"). I'm not proud of those two episodes, but athletics were so important to me as a youth that I wouldn't do anything to jeopardize my ability to compete. Then as a teacher, coach, and especially as a dad, being a good role model took preeminence.

I still wish everyone would quit smoking and be teetotalers. These two bring so much grief into families – mine included. Smoking shortened the lives of my relatives and friends. Alcohol is a poison no one really needs. I'll keep battling the use of these as long as I can.

Please forgive me for "beating around the bush." Next time, I'll tell you what I really think!

Prayer: Control of our actions and our lives is so difficult at times. Please help each of us with whatever happens to be a difficulty. I know my weaknesses are just as big and just as bad as anyone else's, and we can't go on without Your help and each other's. Amen.

Dave

February 20

Revelation 3:20

Sallman's Vision

The great artist Warner Sallman, was inspired by this verse to paint the famous picture of "Christ at Heart's Door." What a fabulous picture, verse, and promise!

Study that picture a moment. Notice how the lighting and the door frame form a heart. Jesus has just knocked on this very sturdy door that has an observation grill, but no apparent latch on the outside. See how Jesus head is cocked to one side as He listens intently for someone (you?) to answer.

At this point take note of a couple other items added by the artist. See the birds nest and the thistles and weeds around this entrance? These may be indicative of inactivity and sins that are a part of our lives.

Is Jesus knocking at your heart's door now? He promised that He would come into your life – and He ALWAYS keeps His promises.

Prayer: Thank you Jesus for your vigil at my heart's door. I know I need you. Please come in and guide me the rest of the way. Amen.

Dave

 **February 21** 

Matthew 25:35-40

Matthew Speaks To All Of Us

Serving in public office is truly an honor and a privilege. So, it is with gratitude and appreciation we approach the impact we have on the lives of the people we serve. It is with humility we make the decisions which can affect so many, and with thanks I have been given an opportunity to serve as the 40th Governor of the great state of Iowa.

My faith has always been extremely important to me, and I believe we can all benefit by regularly worshiping God, asking for His guidance and thanking Him for His many blessings.

One of my favorite and most meaningful passages is from this chapter in the Gospel of Matthew.

For I was hungry ... I was thirsty ... I was a stranger ... I needed clothes ... I was sick ... I was in prison ... (What did or should we do?)

Then the righteous will answer Him. "Lord, when did we see you hungry... thirsty ... a stranger ... in need of clothing ... sick ... imprisoned?

The King will reply. "I tell you the truth, whatever you did for one of the least of these brothers of mine, you did for me."

These are inspiring words for me in both my public and private life, and I hope they provide meaning to you in your daily walk.

Prayer: Heavenly Father, help each of us this day to remember we are Your servants. Guide our words and our actions as we reach out to those in need. Amen.

Iowa Governor Chet Culver

Governor Chet was elected for the final 2 years of my term in the Senate. He is also a former teacher, married to Mari (lawyer), and they have two children. It gives me pleasure to call him "friend."

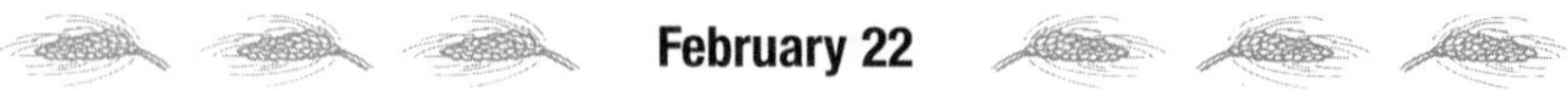

February 22

Deuteronomy 6

STORYTELLING... What's Your Story?

Looking at that title – teenagers, if your parents ever ask you that question after midnight, it's probably not a good thing.

A small child often asks his parent or grandparent to "tell me a story." The elder tells the story and the child listens, taking in every word. That's been going on for generations – many, many generations.

We all remember stories from childhood, school days, adolescence, adulthood, things you heard, and things you saw and experienced. I bet you know some story tellers. Every town has its share of storytellers and every family does too.

To be honest, we're all storytellers. We've all got a story to tell – some kind of story – all kinds of stories. You have your stories and I have mine. Some stories are unbelievable and some are unforgettable. Many of us have a lot of stories, and that's great, because stories make great teaching tools.

What do you want to add to your story today?

Prayer: Thank you Lord that we have heard Your story, and it changes our lives. Please help us this day to reach out and be a positive part of someone else's life story. How do You want me to do that? Amen.

Rob Miedema
Assistant Director of FCA in South Dakota.

I have known the Miedema family for a long time and Rob was the NW Iowa Director of FCA a few years ago. He has also been a teacher/coach and Church Youth Director. He's a fine man and great leader for young people. For the next 4 days Rob leads us on a "Storytelling Mission." Pray and support Rob and his ministry.

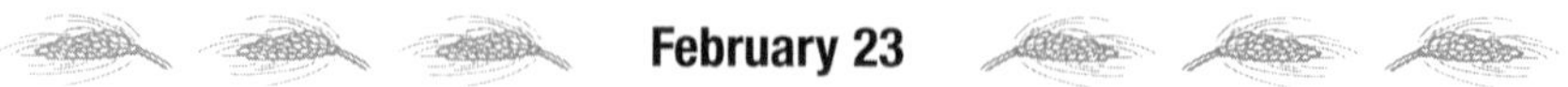

February 23

Acts 8:29-31

STORYTELLING... Stories Instruct

Some people are *known* as storytellers because they tell one every chance they get. These people have stories about their town, the weather, vacations, families, their kids and grandkids. They will make connections about Christmas and birthday celebrations, fishing and hunting expeditions – even stories about their pets, past sporting events at school or on television, and the Olympics. It doesn't make any difference whether they were observers or participants – they can tell an intriguing story about it.

A person's hands can tell a story – what type of work they do, or the life they've had.

A person's face can tell stories too – smiles, wrinkles, frowns, and the eyes.

My Dad is a storyteller. He tells lots of stories of his growing up on the farm during the Great Depression including the farm, the hard work, farming "by hand," planting, harvesting, putting hay up into the barn, farming with horses, milking cows by hand, and the first tiny tractors. I love my Dad and I love his stories.

Who's one of your favorite storytellers? Would today be a good time to contact that person and listen again?

Prayer: Thank you God for listening to our stories and helping us to write more chapters each day. Please help today's chapter include some special time with those we love and with You. Amen.

Rob Miedema

February 24

Acts 8:35

STORYTELLING... Stories Teach

It would be interesting to have all our grandparents and great-grandparents present to tell their stories. There would be stories about immigration – hard manual labor – and starting a new life in a new country.

So many times when I hear the hymn "Great Is Thy Faithfulness," I think of my grandparents. They had that great song played at their 50th anniversary. These were two plain hard-working farm folks. They loved God and knew that God was faithful.

It would be great to have all the missionaries and martyrs to be here with us – the Mother Teresas, Peters and Pauls – and hear them tell their stories of God at work. I know we can read about it, but to hear it "first hand" would be tremendous.

Examine some of your "Christian items." What kind of story do they tell? How about a church with a cross on it? Is the church brick, wood, painted white, and does it have a steeple? Do the people know they can go to your church building and get help, feel loved, receive compassion, understanding, and forgiveness? Hopefully, when we walk out of a church, people know our story. There is a hymn that's called "They'll know we are Christians by our …?" People must know we are Christians by our faith, our lives, and by our *love.*

Some stories speak for themselves. Think about the empty manger, the empty cross, and the empty tomb. What do these stories say to you?

Prayer: Heavenly Father, guide us through another day. Help us tell Your story whenever we see the opportunity. Amen.

Rob Miedema

February 25

Philemon 6

STORYTELLING... Bible Stories

Stories were very important in Bible times also. Most people couldn't read or write, so much of the Bible history – the people, places, and events – the work of God and the life of Christ – were all passed down in the form of stories. These stories were then passed on from generation to generation for centuries. This continues today in many ways.

Wouldn't you like to hear the first hand stories from Noah, Abraham, Moses, David, and Job to name a few? And then in the New Testament John the Baptist, John, Peter, Paul, and the many people that were personally healed by Jesus. Jesus was the best storyteller as He used parables (an earthly story with a heavenly message) continually to get His message across.

When we meet people, what kind of stories do we tell them? Not all stories have

So what story do you want to tell today? Will it only be name, address, job, hobby, and family? Isn't there much more?

Prayer: Each day our story gets a little longer. Please make today's chapter a meaningful one for You, me, and all with whom I associate. Amen.

Rob Miedema

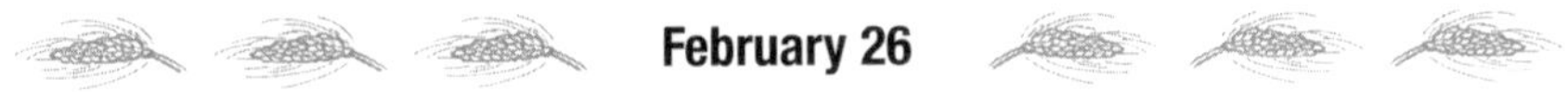

February 26

Matthew 13:3a

STORYTELLING... The Way HE Did It

How often do we tell others the story of our decision to follow Christ, and the stories of our faith? Or stories about God's goodness, abundance, His grace, and mercy in times of trouble? How about stories of healings, comfort in times of pain and sorrow, blessings that are steady and constant and NEW every day? As you contemplate this, here are some thoughts that I've heard or read concerning the topic:

What about our stories when we DON'T speak, and people ONLY see our lifestyles?

Our lifestyle may be the only "Bible" some person ever gets to "read."

People will remember our actions more than our words.

Recent stats show that the number of true believers and church-goers is much lower than it used to be. In many communities it's around 25-40% attending. Many people that have dropped out of churches have never gone back –and their kids have NEVER gone. Many people, young and old, are unchurched and without direction. That's where you and I come in!

God put us on this earth, He didn't have to. I believe He put us here to fellowship with Him and also with each other. We need to help each other, and to be a witness. We can't just live here, enjoy life, and sit in pews. We're not always called to be successful or comfortable, but we are called to be obedient, loving, and faithful.

Many people just won't hear the message or know what to do with it unless people tell (live) their stories. I pray that you may be active in sharing your faith so that YOU may have a full understanding of every good thing we have in Christ. It's not just the hearer who is blessed. We all are, when we share the Good News.

This is indeed the challenge before us – let's encourage and challenge each other to seek opportunities to tell our story – to tell THE story.

Prayer: Thank you Lord for being the great storyteller, and giving us such a great story to tell. Please help us do it, and do it today. Amen.

Rob Miedema

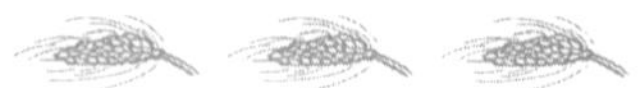

February 27

Proverbs 17:22

A Cheerful Heart

In a Bible study my wife and I attended, we studied this verse and it has since given me a whole new outlook. As a law enforcement officer, I deal with a lot of unpleasantness. In other words, I deal extensively with other people's problems. When they come to see me, something has gone wrong in their life. More often than not, they have a negative attitude created by the situation they are in. I call on this verse in Proverbs often to help me deal with the negative attitudes and problems the individual might be facing.

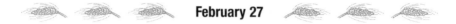

A cheerful heart/positive attitude, no matter what the circumstance, is not only good medicine for me both mentally and physically, it is very often good medicine for the person facing the adversities life has dealt them. In the book of Proverbs, the Lord uses Solomon to give us advice on handling various situations that occur in everyday life. God has something to say about every aspect of your life. Look for His guidance and direction in the decisions you must make every day, pray often, and remember Proverbs 17:22. *A cheerful heart is good medicine, but a crushed spirit dries up the bones.*

Prayer: Dear God, it's not always easy to be cheerful, or even optimistic, but You can help us through any situation. Please help us recognize where we can be useful and bring some cheer into other peoples' lives. Amen.

Paul Adkins
Chief of Police, Sioux Center

Paul and his wife Carol are members of Central and I really appreciate the way he uses his office and position to show our youth, as well as any others, that the police are there to help and can also be part of fun things. I remember him as a little second-baseman, playing for Floyd Valley as I was umpiring. He was a hustling and scrappy player that gave all he had. He does the same thing in his present job and working for others.

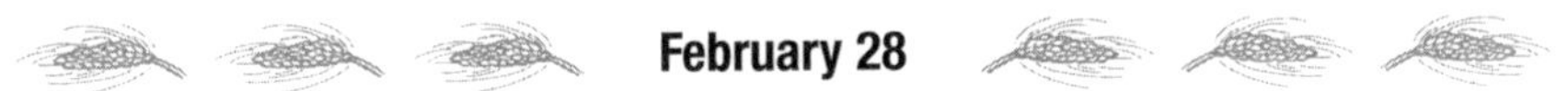

February 28

Ecclesiastes 8:1; Mark 10:21-23; Luke 12:16-21

"People Are More Important Than Things"

The first person I heard make this statement is a good friend, and a former pastor of mine, Wes Kiel. Wes had many good messages, but none influenced me more than this phrase. When you practice thinking about the effects of any action on people, it can change perceptions and outcomes.

So many times we get these two reversed and we use people to get things. I'm not saying it is always wrong to use a person, but he/she should always be made aware of it. For example, I think back to the time I wanted to use a famous athlete to introduce a speaker that was an authority on drug abuse. I told the athlete that I wanted to use him to attract a larger crowd of teens to this speaker. After deliberating for a few days, he called and declined. That was okay too and I understood.

Do any of you ever want to be used, and under what circumstances? Think about it.

Prayer: Thank you for using us. Please continue to guide and direct our lives, and our relationship with others. In comparison to the rest of the world, You have made us very wealthy as we consider our earthly possessions. Show us more ways to share. Amen.

Dave

March 1

1 Corinthians 12:28

Rev. Bob Vander Schaaf

Bob owned Floyd Hatchery in Alton when I first met him. I was a kid that loved all kinds of animals and birds and especially baby chicks. I was in the 5th grade when Bob first hired me to help. My salary? 15 cents an hour. (Remember, this was 1949!) I did any kind of work involving chickens and worked for Bob into my college years. (My top salary was $1.25 per hour – he paid me what I was worth – not what I thought I was worth!) He was the perfect boss, because he would never let the work interfere with my sports practices and games, or any other school or family functions. He was also a great personal example, because he never swore, smoked, drank, and always talked about the importance of family and the Christian Faith. I learned a great deal from Bob about dealing with people.

It was only a slight surprise to me when Bob sold the hatchery and went to seminary. He was destined to become a preacher and he was a good one. His Bible knowledge, sense of humor, and caring for people allowed him to be richly used in the ministry.

Bob taught me much by being a consummate Christian role model and father. He continues to be a great supporter and friend.

Prayer: Thank you Lord for having a plan for each of our lives. Thanks for the way you prepare us to minister for you. Please continue to bless Bob and all those "men of the cloth" that minister to each of us. Amen.

Dave

March 2

John 14:1-4; Proverbs 3:6

God's Promises

After a relatively long life of owning a hatchery, raising a family, becoming a preacher, and then living in retirement, I appreciate God's many promises. There have been many hardships but also many joys. No one could have a better wife, kids, and grandchildren. I have been very blessed.

But, as I write this, I am in my 89th year, and I can't do many of the things I once could. Isn't it great to know that our Lord has gone "to prepare a place for us"? And it has "many mansions" (rooms). God always keeps His promises, so I know what lies ahead. As great as this life has been, I'm anxious to see what He has prepared. There are so many loved ones I want to see again. You know what? I'm going to be looking for you too! May you always acknowledge Him and may your roads always be straight. God Bless!

Prayer: Dear Lord, we do thank you for all you have prepared for us. Continue to bless us as we keep traveling towards your destination. Amen.

Rev. Bob Vander Schaaf

March 3

I Thessalonians 5:16-18; Romans 8:28; Joshua 24:15

Live With The End In Sight

Being the Head Coach of a college men's basketball team involves much more than "X's and O's," and scoreboard wins and losses. The character growth of each of the team members is imperative. Basketball is a great tool to help achieve this goal!

This past year I challenged each player with the following four character builders to be considered:

1. How am I going to let the events in and around basketball shape my Kingdom Character?
2. In every change/bump/disappointment/victory I will ask "How does God want to use this to shape me for marriage/parenting/future service?"
3. Will I recognize in any situation, if God closes one door, HE will always open another for my Character Growth?
4. If God is the Center of my life, my life will be On Center and this will free me from blaming/complaining/ and squirting out negativity on those around me.

As important as games are none are as important as the young men that play them. It is our desire to see young men grow into mature men who will focus on their faith, not their feelings – to see young men grow into men who focus on the finish, not their feelings. When we focus on our feelings we become inconsistent. When we focus on our faith and the finish we become much more consistent and dependable.

The name of the game is character formation and character transformation – for myself, my family, our coaching staff, our players, and the future families of our players. Fame is fleeting – Character Lasts!

Prayer: Thank you Jesus for always being dependable and consistent. Help us become the kind of men and women that You can use to help others. Character counts with You and all of your of people. Amen.

Coach Kris and Ann Korver
Head Basketball Coach, NWC

March 4

Ephesians 2:8-9; Romans 5:6-8; Philippians 3:11; 2 Corinthians 12:9

What's Your Daily Routine?

My daily routine is to read a portion of one of R. B. Thieme's booklets. Currently it is the one titled "The Unfailing Love of God." Within this booklet are many Bible verses of reference that I read. I also enjoy the books by Fleming Rutledge, a female Episcopalian rector, who is on a nationwide speaking tour.

I gravitate to the writers and preachers who have studied the scripture from the original languages and interpret it accordingly. The main theme is one that gives me peace in my life. That's Faith and Grace. I will never be good enough to merit heaven. I have stumbled and erred too many times. But, like Paul and David, two of the best examples of men who God forgave, accepted and loved, I humbly, by Faith, accept His grace and forgiveness.

Prayer: Dear Lord, Your grace is sufficient for each of us. Thanks for loving us unconditionally, in spite of ourselves. Amen.

Jim Kaat

A former great major league pitcher, Jim pitched in four different decades (50's -80's) for 6 different teams. He won 16 Golden Gloves, named to the All-Star Team 3 times, won the World Series with the Cards in 1982, won a total of 283 games with a 3.45 ERA. Jim was a great announcer for the Yankees and still works for YES network. His book "Still Pitching" is a great one. He's been a friend since he visited Sioux Center and NWC back in the '60's and spoke in Chapel. His sister is another close friend, Mil (Kaat) Vander Beek.

March 5

Psalms 51:10

Take The High Road

A balanced stance is a key ingredient for success in sports – a golf stance, a defensive stance in basketball, a hitter's stance at the plate, etc. However, as important as the right stance is in an athletic event, it is even more critical in life. Our life's stance is the set of attitudes, assumptions and expectations that we hold. It's the way we consistently look at people, events and circumstances; whether we tend to be trusting or suspicious, cheerful or gloomy, optimistic or pessimistic, gracious or selfish to list a few.

Our life's stance can be influenced by a number of factors, but there is one aspect of our frame of reference over which we have total control. That factor is simply the decision to take the high road in our journey through life. David understood the importance of a clean heart when he pleaded with God, *Create in me a clean heart...* When our motives are spotless, when our heart is pure, we can begin to live a steadfast life that reflects the will of God.

What does it mean to take the high road? John C. Maxwell in "Leadership Wired" suggests that it is very simple. *Don't keep score. Forgive others quickly. Learn to serve. Don't get even.* It's an amazing road to travel, but it is certainly the road less traveled. It requires us to think and do things that are not natural or common. The good news is that when we deliberately choose to travel the high road, we become instruments of grace to others and recipients of grace for ourselves.

Prayer: Create in us a pure heart, O God. Allow us to be an instrument on Earth in furthering Your Kingdom as we live a life that You expect of us. In your Holy Name we pray, Amen.

Les and Bev Douma
Former Head Basketball Coach and Athletic Director at NWC
Presently the Mayor of Orange City

March 6

Jeremiah 31:24-26

Restful Sleep

"Before you go to bed, give all your troubles to God. He will be up all night anyway."

This is the advice on a plaque affixed to my refrigerator. All of us, at one time or another, take our troubles and cares to bed with us. Scripture has many passages of comfort when you're feeling down or living through low times.

Notably are the words Jesus spoke most often, "*Come unto me all you who labor, and are heavy laden, and I will give you rest.*" (Matthew 11:28)

Prayer: Thank you Lord for untroubled sleep. Amen.

Eda Kroon

Eda is a retired Bank worker and a lifelong member of Central Reformed. Jams and jellies and fudge. (Hint – Hint) It is always worthwhile to listen to what she says. I value her friendship a great deal.

March 7

Psalm 92:14; Proverbs 20:29

Aging

Interesting process, this aging. Oh, I know all the sayings about "it beats the alternative" and "it's not for sissies" etc. etc. etc .. But it's also exciting! I've never wanted to go back to any time in my life. I enjoyed being a kid, high school, college ... and all the decades since. I just started my 9th decade! Right now is pretty good too. Do I qualify for saying I lived in the "olden days"? Let's see – born in 1939 ... before television, space travel, computers, and lots of other stuff. I hope that some of you younger folks will someday be able to also say you lived in the "olden days."

I'm amazed at all the things I've witnessed. Wars, atomic bombs, assassinations, and loss of loved ones, on the one side. But think of the amazing positives – IPods, computer games, replacement parts (I have two new hips), improved communications, the internet ("thanks to Al Gore!"), cars that start in winter, great music reproduction, people live longer, and a myriad of family and friends.

Let's start today and show more appreciation for each day (and all the things in it) the Good Lord gives us.

Prayer: Thank you Jesus for the gift of life. We are so blessed with all of things and people around us. Please keep us safe and guide all of our leaders and those that advise them. Amen.

Dave

March 8

Lamentations 2:19

Pour Out Your Heart

Although I never focused much on the first and last parts of this verse, it is the middle portion, " ... *Pour out your heart like water in the presence of the Lord. Lift up your hands to Him for the lives of your children ...*" that became very familiar to me as my kids were growing up. For 15 years I met on a weekly basis with a handful of other praying-moms to come before the Lord with our joys, cares, and concerns, lifting our hands to Him for the sake of our children. Pouring out our hearts before the Lord with each other became a necessary part of my week, as in doing so I was cleansed, refreshed, and renewed. Many times our prayer requests seemed a bit trite ... Should we bother our God, the same God who causes the earth to orbit the sun, with our simple prayer requests of helping our children remember an assignment, or that they have a good day at school?

Our loving Father is so great and mighty that each and every request of ours is important to Him. Perhaps more importantly is God's desire to hear from us. The author of Lamentations doesn't say "when" or "if" you pour out your heart, but rather commands, "*Pour out your heart* ***LIKE WATER***" – Water! A perfect word that was placed right in the middle of this verse to reflect upon. Water is essential for the survival of all known forms of life. Water cleans my dirty laundry and the mud off my floor. I use it for cooking, and it makes my lawn grow. We bathe in water and at the end of a long day, how relaxing and refreshing a nice hot shower can be. Water is everywhere. It flows freely, and it cleanses, refreshes, sustains, and renews us. As you pour out your hearts like water to the Lord, may God's cleansing power refresh and renew you too.

Prayer: Thank you Lord for caring enough about each of us that You want to know our every concern. Continue to guide us to work with each other and always seek Your will. Cleanse us and renew us this day. Amen.

Shari and Gregg Boone
Members of Central Reformed

Gregg is a life-long member of Central and played golf for me at SCHS. He is a banker and Shari is a music teacher, particularly the strings.

March 9

John 15:5

Molded Clay

I have struggled with an inferiority complex all my life, coming from a large family with a lot of give and take. I was always a follower in school and asking God why. I had a talent but never believed in it myself – until I was older.

I prayed many times for God to make me useable and then to enable me to do what He asked. Learning to trust Him was the key, and accepting the fact that even though I would never be able to do what some of my friends could do – the talents He gave me were just as important in His sight.

He had to take my broken vessel and make it into something useable for Him. As one of my grandson's says when referring to Philippians, "I can do all things through Christ who gives me strength." My favorite verse became the one in John 15. Jesus is the vine, and I am only a branch – if I stay connected to Him, I can do many things.

Prayer: Dear God, keep us attached to You this day, and use us for Your good. With You by our side, much can be done. Amen.

Gladie and Dave Vander Berg
Owners of Vander Berg Furniture and Homes

Dave and Gladie are part of our 6-couple Saturday Night Group. They have become dear friends and are always ready to help.

March 10

1 Peter 5:7

Cast Your Cares...

Thirty-one years ago, our daughter came into this world twelve weeks early. She weighed only 3½ pounds. For two days she was stable and her prognosis seemed good. I thanked God for this beautiful child and felt like "**I**" had everything under control. On a Saturday night I went to bed around 9:30 after my husband left for the motel. Around 10:00 I decided to walk down to the neonatal unit to check on her. The curtains were closed which was an ominous sign that one of the babies was in trouble. I peeked in the door and saw the staff hovered around my daughter's bed trying to resuscitate her. The doctor came out and told me to call my husband back to the hospital right away.

Walking back to my room, I said to God, "I can't do this" and turned her life over to Him. Eleven surgeries and many challenges later God has carried her through the darkest and brightest days.

This is one of the few things in my life that I have completely and unconditionally given to God. The reward was not the daughter I unoriginally expected – but a blessing and miracle I could never have imagined.

Prayer: Dear God, we thank you so much that You can do the things we can only dream of. Please continue to strengthen us and enable us to reach out to others as You reach down to us. Amen.

Maureen Freed
Chair-person Village Northwest Board

Maureen and I have served on the "Village Board" for a number of years. She has been a great leader and I consider her a personal friend. We need more people like her.

March 11

Romans 3:23; 1 John 1:8; John 14:1-6; Galatians 3:26; Romans 2:10; Acts 4:12; Hebrews 13:5

The Way

First, let us think a moment about our predicament, our basic need. By nature and by conduct we are sinners, lost sinners. The Bible tells us that we are sinners (Romans).

Young or old, rich or poor, we are all sinners. There is no difference between us. Every soul has accumulated a mass of sins or guilt that separates us from God and disqualifies us from heaven. We are in desperate need of help. (1 John)

But there is good news! In the evening shortly before His crucifixion, Jesus gathered His disciples around Himself preparing them for events which were about to happen, including His soon departure from the world to return to the Father (John). Please take note of Jesus response to Thomas' question.

<u>Jesus is the way, the only way.</u>

He is the way to reconciliation with the Father because Jesus loved us so much, even when we were yet sinners. He was willing to assume our sins and guilt, willing to suffer the terrible agony of crucifixion so that He might be for us The Way to full recognition with the Father, The Way for us to walk pilgrimages of life, and finally The Way to enter the heavenly home.

By faith in Christ we even now are the children of God (Galatians) and, therefore, also heirs of eternal life and glory. Faith in Him, the Redeemer, is the <u>only</u> way to our desired destination. (Romans and Acts)

But we are still pilgrims here on earth. Someone might ask whether the words of Jesus, "*I am the Way*" have any significance now so far as our pilgrimage is concerned. Indeed they do. He is also The Way for our daily walk and march. Here is the manner William Barclay describes it.

"What did Jesus mean when He said, 'I am the Way?' Suppose we are in a strange town and we ask for directions. Suppose the person asked says: 'Take the first turn to the right, and the second to the left. Cross the square and go past the church and take the third turn on the right and the road you want is the fourth road on the left.' If that happens, the chances are that we will be lost before we get half way. But suppose the person we ask says: 'Come, I'll go with you.' In that case that person to us is the way and we cannot miss it." That is what Jesus does for us. He not only gives us advice, and direction, and counsel. He does do that through His love letter to us – the Bible. He also goes with us. He assures us, "*I will never leave nor forsake you.*" (Hebrews) He takes us by the hand and leads us and directs us personally every day. He does not tell us about the way – He is The Way.

Let us walk in this Way as we daily continue our pilgrim journey, loving Him, fully trusting in Him, obeying Him, praising Him, serving Him. With Him we shall be safe and when our journey here on earth is over, He will welcome us home to be with Him forever. He loves us so very much. We must love Him too.

Prayer: Thank you, Lord Jesus for providing The Way for each of us. Continue to go with us as we do our best to follow You. Amen.

Rev. Henry Eggink

March 12

James 1:22

Just Do It

I asked a group of high school students about their thoughts on "Christianity." A high percentage brought up the word "hypocrite." Why? Because they don't see us live out our faith. Our Christianity has to be so much more than making it to church on Sunday morning and then living a totally different lifestyle the other 243 hours of the week.

The Bible gives us some concrete ways to live out our faith 24/7. Ephesians 5:25 tells us that we as Christian men especially need to love our wives like Christ loved the church. We need to conduct our businesses like Christ is our CEO (Colossians 3:23). John 15:9-17 outlines how we must love others, not just tolerate them, but love like Christ loved.

If we do what the Word says out of love for Christ and not out of duty, we will be the contagious Christians that others desire to be like.

If joy is complete, if we experience the peace that transcends all understanding (Philippians 4:7), we will not be able to walk away from the passage in James. We will "Just Do It!"

Prayer: Lord, help me to live like Jesus so that others will also want to do what Your Word says. Help me to be a witness for You! Amen.

Kelly Hulstein
Board of Directors of ATLAS of Sioux Center

Kelly was one of my students at SCHS. It has been a blessing to watch him as husband, father, and church worker. His leadership with the ATLAS organization is producing much fruit.

March 13

1 Corinthians 14:20

Peer Pressure

Should I or should I not?

Last summer some of my friends and I were playing football. After a while we decided it was getting boring (don't tell Dad!). The other guys said they wanted to go to Alco and run around and eventually get kicked out. I really didn't know exactly what to do. So, I went along even though I knew my parents had told me to "stay in one place." I wish I had known the verse in Corinthians at that time. It reads, "Brothers, stop thinking like children. In regard to evil be infants, but in your thinking be adults." We did manage to get kicked out.

Since that time I have been asked to go to Alco again. I managed to get my friends to do something else equally "fun," and I didn't have to break my parent's rules to do it. Now they won't let me in to Alco without my parents. That's because I didn't do what my parents said. I found out I don't have to be rebellious to have fun.

Prayer: Dear Lord, it's not always easy to take an unpopular stand. Please help us to think straight and make good decisions. Amen.

Ethan Achterhoff
#1 Grandson!

Ethan is a special young man and we love him dearly. He starts his freshman year in 2010 and it has been a joy to watch him grow and mature. Dot and I couldn't be prouder nor love him more. Today is his birthday – let him know you care. "E"– never forget how important and how loved you are by so many people! (Isn't that true for all of us?)

March 14

Jeremiah 29:11

God Has A Plan For You

As our youngest daughter held and looked down at her new nephew for the first time, she commented, "What unlimited potential you have! You have everything in front of you ... an exciting future!"

As parents watching our children grow, we formulate plans in our minds for their future. These plans often include developing good relationships with us and others and becoming involved in a variety of activities, and in seeking to discover their gifts and talents. We are excited when they are successful in meeting their goals and we hurt when they are disappointed. Sometimes our visions for our children become reality and sometimes they do not, but we continue to love them no matter what.

As our heavenly father, God sees in us our unlimited potential and has a marvelous plan for our lives. He created us in His image and we are His children. He yearns for us to love Him, to develop a close personal relationship with Him, and to use the gifts and talents He has given us to fulfill our lives and to further His kingdom. But above all else, and in times of joy and sorrow, He gives unconditional love and encourages us by reminding us, For I know the plans I have for you, plans to prosper you and not to harm you, plans to give you hope and a future.

Prayer: Lord, help us to reach the potential you created in us to further Your kingdom. Amen.

Eileen Vander Wilt
Middle School Teacher

Eileen and Dale have 3 beautiful daughters and several grandchildren. They live a joyful life and continue to be leaders in our church.

March 15

Isaiah 40:31; 1 Corinthians 9:24

Our Race Of Life

On race day, as marathon runners stand at the starting line waiting for the gun to go off to begin the race; many thoughts go through their minds. While some will be thinking, "I am ready. Let's get started." Many others will be thinking, "Have I trained enough? I hope I can finish." Often the negative thoughts have a tendency to outweigh the positive and certainly affect the outcome of the race.

In our race of life, we may also have doubts and challenges that will attempt to detract us from finishing strong. But if we look to God as our coach, we do not have to dwell on the negatives. We can be confident that no matter how short or long our race is, we can lean on Him to carry us through. No matter the obstacles that are placed in front of us, with His help we are able to overcome them. Through God's word, He assures us that He is always by our side encouraging us and lifting us up. We can run the race of life knowing that by putting our trust and confidence in Him as our "coach", we can run and not be weary, we can walk and not be faint, and we will be able to finish "strong," winning the prize God has placed before us. Let us put our trust in Him and run in such a way that we will win and receive the prize!

Prayer: Lord, help us to put our trust in You and run our race with confidence. Amen.

Dale Vander Wilt
Banker and former High School Math Teacher and Track Coach at SCHS

Dale and his wife Eileen are members of Central Reformed. It was my pleasure to work alongside Dale at Athletic Director when he was the Head Track Coach. He was one fine coach. He also helped a great deal with the FCA and is a great supporter.

March 16

Proverbs 20:12

Eyes and Ears

I have experienced all of the following: Multi-tasking while another person is speaking, continuing to do the all-important paperwork as the student is talking directly to me, getting ready for my words of wisdom as another speaks, and hearing I told you that but you weren't listening.

God created us with two eyes, two ears, and one mouth. I think He meant for us to use the mouth less than our ears and eyes.

Let's give that a conscientious effort today.

Prayer: God, when I listen, You provide the fruits of the spirit (love, joy, peace, patience, kindness, self-control, gentleness, goodness, and faithfulness). Thank you, and please help me practice at least two of those today. Amen.

Dot

March 17

2 Chronicles 6:41

Good Ole Saint Patrick

Will you wear some green today? I suppose I will since I'll do my devotions before I dress for the day and that will remind me it's St. Patrick's Day. Green was my mom's favorite color – I guess that means more to me than this day, although we've been celebrating this day since 1762.

Do you know what the good ole Saint did? A lot of it is mystery, even when he lived. Most argue that it was the late 300's. He was a missionary that was captured and made a slave in Ireland. He escaped and returned to Britain where he became an ordained Bishop. He returned to Ireland and served the Church in the very country that had enslaved him. He also banished all the snakes in Ireland for some reason. I didn't even know they had a lot of snakes there. I also couldn't find the "green" connection and why alcohol is such a big item for this day. Maybe you want to do a little more research.

Hey! Today tell people to be happy, wear some green, avoid snakes, honor our real Savior, and share the peace.

Prayer: Lord you give us many interesting things to do, see, and celebrate on this great earth. Help us always to honor You and Your very special people. Amen.

Dave

March 18

Revelation 7:9-12

John's Vision

God's future family is so diverse. We speak different languages, eat different foods, and play different sports. Yet, we are all brothers and sisters in Christ. We have one Heavenly Father.

I am often grieved that while we are on earth God's family is so divided. We avoid worshiping together because our preferences are different. We separate from each other because we cannot agree on matters of little eternal significance. Often we miss out on family gatherings because we cannot admit we are wrong. We are all part of God's family on earth, but it doesn't always look that way.

John's vision is indeed exciting. It assures me that we won't always be a divided family. One day we all, as forgiven sinners, will gather at God's throne. We will sing praises to our God.

Until then, we have a mandate to promote unity among God's people. They are in the high rises of overcrowded cities. They are in the mud huts of the Sudan. They are in rehabs and prisons throughout our nations. They are everywhere!

It is my prayer that as we see John's vision of our future family, it will have an impact on how we treat our present family, whether they are within the walls of our home or in our world.

Prayer: Lord, help me to see people as part of my eternal family. Let us continually grow closer together in love and understanding. Give us compassion and forgiveness. Amen.

Rod and Carol De Kruyf
Members of Central Reformed

These two are ministers in their own right. Rod ministers to many addicted people and leads them to Christ and another life. He and Carol also have a ministry at Crown Pointe in Sioux Center. These two don't just talk – they put their words into ACTION. I've never seen them without a smile and cheerful greeting. God bless them.

March 19

Matthew 6:25-34

Worry

If I were to name the one thing that I have battled with the most throughout my 25 years, it would have to be worry. I am a worrier. Whether it's dwelling on events of the past or uncertainty about the future, worry is something I battle daily.

In Jr. & Sr. High School, and at NWC, basketball was undoubtedly what caused me to worry the most. Missed shots – that is where my attention was focused. I wasn't worried about missing shots before I took them; it was *afterwards* that those misses really got to me. For example, if I had made ten shots and missed four, those four shots drove me absolutely crazy. My life, for a period of time (usually until the next game, and a chance to do better) revolved around my thoughts of those missed shots. The perfectionist within me took control of my life, and I was always worried that I wasn't playing or shooting the way that I was capable of.

Now my playing days are behind me. But my tendency to worry certainly is not. I worry about the future, since I don't know what it may hold. For the first time in my life I don't have a major long-term goal that I am pursuing. No longer a basketball player, I don't have those goals that caused me to spend so many hours in the gym seeking the next victory, championship, and being the absolute best player I could be. I don't know what God has in store for me; I don't know where He is leading or what lies ahead. That is scary, especially for someone who always likes to have a specific plan and goal in mind.

But I know that is not the end of the story. I know I don't NEED to worry. I know that God has a great and wonderful plan for my life. I know that He will use me in ways that I cannot imagine as yet. I know what I need to do – I need to trust Him. If I hand all my worries over to Him, He will gladly take over. But that's easier said than done. Each day, I try to rely on God's promises and I do my best to let Him lead me down the path that He knows is best for me. I still struggle, but I know that I am not going through this alone; God is with me, and I can fully trust Him.

Prayer: Dear Lord, please take the worry from my heart, remove the uncertainty from my mind. Help me to trust in You more and more each day. Help me to know and truly believe that I don't need to worry because You will take care of me always. Lord, I know that You have a plan for my life and that Your plan is the best one for me. Even if I don't know what the future holds, You do. Help me to fully rely on You when I am feeling scared or anxious. You are an awesome God. Thank you for loving me and protecting me always. Amen.

Deb Remmerde

Deb is a 4-time 1st Team All-American. She averaged over 28 points per game for her career and helped win two National Championships, while earning the NAIA National Player of the Year honor. She holds a great number of records and is the best free throw shooter ever. She made 133 consecutive free throws in college competition and that is the best at ALL levels of basketball male and female! She's made over 100 consecutive 3-pointers (in practice) which I think is incredible. 162 consecutively is her record. She is also a 2-time Scholastic All-American with a near perfect 4-point average. Deb is presently pursuing a higher degree at SDSU in Brookings and assisting with the Women's Basketball Team. Suppose maybe she can help them with their shooting?!

March 20

Romans 10:9-10

That's All It Takes

It's really pretty simple, isn't it? It doesn't say do lots of good works, don't swear, and smile a lot or anything else. Just believe, confess, and know that Christ died for you and rose again. It doesn't then say that you might be saved – it says you **shall** be saved! We can't earn our salvation – but we know now how to get it and accept it.

Although insuring salvation looks easy, and it is – living the Christian life is a real test. That's why we need each other, God's Word, and a spirit of thankfulness. It's our thanks for what He has done for us (died on the cross), that makes us want to do good things for Him and for others.

May you enjoy your Christian walk and feel secure in His love.

Prayer: Dear Lord, thank you for all you did for us so many years ago. All of our sins have been committed since then and you have forgiven them. Help us forgive ourselves and others. Motivate us to be the kind of men and women you want us to be. Amen.

Dave

March 21

Philippians 3:7-8

Identity

What is my identity? I always thought I knew. In my mind, I know who I am in Christ – I know He is my all in all. But how do I know that's really what I believe? A trying experience during my junior year of college caused me to reevaluate where my true identity lies.

I enjoy shooting baskets, and ever since middle school, people have told me what a great shooter I am. Running down the court, the defender would call out, "I got shooter" and close out on me. Looking back, I can see that as life progressed, I took more and more pleasure and solace in this identity.

However, all of a sudden in the middle of my junior year of college basketball, I could not shoot anymore! I was shooting poorly in games so I would go in and shoot and shoot and shoot to get back into my rhythm. But no matter how hard I practiced and tried, I kept missing. It was so frustrating because I had worked the entire last year no, my entire life, and now I was *getting worse*! It was so hard for me because I felt I was being an unreliable teammate, who could not perform as I should. I was letting my teammates down and was angry at God for taking away what I had worked so hard for.

It was a lie. I *am not* a shooter – it is just something I *do*! There is a huge difference. Who I am is not defined by what I do. My task is to simply lay my will down and let Christ reign in me. My identity is not found in how I *perform* but in what Christ has done for me. I had been using my identity as a shooter to find fulfillment in life – I had let it become my identity and life source. God revealed my idolatry to me and gave me the renewed focus of letting my life flow out of its true Source!

Prayer: Dear Father, reveal the idols in my life – the things and people in which I place my identity. You are my identity and my life and will love me no matter what. Teach me to daily submit to You and let You live through me. Thank you for Your grace. Amen.

Becca Hurley
Two-time NAIA All-American. NWC National Tournament MVP for the National Championship Team

March 22

Philippians 4:4

True Joy

Athletics can provide many exciting and happy times throughout a season or athletic career. Scoring points, breaking records, winning championships ... it doesn't get much better than that, right? In my own experience, those are all things that made me happy for a time, but I found out they don't last. The next generation of players comes and scores more points, breaks your records, and continues to win championships. That is why it has become so important that I do not seek happiness in the events of my life, but rather to experience the joy in Christ that will remain consistent through the good times and the hard times.

What a privilege it is to have Christ live with me. How can I not be joyful in all things when I reflect on my holy, powerful, and majestic creator? God wants to make His presence known to all people, and if we allow Him to take root in our hearts, we can experience His true joy. That way when we face unpleasant circumstances, or things really go our way, we can rejoice that no matter what the outcome, God is present in our hearts.

Prayer: Dear God. Make a home in my heart so it will be filled with your presence. Let my heart know true joy, so that my attitude will not be based on my circumstances, but in the full knowledge that You are my personal Lord and Savior. Amen.

Jaime Woudstra

Jaime is a 3-time All-American and also played an integral part in winning a National Championship for NWC. She played both ends of the floor exceptionally well, she had to, and her Dad was the Coach. Jaime works in the financial world and is located in Denver.

March 23

John 6:37, 40; Revelation 3:20; Luke 15:10

Salvation Applied and Received

Victoriously the Risen Savior has returned to Glory. But He has not forgotten the needy sinner whom He loves and for whom He died. Mysteriously (mysterious to us but not to Him) through the Holy Spirit, He touches, moves and speaks to our minds and hearts. Perhaps you have felt that touch of His love in your heart. As He spoke to the needy when He sojourned here on earth, He still speaks to us, graciously calling them and us to Himself. (Review the passages in John and Revelation)

The Savior comes to us with His call of love, with His gracious invitation to open the door of our hearts allowing Him to take full possession there. He awaits our response. We cannot be passive longer. We must act.

His invitation is personal. No one else can speak for us. This is the greatest the most important decision or choice we shall ever make. It is the first step, the most significant step, in the conversion process. Fullness of life here and life eternal hang upon it.

This choice is urgent. Perhaps we have been confronted with it before but we fail to respond to it affirmatively, we brushed it off at least temporarily. Let us not do that again. "This is the day of salvation, the acceptable time." Tomorrow may be too late. There may not be another opportunity. Just say, "Jesus, I come to You. I accept Your invitation. I open the door of my life to You. Please come in and take charge. I love You. Be my Savior and Lord; my only hope for time and eternity."

A glorious new life has begun! Jesus assures us in these words we read in John. And we may be sure that the angels in heaven are rejoicing because you have responded to the Savior's invitation as you have done. The passage in Luke verifies that.

Prayer: Thank you for Your saving grace. As we take this step help us to walk the walk. Amen.

Rev. Henry Eggink

March 24

1 Peter 5:7

Second Chances

I was born into a loving and caring family with a Christian atmosphere. At about the age of 30 I decided the world owed me a little more. I chose to try alcohol. After my first experience with it, little did I realize that one day I would become an alcoholic. I struggled with an alcoholic life style for 25 years, and many times asked God for help. But my prayers seemed to go unanswered.

The miracle I was looking for happened when I quit trying to negotiate with God on how to fix my problem. The solution was simple. No bargaining, just complete surrender. I was 54 years old when this miracle took place and because of it, I exchanged 25 years of fear, discontent and chaos for 25 years of serenity, comfort, and most of all, a beautiful relationship with God. What a deal!

Prayer: God, thank you for second chances, because of Your grace, I get to start over every day. Amen.

Wayne Juffer
Retired Mail Carrier and full-time Christian worker
He's a life-long member of Central Reformed

They don't come any better than Wayne. He has a heart of gold and is the complete testimony to the fact that "Jesus changes lives!"

March 25

Proverbs 24:3-4

There's No Place Like Home

"There's no place like home, there's no place like home." You remember Judy Garland's magic words that would take her out of Oz and back home to Kansas.

What makes a house a home'? It's not the size of the house, or the furnishings. It's more than drapes, carpet and a T.V. Even if your house burned to the ground, your home wouldn't be destroyed.

Your home is the people who live in your house. It's the memories you have and the character of those people. A home is not built on what we have or don't have, but on what we are.

Every home has a different personality. I believe the wife and mother usually sets the tone for the home. Her moods affect the entire household. There have been times when I've wished it wasn't true, but I've discovered that it is.

This passage in Proverbs speaks of "Wisdom", Understanding", "Knowledge", and 'Treasures." I notice that there is no mention of money. I don't believe the last line is talking about antiques. Treasures are things money can't buy. Things like; watching your baby take his first step, listening to your child say "ma-ma" or "da-da," laughing so hard at the dinner table about something that happened that day that you choke on a sip of water, answering questions like "Mom, how do you know if you're in love?"

Treasures are beautiful moments that happen every day when we look for them, as we put Christ first in our homes.

Prayer: Dear God, we're so happy You are in our homes. Help us to continue to build memories, love, and a place where all are welcome and want to be, especially You. Amen.

Pat Estes
Proprietor of Pat's Jewelry

Pat and Bill have been our neighbors and friends for over 40 years. They are a great couple and have raised a mighty fine family of Christians.

March 26

Matthew 6:33; Luke 12:31

Work

I hate to tell you how many times I put my work above everything else in my life at the time. I know it's supposed to be God, family, and then whatever priorities may come along, but that word "successful" always got in the way. I wanted to be a great player, a great teacher, a great coach, a great prof., a great legislator, etc., etc., etc. All of these fell under the category of "work" but I loved them. However, as you can see, I was majoring in minors. What does the Bible say we should seek FIRST? Yes, the Kingdom of God. Then "EVERYTHING will be added" (capitals added for emphasis).

What a hard lesson, and it has taken me so long to learn. Faith and Trust in the One who can do everything is the answer. "Oh ye of little faith ..." I should have practiced what I preached.

Prayer: Heavenly Father, time and time again we fail You. Thank you for Your forgiving heart. Help us keep things in perspective and remember people are more important than things. Amen.

Dave

March 27

Matthew 5:14-16

Your Influence

As followers of Jesus, God's people, we are called to be: The Light of the World. Jesus commanded that His people be a reflection of what He Himself is: *The Light of the World.* Ours is a reflected light. What a privilege and honor is ours. Too, what a responsibility is ours – to reflect Him accurately. That is possible only when our lives are fully yielded to Him.

Let us pause to notice a few things about light.

A. First, a light is to be seen.
   Jesus himself emphasized that. A person's Christianity should be visible to all, always. It should show in the way we treat other people, in our work and in our play.

B. A light should guide.

So many around us need our guidance; they are looking for it. This is true especially for children and young people. They have a tendency to walk in our footsteps. Many need someone to take them by the hand, to point out the dangers along the trail. Most of all they need someone to direct them to Jesus, to assist them in coming to know Him, love Him, and trust Him. What a glorious privilege this is for us. Yes, you can be an influence which has eternal significance. We are promised that, in some marvelous way, through the operation of the Holy Spirit within us, we will become a source of new life for others.

Prayer: Jesus, help us never to be afraid to stand up for You. Please give us the opportunities today. Amen.

Rev. Henry Eggink

March 28

1 Timothy 6:10-11

Love People – Use Money (Not the Reverse)

To be honest, I don't know where or how this phrase came to me. It's somewhat like the "People/Things" analogy (Feb. 28 devotional), but still has some differences.

I think my Mom taught me the most about money. She said, "Some money is a necessity, but don't make decisions based on how much money is involved."

You can't out give the Lord. (Ray Hildebrand taught me that – see Nov. 1 & 2) If all of us would just give a tenth of our earnings, every church and charity would have more than enough funds to carry out their actions of love. God is love. We can love others because He first loved us.

Starting now, let's share our money and time (we should tithe that too), to show our love for God's people. There are tremendous needs. Let's help with at least one of those today!

Prayer: Heavenly Father, help us to be better managers of all you give us. We know it really isn't ours, but sometimes we forget that it ALL comes from You. Thanks for giving us so much! Amen.

Dave

March 29

John 14:1-4

We All Crave Assurance

Recently I read a book about heaven and a book about hell. We hear more, and talk more about heaven; and it actually seems to be considered politically incorrect to talk about hell – but we need to. Thinking about heaven and hell forces me to contemplate my own future after death. We know death is inevitable for all of us. I for one, am eternally grateful to have the assurance of eternity in heaven (1 John 5:13), because Jesus died for my sins.

It is Holy Week as I write this in the Iowa Senate chamber, and it seems that each passing year I am more grateful for Christ's sacrifice so that I can spend eternity with Him in heaven.

I also feel more urgency in telling others about God's gift of salvation. The older I get, the more aware I am of God's consistent and omnipotent presence through the Holy Spirit in my everyday life. I am constantly challenged to better focus my attention on Him, and to listen and obey throughout the day. I have a long way to go and I do not know how much time I have here. I want to be in His will for my life, for that is the best place to experience His peace and joy.

Prayer: Thank you Father for your many kept promises. You continually give us eternal hope. Our assurance of salvation enables us to reach out in confidence to others. Help us do that. Amen.

Nancy and Dave Boettger
Iowa State Senator, District 29

Nancy and Dave were active participants in the Thursday morning Bible Study. It was great to work with Nancy on a variety of issues, but particularly on Education. Dave served as her Clerk and they make a great team. I'm happy for their friendship and grateful for their service.

March 30

Proverbs 16:9

Who's In Control?

At every age, we are planning for our next move in life; we plan the simple mundane things like, what we will eat and what we will wear, to the more complex plans of our occupation, marriage, kids, retirement, and distribution of wealth when we leave this great earth.

As we plan and decide the most basic to the most serious things in life, it is more likely to create a plan that seems to provide the best benefits for ourselves. Then we set the agenda to fulfill that plan. However, our plan may not match the course the Lord has set out for us.

I have seen the Lord correct my course of action many times. My plan and actions didn't turn out to be the plan of the Lord. Quite often these path corrections were quite painful in my life. After time passes we often understand, as we look back, that the Lord's plan was much better and that the correction, which seemed difficult at the time, was actually a valuable learning tool.

Through these tough experiences, it has made my faith stronger and has helped me understand that I am not in control. The Lord has an awesome plan for each of us. It doesn't matter what your age may be. Your plan for earth is not complete until the day the Lord calls you home.

Today, when challenges begin to win the day, remind yourself that your life instructor (the Lord) is teaching you some vital lessons which will help grow your faith and give you a closer walk with your Heavenly Father.

Prayer: Let it be our prayer each day that we seek Your will to be done. Also help us to mean it. Amen.

Randy Feenstra
Iowa State Senator, District 2

Randy was elected to the Senate in 2008 when I retired. He lives in Hull and is doing an excellent job.

March 31

Matthew 19:13-15

Children

Kids are life changers. Dot and I have two and now have two grandchildren. What a blessing they are. Does that mean they never got in trouble and we didn't worry about them? Of course not, and we still worry from time to time. But kids add purpose and additional meaning to life. We found that when your kids are happy, you are happy; and when your kids hurt, you hurt!

It is never easy to raise kids, there is great responsibility, and many questions are raised. When do you stop making decisions for them and let them decide on their own? Are they really adults at 18? How about the issues of cars, individual finances, hours, study time, bedtime, proper attire, dating, and college selection, to name a few. Does anyone have all the absolute right answers for any of these? There's only one that I can think of. Make Jesus your partner with all of your family decisions, and keep all lines of communication open. Do we ever stop being a parent?

Prayer: Thank you Lord for our kids. Bless them with good health, great purpose, love for others, and love for You. Amen.

Dave

April 1

1 Corinthians 12:28

Don Protextor

"Pro" was my college baseball coach at Morningside from 1958-61. He gave me a chance, was an encourager, and without his willingness to grant me a scholarship, I could not have finished.

I made several "bonehead" decisions while in college and "Pro" helped me through them. My college years were good in many ways, but also very traumatic. Baseball was my "god" (and that's not good). That mentality did allow me to become reasonably effective at the game, and it kept me from smoking and drinking. But, I wasn't focused about the future. I just wanted to play professional baseball.

So a lack of focus, a few bad decisions, and the fact that my Dad died suddenly from a heart attack in the fall of my senior year, put me in a rather sorry state. I needed a man who understood. "Pro" was that man. He taught me some things about coaching, being a man, and helping when a need is there. I've tried to follow his example in many ways.

Tragically, we lost him to a heart attack in 1983. I'm happy I told him how important he was to me. Do you have someone you should get in touch with today?

Prayer: So many times things happen and I don't try to consider what Your plan is. Please help me be more discerning and concerned for the welfare of others. Amen.

Dave

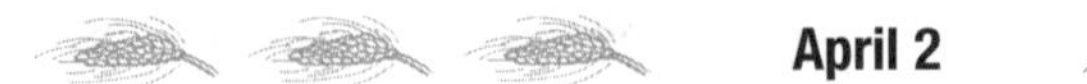

April 2

Matthew 16:21-23

Self Pity

Ready:

When athletes or any one of us feel sorry for ourselves we fail to put our trust in the Lord. It is a retreat into our "pity pot" and we seek to draw others into the pot with us. We may feel this way when we have to go up against someone who is bigger and stronger and faster than our own skills. Or we may feel this way when we are disciplined by a Coach, parent, school authorities or even the Law Enforcement Officers.

Self pity is a sign of immaturity and it is saying that God is not sufficient for all of my needs. When I can be successful in drawing others into my "Pot" I find refuge and it causes me to go there each time I have adversity. All of us are guilty of self pity at times and it cripples our spiritual life. Theologian Oswald Chambers says "we are hindered by self pity because it only serves to weaken us as a person." That scripture passage in Matthew says it is "Satanic."

"The first thing God does is to get us grounded in the strong reality of truth. He does this to bring us into submission to Him for the purpose of redemption. Why shouldn't we experience heartbreak? Through those doorways God is opening up ways of fellowship with His son. We sit down at the door of God's purpose and enter a slow death called self pity. And all of the so called Christian sympathy of others helps us to our death bed. But you can be sure God won't." (Oswald Chambers)

Self pity will not allow you to be used for God's highest purpose. Self pity is inward growth, it is a form of selfishness. If you are an athlete it will retard your effort to be a "team" player. Do not allow God to be stunted through the indulgence of self pity.

Go:

1. Where have I indulged in self pity in my life?
2. How does this indulgence affect my attitude?
3. Am I willing to let God be the source of my strength?
4. How is self pity Satanic?

Workout:

1. Read Jeremiah 1:8
2. Romans 8:35
3. 1 Peter 1:19

Prayer: Dear God, there are so many times we wallow in self pity. Forgive us and motivate us to look for paths of worthwhile efforts for You. Give us strength of purpose and the energy to help others. Amen.

Gordie Fosness
South Dakota FCA Assistant Director and former College Coach

Gordie is a long-time friend and great leader of young people. He has always been a strong Christian example for his peers and athletes to follow.

April 3

Psalm 118:24-29

A Special Gift

Imagine waking up one morning, walking into your kitchen and on the table is a beautifully wrapped gift box! On the box is a gift tag reading: "To (insert your name) From: Your Heavenly Father."

That is exactly what each one of us receives each morning: the precious gift of a brand new day! Think of some of the special gifts that you have received from family and loved ones. Do you toss the gift in a corner or put it on a shelf never to look at or use again? No! You enjoy it, you show it off, or you use it! That is exactly what we are to do with each new day given to us by our Father. We are to bask in His love and use the day to His honor and glory. We are to use the day to serve those around us: family, friends, and co-workers.

There are days when we feel that we do not have the energy to be a servant. There are days when we feel that we cannot even put one foot in front of the other. On those days, and every day, we need to cling to the promise from Philippians 4:19: "And my God will meet all your needs according to His glorious riches in Christ Jesus."

Enjoy this new day remembering that you are not walking alone. It's a new day to live in the joy of the Lord!

Prayer: Oh Heavenly Father, thank you for this new day and for the opportunity to serve You and my neighbor. May I celebrate this new day and live in the joy of Your presence. In Jesus name, Amen.

Tom and Carol Van Den Bosch
Head Volleyball Coach at Dordt College

This is a great couple. Tom is one of the finest coaches I know. I watched him when he coached at Hull Western Christian and I was an official. He is prepared, knows the rules, and teaches his girls well. Above all – he is a gentleman on the sidelines. He's won many state championships and is now doing a tremendous job at Dordt. Ironically, Tom and Carol are the proud parents of the NWC volleyball coach, Kyle. Successful coaching runs in the family.

April 4

Psalm 116:6

The Lord's Protection

Over the course of the past three weeks my beliefs have been tested. Our son was going through a rough patch in his life. He had been doing so well in a rehab center, when a misunderstanding forced the doctors to throw him out. He reached out to me to come and get him. I put my mistrust aside and drove the 45 minutes to get him. As I was driving, I prayed to God to give me strength and bolster my trust in Him.

I wasn't sure what to do with Christopher after I picked him up. As we were traveling, a new friend of mine just happened to call. When she heard what had happened to our son she opened her heart and house to our son. She had never met Christopher and I really don't know her very well outside of work. I did know she had a strong relationship with God. I felt the presence of God next to me in the car at that very minute. I was scared for my son and didn't want anything to make him feel that all his hard work this past month, had been in vain. He agreed to go to this stranger's house and stay there until we could get him back into rehab. During the next two days I began to read my Bible again. I found strength in His words and knew that I had to put all my faith in Him. God had a plan and I needed to allow Him to take the lead. Not only did the words I began to read save me, but through His power, my son also found God. Christopher finally found his "higher power" through a complete stranger. Every day since then, God has shown His presence in my life. I have learned to just "let go" and "let God" take the lead.

May you open your heart and soul to God. Let Him take the lead because God will save you even when you think there is no hope. The presence of God will surprise you and warm your heart when you least expect it.

Prayer: Thank you God for using Your people to help others in need. Thank you for always caring for us regardless of where we are, and what we are doing. We need each other and we need You. Amen.

Brooke and Paul Ondrus
Retired Teachers in the Chicago area.

Brooke and Paul are the third couple with our son Dick's group. What great friends they are and we are so thankful for that. We all need good friends and we need to be good friends as Brooke told us. May God bless them and Christopher. Please pray for all of them.

April 5

Proverbs 17:17

Memories

Does one ever get too old to keep making memories? I hope not! And I don't think so. There are so many things I'm still looking forward to. I never did really make a "Bucket List" but there were a few things I dreamt about.

Going to the St. Louis Cardinals Spring Training in Florida was one. Another was to visit all 50 states. (Did the first but still haven't set foot in Oregon). There are a few family goals that lie ahead, but there are many great past memories to treasure.

All of the memories involve people we love: *The grandkids' special trips when they reached the age of 12; Many special trips for major league baseball; The family Amtrak trip to Florida; Visits with friends on a daily basis.* These are just a few.

What memories are you planning to make real soon?

Prayer: Once again we stand in awe of You and this great earth. There are so many opportunities, and so little time to do them. Please grant us wisdom, time, and love for each other. Amen.

Dave

April 6

Galatians 5:22-24; Romans 8:26; Romans 5:5

Holy Spirit

The Holy Spirit is like the wind. You cannot see the actual wind but can see its effects – swaying trees, blowing snow, smells wafting, etc. The Holy Spirit is the presence of God in our lives, carrying on the work of Jesus. How is this displayed in our lives? Can others observe the effects?

1. The passage in Galatians speaks of "In warding – granting the fruits of the Spirit." We are exhorted to seek these fruits of love, joy, peace, patience, kindness, goodness, faithfulness, gentleness, and self-control. Which do you feel you possess and which are you striving for?
2. Romans is "Upwardly – praying for us." Many times it is hard to find the right words and we really don't know how to pray. Isn't it a comfort to know that at those times the Holy Spirit speaks for us.
3. The second passage in Romans concerns "Outwardly – pouring God's love into our hearts." God, who is the essence of love, pours it out for us and fills our hearts with it. Rest assured, God always keeps His promises.

Prayer: Heavenly Father, thank you for the daily grace and love You pour upon us. Amen.

Dot

April 7

Matthew 28:20; Matthew 9:12

All the Way

A Christian physician of South India tells how one day an old Indian woman came to his clinic. As she was being helped to the examination bed, the doctor asked, "Have you come alone?" With a beautiful glow on her face, the woman looked up at the doctor and said, "No Manka (God) came with me."

Life calls upon us to travel many hard and lonely roads. We may be called upon to walk the road to a hospital room, to a sick-bed, to a cemetery lot where the body of a loved one is being laid to rest, to some difficult assignment which fills our heart with fear. Perhaps we may be called soon to walk to the door of death itself, but we need never walk alone. God will go with us. He is a Companion on every road as Jesus said in Matt. 28.

We have many needs of body, of mind, and of soul, but we do not have a single need in which Jesus is not ready to help us, to care for us, to sustain us.

What is burdening your heart today? Are you worried about providing for your family, or about some pain which throbs even now in your body, or about a wayward child, or about a difficult task you may face tomorrow? Or are you concerned about your sins and your soul's eternal welfare? Whatever it may be that concerns you, look up into the face of the Christ, the Christ who was willing to die on Calvary's cross, and see His infinite love for you. We have a Savior, a Friend, who loves us and has marvelously demonstrated that love. Realize that "*greater love hath no man than this, that a man lay down his life for his friends.*" The apostle Paul reasoned thus, "*If God spared not His own Son, but delivered Him up for us all, shall He not with Him also freely give us all things?*"

His care embraces our every need. He is our only hope for body and soul, for time and eternity. But it is not until we recognize our need of His help, until we recognize that we in ourselves are lost and helpless sinners, it is not until we fall to our knees before the Savior and have no other hope, that we begin to see the marvelous glory of His cross and the redemption He there wrought. It is then that we come to know His saving presence.

Will you ask for His presence now?

Prayer: We do ask You to be the kind of presence we have just read about. Thank you for always being with us and for saving us. Amen.

Rev. Henry Eggink

April 8

Philippians 3:14; 1 Corinthians 9:24

Sports

Does God like sports? I think so. The Bible says we are created in His image, we seem to like sports, so He does too. Paul used several Track examples in his epistles, and you can find other references to sport throughout the Bible.

I love many sports but never cared much for the Olympics. I like the Special Olympics but that's for a completely different reason. I tend to like professional sports better than high school and college. I know that puts me in the minority, but that's okay too. The Olympics always made me frustrated and mad as a kid. We (the Americans) always lost to the Russians. I hate to lose and it never seemed fair, (besides they didn't play baseball!). They could use pros and we had to only play amateurs. That has changed now thank goodness. The Olympics I enjoyed the most was when the "Dream Team" just clobbered everybody in basketball.

Hey! You have the right to like what you want and have dislikes as well. Find something positive that turns you on today and go for it.

Prayer: Dear Lord, thank you for diversity and excitement. Bless each one of us today with a feeling of well-being and love and acceptance for others. Amen.

Dave

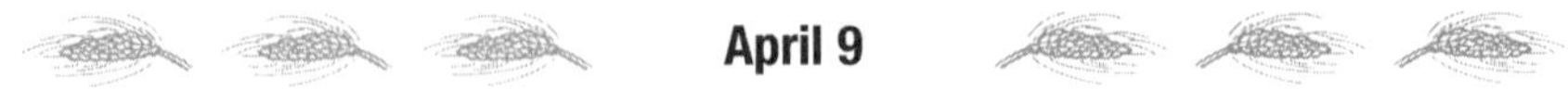

April 9

Mark 1:35

Day's A-Dawning

In the wisdom of God our time on earth is divided into days and nights. Every morning opens the door to new beginnings, new challenges, new opportunities. And what happens during the course of the new day is determined pretty much by what happens during the first half hour after our awakening. It is in those moments that the sails for the day's voyage are set. It is then that the direction for the day's journey is determined. It is then that the pitch is set for the hours which are to follow.

Bred with the conviction that his time, his talents, his possessions and yes, his very life, come as gifts from God, a Christian feels a keen sense of obligation to use them correctly. He wants every day to be lived in the circle of God's will. For this reason the dawning of each day will find him in prayer seeking God's guidance and help for the activities which lie ahead.

Jesus, our Savior, has given us an example in this matter of beginning a day. Concerning Him it is written in the passage in Mark that our days should start with solitary prayer. This is not an isolated instance; several times we find this recorded in the New Testament concerning Jesus.

Each new day is a challenge. Within its limits are 24 hours, or 1440 minutes. The amount is the same for every person. Men and women may differ with respect to talents and abilities, but each day gives to every person the same amount of time. On that score we are equal. How that time is utilized each individual must determine.

Time is something we cannot hoard; it must be spent. And once spent, it can never be recalled to spend again. It is gone forever. But its fruit, whether good or bad, is not gone forever. It has eternal significance in our own lives but also in the lives of others. In the spending of each hour something is happening to others, but also to the spender. His/Her life has been shortened by that amount of time and his feet have traveled upward or downward. There can be no standing still. This thing called "time" is so precious and the results of its use are so momentous that we dare not launch a new day without first seeking God's guidance in its use.

Not only is each day a challenge, it is also a mystery. We know not whether it will bring joy or sorrow, good or ill, pleasure of pain, life or death. And it is surely true that we cannot be prepared for what the long hours may unfold unless we have placed our hand in the Lord's hand.

Prayer: Dear God, we know You can make this day good. We can make it bad. Stay with us each step of the way. Amen.

Rev. Henry Eggink

April 10

Proverbs 18:24

Friends

"There's nothing like old friends, so be sure to make lots of them while you are young!" I tried to find who said this but failed. It sure is true. "Google" *friends* sometime and read the quotes. This is one way of reminding us of important friends we've had or have. What a treasure they are. Hopefully this inspires each one of us to be better and loyal friends. We really do need each other.

Many of us are also married to a great friend. Friends have fun with each other, help, share, laugh, cry, and forgive each other. Sometimes it's just important for us to be there. Right now, think about your friends, pray for him/her/them. Someone might need a call or a note from you. Do it now! If you wait until tomorrow, it won't happen.

Prayer: Thank you God for our many friends that care about us. Thanks too, for being our friend. It is always safe to trust You. Amen.

Dave

April 11

Psalm 139:16b; Isaiah 55:8-9; John 15:13; Romans 5:8

A Wonderful Life?

There are countless examples all around us and in our own lives of extreme suffering, pain, and loss that would make us question that God loves us and has a wonderful plan for our lives. When we hear that, our expectations of what "Wonderful" looks like is often far from the plan that God has for us. The passage in Psalms says "*each day is ordained before one of them comes to be.*" It tells us that God foreknew the trials that would come our way and although having the power to change our course, He allows it to be our reality. How can that be wonderful? How can that be love? God's definition of "Wonderful" more often than not resembles the abundant life Paul embraced, even though he endured imprisonment, persecution, and was beaten and stoned.

When God says that "*My ways are not your ways, my thoughts are not your thoughts,*" He tells us His love and wonderful plan can only be understood by looking to the cross. John says "*no greater love is there than to lay down your life for your brother.*" We find the "wonderful" again in Romans where Christ died for sinners and the unworthy. If there is anything that I can identify with in Paul, it is that like him, I am the worst of the worst. How could I be worthy of such a plan? To redeem the exceedingly sinful nature by having someone else pay the price for what I have done, the penalty I deserve? When I think of the love I have for people in my life, there are only a few that I would be willing to die for. But Christ died for us while we were still sinners and unworthy, a prevenient grace that is beyond comprehension and truly makes God's wonderful plan for our lives a reality. I often wondered why God would come up with such a plan. If I were God, making the rules, I think I would have come up with something far less costly to the one that I love most dearly. Certainly, a love beyond understanding, a "wonderful" plan indeed.

Prayer: Thank you for Your wonderful plan for all of us. This is such a great world and a great opportunity for joy. Please enable us to reach out and be a positive part of Your plan. Amen.

Brian Hansen
Retired NFL Punter (15 years), South Dakota Director of the FCA

Brian is from Hawarden, Iowa and was an outstanding punter for the University of Sioux Falls. He then played for 5 NFL teams in a 15-year career that included being selected as the Punter in the Pro Bowl. He is an outstanding speaker and a great representative for the FCA. Contact him at 1-800-322-1646.

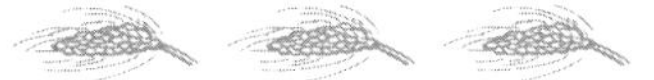 **April 12** 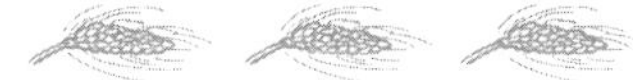

Matthew 28:20; Romans 8:38-39

We Never Walk Alone

Dr. Clyde Meadows tells about a young soldier who, during WWI, was assigned a difficult and dangerous detail. It meant almost sure death. On his way to the assignment he passed the chaplain, and paused a moment to say, "Chaplain, I've been assigned a very dangerous detail. Will you pray for me that I may be saved from death?" The Chaplain replied, "My comrade, I can't pray such a prayer, for you are being sent deliberately into the very presence of death. But one thing I can do; I can go with you and pray that the Lord will be with both of us." Side by side the chaplain and the soldier lad went into dangerous No Man's Land.

So it is with us. Our Lord does not promise us ease or freedom from dangers, problems, troubles, and pain. But he has promised to always be with us. Concerning one thing we can always be sure, namely, the presence of the Divine Companion. We never walk alone.

The sailor in his lonely ship at sea may know His presence; the pilot in his plane among the solitary spaces of the sky may know His presence; the minor in the dark chambers of the earth, the farmer on his isolated homestead, the sick on hospital beds, the lonely stranger walking the crowded streets of the great city – all may know His wonderful, living presence.

Our greatest need is not to find God; it is simply to recognize Him. He is here, waiting for us to touch Him with the hand of faith. Whatever lonely spot may lie ahead in life's journey, God will be there. Whatever difficult experience may await us in the unknown future, He will be at our side. Nothing can separate us from Him and His love.

You need never face a task alone. If you have surrendered your life to the Christ, a new partnership has been established. From that moment on, it is God and you. You and God are a majority. We never walk alone.

Prayer: Embolden each of us to act in such a way that others may be drawn to You. Amen.

Rev. Henry Eggink

April 13

Proverbs 11:25

Arnie and Jack

Hey golf fans – you know who I'm talking about. These are a couple of national treasures. Both of them were great on the course, but they accomplish other goals in different ways. That's okay.

Many years ago at the PGA in Chicago, my son Dick and I watched the following:

We were in the parking lot where the players come in. Jack arrived first and he chose a parking spot as close to the clubhouse as possible. Autograph seekers surrounded him and he greeted them with a smile. He instructed them not to stand in front of him and he signed three or four autographs as he walked to the door. He was courteous and friendly.

Some minutes later Arnie arrived. He parked under a tree and opened the trunk. He took out his clubs, visited with everyone, posed for pictures, and signed every autograph. He stayed out there about 20 minutes.

Both men are great salesmen for the game of golf. They just go about it a little differently. How do you let people know you care about them?

Prayer: Heavenly Father, thanks for making all of us different, yet still in your image. Guide and direct our paths in ways that draw us and others closer to you. Amen.

Dave

April 14

Matthew 7:13-14

Narrow Passage

Occasionally one encounters an individual who has the erroneous idea that a person can be a Christian and still do completely as he pleases, that Christianity is easy and that anything goes.

Nothing could be more false. The Bible never presents the Christian life as being easy. Rather, it speaks of it as a warfare. The Bible never presents the Christian life as being an undisciplined life. Quite the contrary is true. Let it be said with emphasis that the Christian life has its disciplines, and they are rigid. You read what Jesus said in Matthew 7.

That obedience and discipline are required in the Christian life is not strange. Observation discloses that every worthwhile endeavor has its disciplines. Consider the following example:

Here is a young woman who aspires to be a concert pianist. To become that, a price must be paid. She must submit herself to rigid discipline. Hour after hour, day after day, year after year, must be devoted to practice. Meanwhile her friends who have no worthy aspirations are not so limited. They do what and go where they please. They appear to have full freedom; she does not. But wait, as the piano student yields herself to the discipline something splendid is happening to her. Gradually her talents are developing. Slowly she is moving into the wonderful new world of music. One day she will step upon the concert stage, and it will become apparent that what once appeared to be a narrowing procedure in reality opened her life to new freedoms, freedoms her friends will never enjoy.

So it is with life. It is only when we yield ourselves to the Savior and to His will for us that we really begin to live. It is then we really begin to perform. It is then that our lives open to freedom such as we had never known before.

It is paradoxical but true that the life surrendered to Jesus the Christ is the free life. The gate through which He calls the pilgrim to enter is narrow, and the way is hard, but it opens to fullness of life.

Prayer: Lord, we ask for that freedom that can only come from finding You. Help us use that freedom to inspire others. Amen.

Rev. Henry Eggink

April 15

John 1:12; Psalms 25:14-18, 20-22

Memorial Service

I attended a memorial service today for a relatively young man (63). I'm sorry to say, it's a man I'd "given up on" (Interpret that as "stopped praying for quite a long time ago"). That's a sad commentary on me, isn't it?

Paul was a great baseball player that I coached back in the early 1960's. He signed a Yankee contract after high school but was released for disciplinary reasons. He went on to live a very undisciplined life for many years, and eventually wound up in prison. I lost track of him.

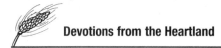

Read his poem and you'll know why I rejoiced today and the tears I continue to shed, are tears of joy.

BEHIND THE WALL

Three hundred men lay sleeping,
three hundred souls don't rest.
Each heart has its own rhythm deep within his chest.

These walls are old and knowing.
They have seen us come and go.
Chained, cuffed and strutting, gangster walking slow.
We walk the wall, known main line, been doing it for years.
Showing men's courage, hiding men-sized tears.

They lock you down in irons, in cages made of steel.
Even though your wrists are bleeding, it's the inner pain you feel.
When the man takes his arm around you and chains start to fall.
When the smoke has cleared away, you're still behind the wall.

So many men are searching and looking for the door.
Even though they make it through, they still come back for more.
For many years I stumbled and played a losing game.
Would I ever be the ruler, or would I bare the pain.
I thought I could make it, I thought I knew it all.
But all my years of thinking, I'm still behind the wall.
As the years rolled slowly by, nothing seemed to change.
All the world would slowly pass, as I slowly went insane.

I knew there was an answer, somehow I'd find the truth.
I knew that I could make it; I could be the living proof.
Then I heard of Jesus in the jail that day.
How He changed so many lives, of all who came to pray.
He became my Savior, He became my Lord.
Now I'm serving Jesus. I'm giving Him my all.
He gives me peace and freedom, even in my cell.
He promised me eternal life from sin, death, and hell.

I've never been so happy, since I heard my Father's call.
Because all the world is living and lost behind the wall.

By Paul A. Bruinsma (May 14, 1946 -December 25, 2009)

Isn't it great to know that Jesus continues to change lives. I can't tell you how much I hope that maybe I helped "plant a small seed" with Paul. The most important thing is that he heard the Word and finally made the right choice. I'll never "give up" on anyone again. Is there someone out there that you should "remember" today? I'm anxious to see Paul again.

Prayer: Thank you Lord for never giving up on us. Thank you for salvation and thank you for Paul's friend that sent this poem to his family. Amen.

Dave

April 16

Romans 8:15; Galatians 4:5; Ephesians 1:5

Adopted? Aren't We All?

Adoption is an amazing thing to be a part of. My wife and I, after being married for a few years, were told we were unable to have children on our own. We talked about it and prayed fervently. We decided to call Bethany Christian Services and start the adoption process. A few years and many tears later, we were able to bring Laura Lynn into our family. What a blessing!

Much to our surprise a few months later, we found out Karen was pregnant with Rachel. So we have Laura (adopted) and Rachel (biological) and both treated the same – with lots of love and care.

Isn't that what happens when we become Christians? God waits and waits until we hear His call. After many tears, God joyfully takes us into His family, treating us as if we were His own flesh and blood. This acceptance comes with all the joy and the inclusion of eternal life.

I thank God daily that He allows us to be adopted into His family. Aren't you?

Prayer: Heavenly Father, we are so thankful to be Your children. You bring us great joy, acceptance and love. Amen.

Dave and Karen Hulsart
Proprietor of Dove Christian Book Store and Karen is a Loan Officer at Iowa State Bank.

Dave was a fine football player and now he not only assists with the Softball program as an Assistant Coach (he's a retired Head Coach) but he also volunteers with football statistics and sits next to me on the bench as he is the Timer at the Men's Basketball games here at NWC. He is a great friend and I thank him again for helping distribute and promote this book.

April 17

2 Corinthians 4:18; Revelations 7:9; Revelations 21

Where Are The Potholes?

Yesterday as I took a walk around the city where I live, I felt like crying when I see all the pot holes and litter lining the road. The Lord then reminded me that this is not how He desires the world to be either. For a moment, I felt joined with Him in grieving for our fallen world.

Upon turning the corner, I stepped onto a newly paved road. The road looked great to me, and I felt satisfied. But the next thought the Lord impressed upon me was "I can do even better than this. Just you wait."

We need the Lord to help give us a different perspective on things around us. In our own strength we often get discouraged by our circumstances, or we are far too easily pleased by what this world offers.

The Lord has a plan that is bigger than anything you or I can imagine. The passage in Rev. 7 talks about the "*great multitude ... from every nation ... before the throne ... wearing white robes holding palm branches.*" As we walk more and more closely with God, He will give us the ability to see things from His perspective more often.

Everyone has pot holes and litter in his/her life, these separate us from God, but Jesus Christ paved the way for us to restore this relationship and to experience eternal life. I don't want to miss out nor do I want anyone else to miss out on that party. One day we will be walking around on streets of gold. Just you wait!

Prayer: Dear Jesus, thank you for preparing the way for us and taking all of the hazards out of the way. Truly You are the answer. Keep us on the straight and narrow path. Amen.

Kim Hiemstra
Missionary with Campus Crusade for Christ in South America

Kim is a member at Central Reformed and is devoted to Christian Missions. Pray for her and give her all the support you can.

April 18

Luke 22:31-32

Christ Prays For Us

Jesus is approaching the end of His life. The disciples are gathered with Jesus and have finished celebrating the Lord's Supper after the Passover. Jesus is talking about leaving and the coming of the kingdom of God, but He also discloses the fact that there will be a traitor in the group.

Who is it? It is interesting that the discussion immediately jumps to who will be the greatest in the kingdom. This suddenly becomes a discussion of self promotion. This is not the first time this issue was raised (Luke 9:46, Matthew 19:1-4). What also is interesting is they are attempting to tell Jesus who is the greatest. Peter, I am sure, was in the midst of that discussion.

Jesus then directs his attention to Peter. Peter was the leader. He was the first to respond when the question came up as to "who do men say that I am?" Peter's reply was that "you are the Christ, the Son of the living God." (Luke 9:20) In the context of this discussion, Jesus tells Peter that he will be entrapped by Satan, but Jesus as our advocate will pray for him – and when he turns again, he is instructed to strengthen his brothers. The self defense of Peter was an immediate response to Jesus' comments, probably using the same argument he used to promote himself in the kingdom conversation. He will do anything for Jesus.

Jesus stops him in his tracks. What is really significant in the prayer of Jesus? It was "I have prayed for you, that your faith might not fail." The prayer was not that Peter would avoid all hardship, avoid all difficulties, avoid all doubts, and be comfortable and quiet in his spiritual life. It was that he would retain his faith that Jesus was the Christ, the Son of God as stated in his original confession and faith in that pronouncement would not fail. I am sure the comfort of the promise of Christ came back to Peter many times, after his repentance and after he humbled himself. In particular, I suspect it was very present when he repented for the three times that he denied Christ shortly after this conversation. He became a spokesman, leader and a key member of the New Testament Church. He also strengthened his brothers and sisters as the Lord commanded.

Do we have the same comfort of knowing that Christ prays and makes intercession for us when we go through difficulties? Do we feel that way when our hearts are broken or when we have rejected Christ? When we reject Him or even think that we do not need Him, we must remind ourselves that even as Christ was an advocate for Peter, he is an advocate for us (1 John 2:1).

Prayer: Dear Lord, help us to share the power and assurance of that message to strengthen others. Amen.

Lloyd Bierma
Lawyer in Sioux Center and Board Member of ATLAS of Sioux Center

April 19

Exodus 12:1-14

The Passover

There are so many interesting stories in the Old Testament. Actually my favorite is the one about Joseph and his brothers in Egypt. It brings tears to my eyes every time when he reveals himself to his brothers and shows love and forgiveness. But the Passover is another dandy and it really makes me think how I would have reacted to the order. I get so blame mad at the Israelites so many times when they question and rebel after they have been freed – but while they are actually slaves is a different story.

Remember all the different plagues that the Egyptians have endured? But each time, Pharaoh "hardens his heart" and breaks the promise. Now comes the "coup de gras," but it takes some real faith on the part of the Israelites. Notice all the ritual they have to go through. If the blood isn't on the doorposts, all of the "firstborns" will die. I'm not a very skeptical person, but would I have had some doubts after all the other failures? I'd like to think not, but I've had the benefit of reading about all these happenings and the recorded history, so I know how the story ends. What if I had lived at that time? Would I have scoffed at Moses and Aaron?

You know, we really don't have any excuses. We've read the last chapter and we know how the book ends. The Bible tells us we are to honor the Passover each year and never forget its significance. It is Jesus shed blood that has saved us again. He did it "once for all" but that was enough. We can take that promise with us to the Promised Land.

Let's honor the Passover and all it means to us. This Easter week is so special.

Prayer: Thank you dear Lord for saving each of us because we believe. Continue to strengthen our faith in You and in each other. Amen.

Dave

April 20

Ephesians 2:8-9

Grace

Isn't it hard to receive a gift when you haven't given one and aren't "obligated" to give in return? Don't you feel you have to "earn'" a gift? Yup, me too! But that isn't the way God is. He gives the greatest gift possible and it's free. He gives us eternal life in a perfect Heaven, because of our belief in Him and our faith. Grace can't be bought or earned. He just wants us to believe in Him.

There's no time like the present to start building or receiving that saving faith. Isn't it great that Jesus paid the price of our salvation on the cross? There's nothing we can do but accept the free gift. He doesn't want us to boast or think WE did anything. He did it all.

Prayer: We can't thank you enough for the free grace. Help us accept it as the gift it is. Let the good things we do and try to do, reflect our love for You because You first loved us. Amen.

Dave

April 21

Romans 8:28

Sad Yet Heartwarming

My 50-year-old nephew has A.L.S. (Lou Gehrig's disease). It's a terrible disease as you all know. But here's some good stuff as the passage above predicts. (By the way, you can read my nephew Steve's devotional on May 5). Steve loves baseball and is a big fan of the Chicago Cubs. (Some might say that is a contradiction in terms – but that comes from a St. Louis Cardinals fan!).

As Steve was growing up, Ron Santo was the Cub 3rd baseman, and Steve's favorite player. I think Ron should be in the Hall of Fame as a player, but he's definitely in the "Hall" as a compassionate person. He's signed a bunch of memorabilia to Steve and then arranged a special meeting in the Wrigley Field parking lot in June, 2010. At this meeting Ron signed everything, took pictures with Steve and his family, was as congenial as anyone could be and wouldn't be hurried. It was one of the most memorable days of Steve's life. Ron Santo's parting comment was "I'll be praying for you big guy!"

Two other Hall of Famer's, Ryan Sandberg and Cal Ripken Jr., have sent special items to Steve. These famous people took the time to reach out to someone and give him a "lift:" Let's each of us think of, pray for, and reach out to "make someone's day" today!

Prayer: Heavenly Father, please use each of us to provide special times for those who have special needs. Help us be more thoughtful and thankful. Thank You for our many blessings. Amen.

Dave

April 22

Matthew 27:35-46; Mark 15:24-39; Luke 23:32-46; John 19:18-30

Good Friday

It's always been hard for me to think of today as "Good" Friday. Have you read about the agony of what it's like to die on the cross? It's brutal and horrendous! I described what a person being crucified goes through one time in a speech, and a man passed out! That wasn't my goal at all, but I did want everyone to realize what our Savior experienced.

I know the "good" part comes from the fact that Jesus shed His blood so we don't have to. He died in our place and did it long before any of us were even born. Our sins are forgiven before we ever commit them, all because we believe. That's grace! That's forgiveness! That's good!

Now let's do our best to live our lives the way He wants us to.

As Tony Campolo says – "It's Friday – but Sunday's coming!"

Prayer: Jesus, there is no way we can really comprehend what you endured for us, but thank you! Amen.

Dave

April 23

Psalm 30:5

Joy in the Morning!

Life's experiences have helped me to understand the truth and depth of the words in this Psalm.

When stricken with the news, "Your daughter has been in a serious car accident and is being transported to a larger hospital," my heart raced with the possibilities of what might be. With God at our side, we endured the anxious hours and days until we felt the assurance that she would be restored.

A few years later there was another announcement to rob me of my joy when told, "It appears to be a malignant tumor." Again my thoughts threw me into a frenzy over what would be the outcome. Going into surgery with God at my side, the outcome was encouraging. I again experienced Joy that God alone can give.

A third experience to bring about weeping was the sudden loss of my life partner for fifty-five years. He was suddenly taken from me. I wondered if joy could come in the morning? Life goes on and I know that God never forsakes those who love Him and whom He loves.

I'm reminded of Mary the mother of Jesus, who must have wondered why her joy was taken, but must have come to the realization that "joy" comes in the morning.

Prayer: Heavenly Father, may each of us enjoy "joy" in the morning, as we pass through life's valleys. Thank you for loving us. Amen

Esther Plantage
Retired Elementary Teacher

Esther is in my adult Sunday School class, is a good friend, and is the Mom of Anita (you read Anita's devotional on Jan. 21). She's a very special lady.

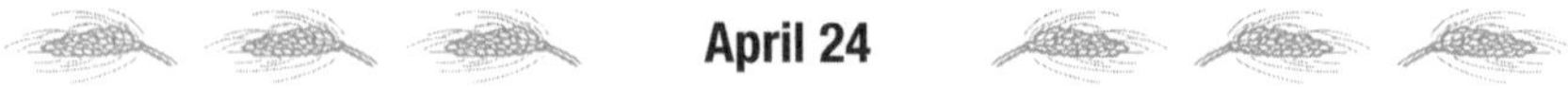

April 24

Luke 24:6

Celebrate Easter Every Day!

Have you ever wondered what it would be like for someone to die accidently and your life is either saved or changed because of it? Have you ever had someone come up to you and offer you an organ from their body that again would keep you alive?

I have personally experienced this twice in my life by having two kidney transplants. One was donated by a family who lost a loved one. The most recent was by a family friend that donated one of her kidneys knowing that it would leave her with one – needless to say, I live the Easter celebration daily in my life.

Isn't this what Jesus did for us on the cross? He died so that sinners could live life eternal. Please join me in celebrating Easter every day, and thank God for what He has done in our lives.

Prayer: It is indescribable the way you love us. Thank you for medical miracles. Thank you for hope and for people who make uncanny sacrifices, But Yours will always be the greatest. Amen.

Dave Hulsart
Owner of Dove Christian Book Store

Dave was an excellent football player in high school and college. I'm glad he came to NWC. He has a real servant's heart. Dave helps with the football team's statistics and is the Official Timer at all of the Men's Basketball games where we sit side-by-side as I announce and score. He's definitely one of the good guys and he's helped a lot with getting this book to you. He and his wife Karen live in Orange City and you read another of Dave's devotionals on April 16.

April 25

Romans 8:28

A Song For the Road

So things haven't been going too smoothly for you as you are walking the road of life. There have been disappointments, heart-aches, sorrows, and perhaps physical suffering.

Three alternatives open to a traveler in such circumstances as yours. Firstly, one may become bitter and rebellious. Some people do. Secondly, one may become stoical in spirit and simply resign himself to his hard lot. You know, an individual can dull his feelings so that he can endure almost anything. Thirdly, with humble trust and love in one's heart, one can rededicate oneself and all that he has, including sorrow and pain, to a Heavenly Father whom we believe knows what is best and will allow only that to befall His children.

Perhaps you have heard the story of George Matheson. He was a brilliant young man with a promising future. Already he was becoming well established professionally. Soon he was to be married to a beautiful, socially prominent young woman. He seemed to possess everything a young man could desire. But one day his eyes began to trouble him. He consulted a specialist and was told that soon he would be completely blind.

He felt that he must tell his sweetheart the tragic news. When he did, she broke the engagement saying that she just could not bear the thought of spending the rest of her life with a blind man.

The bottom had dropped out of everything for George. But in the quietness of his little room he laid his disappointment and sorrow at the feet of his Savior and yielded completely to His will. He gave himself anew to Him. And then came a song! Here is part of the song which was born that day:

"O love that wilt not let me go,
I rest my weary soul on Thee;
I give Thee back the life I owe,
That in Thine ocean depths its flow
May richer, fuller be.

O Light that followest all my way
I yield my flickering torch to Thee;
My heart restores its borrowed ray,
That in Thy sunshine's blaze its day
May brighter, fairer be."

You see, even disappointment and sorrow and pain, when truly laid upon the altar of dedication to God, can bring a song which will live to bless the lives of countless other travelers. God can use them, if we will let Him. The Bible is replete with examples like this.

Prayer: Dear God, it's so easy to get down. Thank you for raising us up and please help us do that for others. Amen.

Rev. Henry Eggink

April 26

John 20:17

Change

In this passage Jesus' mother Mary has discovered the resurrection of Jesus. Mary clings to Jesus with thoughts of, "you're back!", "you're alive again!". But Jesus reminds her not to cling to him, that this is not the second coming. Mary wants things to go back to the way they were before the crucifixion, but change always occurs.

We kiss a baby's belly and hear their squealing belly laughter, and we want time to stand still. Jesus forced change on earth, he was a rebel, changing what the Jews could eat, who he associated himself with, etc. We need to look at change as a gift from God.

In the past few years has your job, housing, school, or people you spend time with changed? If not, go out and discover a new adventure. Pray that God will lead you.

Prayer: Lord, we have found that change can be very difficult, and it can also be good. Even then, it is not always easy. Help us to understand Your ways and Your will for us. Thank you for always loving us. Amen.

Mike and Pam Hulstein
Self-employed Entrepreneur and Trucker while Pam heads up the Nursing Dept. at Dordt College.

Mike, Pam and their family are great friends. Mike was my batboy years ago when I coached at SCHS. We've enjoyed many trips to Branson, MO with the Posts and the Hulsteins to watch our beloved Red Raiders play basketball in the National Tourney.

April 27

1 Corinthians 15:51; 2 Corinthians 3:18; Philippians 3:21

Jesus Changes Lives

Do you like change? What if I said "keep the change"? That changes it a little, doesn't it? (And I'm not sorry about the pun!). It seems the older we get the less we like change. Why is that? Are you stuck in your ways? Are you predictable?

Here's a change that's good. Jesus continues to change lives. That's a fact you can rely on. Following is a true story: Well over 30 years ago I was playing golf with a friend. It was not a pleasant day weather-wise, but I'll never forget it. Knowing that I attended church regularly and led the FCA chapter in town – Bill asked this question. "What do you think about this religion business?" After confirming that I was a strong believer and why, I told him the story of Gideon and the fleece. I don't remember exactly what we shot on that first nine, but I know it wasn't great. Since the weather and my golf were both miserable, I said I'd had enough and went home. That night I got a call from Bill. He said, "You know that story about the fleece – well after you left I said to God, 'If all this Christian business is true, let me shoot par or better on the back nine.'" Bill, who didn't attend church regularly, and said he wasn't sure about being a believer, experienced a significant change. He said, "I shot 35 (one under) on the back!" He had shot in the mid-40's on the front. From that time on Bill and his wife Pat (she has a devotional in this book too) became strong believers. They have been missionaries and great Christians ever since. Yes – Change is good! (Read Bill's remembrance of this story April 30.)

Prayer: Thank you Lord for changing us to know and understand Your ways. Help us to continue to always change for the better. Help each of us to be positive instruments of change in the lives of Your people. Amen.

Dave

April 28

Proverbs 5:21

E Pluribus Unum (Out of Many, We Are One)

I always saw this on our money but never really knew what it meant, so I "Googled" it. There are over 300 million people in the U.S. Of course each of us is just one of that big total. How many people influence you? How many do you influence? America is one country where one person can and does make a significant difference. Think of all of the inventors, teachers, presidents, hall of fame athletes, musicians, relatives and friends that have been singled out for personal contributions and excellence. They were just one of many. Think about your parents and about the individual differences you can make with your own children.

You are also important as a voter. Many elections have been settled by one vote. If just one voter per precinct had changed in 1960, Nixon would have defeated Kennedy. Would that have changed history just a tad?

You are important!

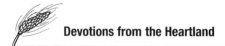

Prayer: Thank you Lord for making us individuals with our own personalities. Thank you too for helping us to influence others, we hope positively. Thank you for all of those great individuals that have made our lives better and been great examples for us to follow. Amen.

Dave

April 29

Judges 6:36-40

How About Fleece?

Have you ever tried what Gideon did? Oh, I don't mean actually using wool the same as he did. God will "tell" you what decision to follow if you ask. Of course it involves prayer and seriously seeking His will, with the understanding you will do what He says.

How many times aren't we betwixt and between, not knowing what to do? God wants to help – and He will. Should I move? Should we buy this house/car? What school/college should be selected? He WILL answer your prayer.

After you have received counsel from family, friends, and those you respect. After fervent prayer, and yet the answer isn't real clear, try a fleece. Think of something that is within the realm of possibility and turn it over to God. It's always safe to trust Him.

Once the decision is made give yourself a day or so. Your "comfort level" will let you know it was the right one. (See Bill Estes devotional for April 30 for a real life example.)

Prayer: Thank you Lord for caring enough to help us with answers. We really do want to follow Your will, but sometimes it's tough to see the exact path. Please guide us. Amen.

Dave

April 30

Judges 6:36-40

The Fleece

Over 30 years ago at the beginning of my Christian walk, I was playing golf with a close friend. As we played, a number of spiritual items were discussed. He brought up the story of Gideon and the fleece and after hearing the story I decided to give this "fleece" a try. I wanted to know if it was okay with the Lord to test him with these kinds of questions.

The weather was terrible. The temperature was in the low 50's, with wind gusts of 25 to 30 miles per hour. We had finished the first nine with neither of us playing well. I finished with a 45 (bogey golf) and I'm not sure he played any better because he said he'd had enough for the day and was heading home. But I decided to play another nine because of the fleece story. My prayer (fleece) to the Lord was if it's okay to question or seek answers this way I needed to shoot par or better. I knew this could only happen with the Lord's help because of all the circumstances. Would you believe that every drive was right down the middle and my iron shots attacked the pin?

In that cold and wind I saw the Lord perform a minor miracle as I finished one under par! That answer solidified my Faith and continues to strengthen me today. I know the Lord is interested in me personally and will answer the honest prayers of our hearts. Praise His name.

Prayer: Thank you heavenly Father for listening to us and showing us your way. Please continue to give us answers and give us loving and forgiving hearts. Amen.

Bill Estes
Dentist

Bill and I have been league golf partners now for over 40 years. Of course he is also my dentist. Would you also believe that since the fleece worked so well for Bill – it also solidified my faith as well? It sure did! Bill also serves on the ATLAS of Sioux Center board.

May 1

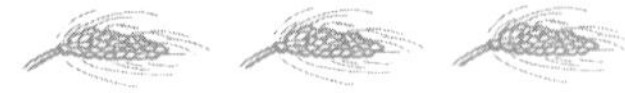

1 Corinthians 12:28

The Gift of Administration

Chuck Irwin is the best administrator I ever worked for. He was the Superintendent of Schools in Sioux Center for 17 years. He was the most "going-to-meetings-person" I have ever known. That, plus the fact that he read extensively about education and current happenings, enabled him to always be "in the know." That's a great quality for a leader of people.

His door was literally always open and one could talk to him with great confidentiality. I did that often as a young teacher/coach. That's also how he got started in education, as a teacher and coach. He was also a man with a great sense of humor, loved to play golf, fish, and attend athletic contests. He also attended every musical and theater production at the school.

Chuck and I became great personal friends over the years, and did many things together. We still do.

I learned the importance of knowing my subject, being straight forward, and keeping the lines of communication always open, from Chuck. Work can also be fun. I think it should be, and he helped make it that way. We need more people like Chuck Irwin.

Prayer: Lord, I personally thank you for Chuck and Angie. Bless them and their large family. Help us to learn from great examples and then be one ourselves. Amen.

Dave

May 2

Isaiah 58:3

A True Fast

I was on the Island of Hispaniola, in the remote Haitian village of Betay, when these words of Isaiah leapt off the pages of scripture. In a culture with so little, a country oppressed and exploited how could people be so happy and content?

The essence of this passage in Isaiah is appearance. We become proficient at creating an appearance of righteousness and grace while retaining an inner spirit of superiority and demanding expectation.

After reading Isaiah 58, practice its message today. Humble yourself. See the people who serve you today. Look them in the eye and thank them – in the coffee shop, gas station, restaurant, grocery store. They are there to serve God, not you. This just happens to be their venue to serve Him. Aren't our jobs, tasks, positions, just the same?

Prayer: Heavenly Father, thank you for helping us be aware of our surroundings and people you have placed in our lives. Keep us humble, serving, and loving. Amen.

Pastor Van Rathbun
Central Reformed Church

Van is our senior pastor at Central and is doing a fine job. He and his wife Teri had four biological children and then adopted three more international kids. What a great family!

May 3

Mark 1:17; Matthew 28:19-20; Acts 20:24

So You're Saved … Now What?

Are you ready and willing to make your life count as a Christian? In the Gospel of Mark, Jesus Christ calls each of us to "*Come, follow me ...*" When summoning the first disciples to trust His leading on this incredible journey of faith, these men immediately dropped their nets and followed. No longer would they be doing what they were used to, which was catching fish. They were being commanded to be fishers of human hearts.

A true disciple's heart most certainly enjoys having a personal relationship with Jesus. But this joy must also lead us to share this fellowship with others by confessing Him as Lord. The Great Commission, which pertains to believers, states that we must "*Go, and make disciples...*" How else will the ends of the earth hear the Gospel and the message of eternal life unless Christians are willing to deny themselves, speak up, and share the good news of Christ's amazing love?

Oswald Chambers said, "Why has God left us on the earth? Is it simply to be saved and sanctified? No, it is to be at work in service to Him. Am I willing to be of no value to this age or this life except for one purpose and one alone, to be used to disciple men and women to the Lord Jesus Christ? My life of service to God is the way I say 'thank you' to Him for His inexpressibly wonderful salvation."

Following our Savior in obedience isn't necessarily supposed to be easy; nevertheless, we obey because we love God. We owe Him our entire lives because He gave us His. We must be ready to count the cost. Run the race. Fight the good fight. Let go of comfort and complacency. Be willing to truly listen to the Lord's voice while walking forth in faith. And we must believe that our God is right there with us every step of the way. Because He is!

Prayer: Thank you Jesus for always being there for us. You lived and died for us help us to do the same for You. Amen.

Haley Janssen

Haley lives in Des Moines and is the daughter of Paul and Sheila. She is a past Tulip Queen and has a real heart for missions.

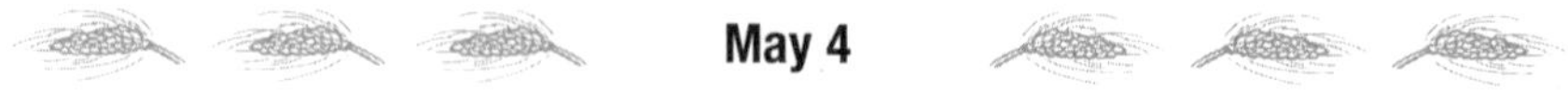

May 4

Zephaniah 3:12

Today's Mile Today

A tourist, no matter how distant his destination, must travel one mile at a time. This is, of course, a very obvious fact, but it is one that we pilgrims on the road of life frequently forget. Too often we try to travel tomorrow's mile today, failing to remember that no far away mile can be crossed until those preceding it have been successfully traversed. Life must be lived one day at a time.

Because this is true, a Christian concentrates his best efforts upon today. In his prayers he does as Jesus told him to do, asking only for today's need, "*Give us this day our daily bread.*" A Christian will give to today his best and leave tomorrow in the hands of his loving Heavenly Father. He will not be anxious or unduly concerned about tomorrow's mile. He lives a life of trust and peace– day by day, one at a time.

Life for the Christian is like a chest of drawers – 365 drawers. Each drawer contains instructions for that day. He does not try to open them all at once. That would create confusion. Each morning he opens the appropriate drawer, receives his instruction and in His Master's yoke does the work he is called to do. This he does not in his own strength, but in the Master's. He does the best he can and, when he lays himself down to rest at the close of the day's journey, he dedicates his efforts to his Lord, and he knows all is well. Tomorrow he will awaken refreshed to travel tomorrow's mile in the same spirit he traveled today's. His life is characterized by humble, simple trust.

Had you been out on one of the beautiful lakes of northern Minnesota a number of summers ago with a group of Iowa fishermen, you would have witnessed a touching sight. As those men fished, they allowed their boat to silently drift. At last it drifted into a quiet bay. The men noticed a movement in the reeds along the shore. A mother mallard duck stepped out, surveyed the lake, signaled, and out of the reeds tumbled a whole brood of ducklings. They ran and swam about, having such great fun.

The men forgot about their fishing. Here was something few are privileged to see. In his rapt attention, one of the men brushed against an oarlock and a slight sound resulted. The mother duck gave a warning signal. All movement on the lake stopped. Every little eye was upon the mother; every little body was at rigid attention. After a time, the mother, having determined that there was no immediate danger, again signaled. The ducklings resumed their play and did so with as much abandonment as before. They knew their mother was watching over them.

One of the men, a devout Christian business man, quietly said to the others, "Fellows, if we would only trust our Heavenly Father like that – trust Him who promises to care for us – how rich and wonderful life would be. How the burdens of today's living would fall away!"

Let us trust the future to our God and Father. Only when we do this is there a possibility of true happiness today. Only thus can we cross successfully the mile which we call "today."

Prayer: Heavenly Father, please increase our sense of trust. It's so easy to remember the mistrust and so difficult to trust in others. Give us strength for today. Amen.

Rev. Henry Eggink

May 5

Matthew 6:34

God Promises Eternity

When the doctor came in and said I had ALS (Lou Gehrig's Disease), it was like somebody had jumped on my chest with both feet! I couldn't breathe. For the next few months, if I thought about being sick, I got that same sensation. All I could think about was that I was going to die.

I had been going to church, and doing my daily devotions. I wondered why God had done this to me. It's been over 5 years now. I'm able to think about it and not hyperventilate. I live by Matthew 6:34, and try not to worry about any of the tomorrows. We all must live one day at a time. He gives us the strength to handle that. This verse gives me peace.

When I see how many people care about me, it's a humbling experience. **God doesn't promise tomorrow, He promises eternity!**

Prayer: Dear Lord, thank you for the gift of life. Thank you too for the love of family and friends. We can do nothing without you but so many things with you. Amen.

Steve Scholten

Steve is our nephew, son of my sister Colleen and Rod Scholten, and brother to Nancy Speer who is married to Stan. Steve has been through a lot in his young life and is an inspiration to all of us. He has a wife (Nancy Ann) and two daughters (Nicole and Allison). So far a couple of grandchildren make life more exciting and pleasant. There is no cure for ALS yet. We continue to donate and pray for that discovery. Someone said recently that Steve is showing us how to die – that's not true – he's showing us how to live! Please pray for him and his family right now!

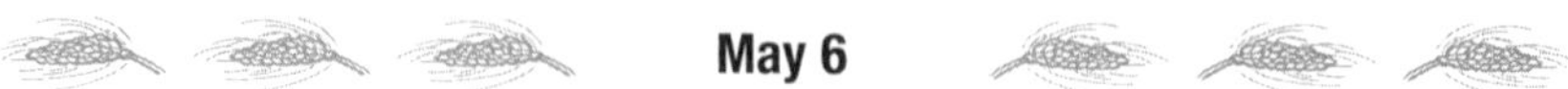

May 6

Mark 1:16-18

Extraordinary Measures

Do you like to read? I really do, but it has to be a pretty interesting or exciting book or article in order to keep me engaged. I can really enjoy the first few chapters of a book, but if it gets wordy or bland, I'm very well known to set the book down for a month or two before I pick it up again. Sometimes I even feel that way about reading the Bible, but the more and more I dig into it, the more things that I'd first consider "boring" are really coming to life! It speaks to my heart!

In the passage in Mark noted above, Jesus calls the disciples to follow Him and says, "I will make you fishers of men." I have heard and read this story A LOT growing up, but today it hit me differently. When Jesus calls us, no matter what we do, we should gratefully and wholeheartedly choose to follow! And when He calls us to follow, he is looking for people who are willing to let go of the ordinary and look for the extraordinary!

Sometimes we are called to make big changes, like leave our work or move away from our families to go where He wants us. Other times we are called to stay right where we're at and go about our ordinary lives. In each of these circumstances, God calls us to live it with a different perspective. If you are a teacher, remember you're making an impact on a child's life. If you work in a business, remember the big picture is we're working for God's Kingdom. When you're doing laundry, washing dishes, or scrubbing floors, remember it's a holy God we serve.

As we strive to be more like Jesus, listen to where He wants *you* to go, and follow Him. I pray we can always stay focused on the big picture, the extraordinary measures we must take in order to wholeheartedly follow Him. Let Jesus open your heart and use you!

Prayer: Dear God, please give us open eyes in our communities. Help us to not be so focused on our specific jobs/tasks that we lose sight of the big picture. Remind us that we are "fishing for" lives that we can touch to be transformed by You. Amen.

Ashley Egdorf
Administrative Assistant of ATLAS of Sioux Center

Ashley's unique combination of brains and heart has been such an asset to the ATLAS of Sioux Center team. Both the staff and those who come in their doors realize that this ministry would not be the same without her there!

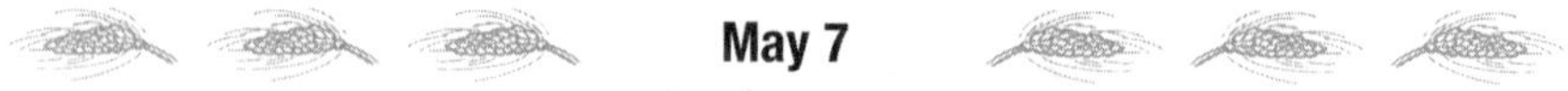

May 7

Psalm 103:17-19

The Covenant and The Kingdom

As I reflect on the legacy of my father, the late Rev. B.J. Haan, who was the first President of Dordt College (1963-82), there are two words that come to my mind. Both of these words happen to be found in this portion of Psalm 103. They are *covenant* and *kingdom*. These are two prominent biblical concepts which my father continually underscored as a pastor and a college president.

Covenant describes our total life situation as creatures of God, defining our relationship in faith and obedience to God, which in turn defines our relationship to other human beings, and to the world in which we live. It lays the basis for an all-encompassing Christian way of life. God has a special relationship "with those who fear him." Even though we don't deserve it, He graciously promises to be our God forever. He will take care of us as we put our faith in Jesus and humbly seek His will. Like the song goes: "Trust and obey, for there's no other way to be happy in Jesus, but to trust and obey."

Whereas covenant has to do more with a person's relationship with God, the concept of God's kingdom is much broader. Like the psalmist says, the Lord's kingdom "rules over all." One might say that while the concept of covenant inspired my father as he served as a pastor within the church (the "covenant community" as he liked to call it), it was the concept of kingdom that motivated him to be a leader in the area of education. Education involves learning about all the various aspects of God's world, and training in and for all areas of life. A favorite quote my father would like to use were these words uttered by Abraham Kuyper. "There is not one square inch of all the universe of which Christ the Lord does not say, 'This is mine.'" Every sphere of life falls under the Lord's rule, and in every sphere of life we are called to kingdom service.

Prayer: Father God, I praise You and thank You for Your precious promises. Help me to be a covenant keeper just like You. Rather than vainly building my own little kingdom, may Your Spirit keep working within me so that I may faithfully serve You with Your Kingdom. For Jesus sake, Amen.

Rev. Bernie and Brenda Haan

Rev. Bernie is the pastor of Faith Christian Reformed Church in Sioux Center. I hear nothing but good things about him. I am so pleased that he would write this thoughtful message in honor of his dad. His dad was an icon in the church, college, and in Sioux Center. I enjoyed playing golf with him because "you never hit a bad shot!"

May 8

1 Corinthians 9:24-27; 1 Corinthians 7:14

His Word Has The Answers

There are many different Bible verses that have been important to me over the years. It seems, whether I am going through difficult or joyous times, there is always a verse to turn to. These verses either explain, justify, or better yet, help me to realize the true meaning behind the situation.

In late 2006, my brother Dewey and his wife Heather, were expecting their third child. Prior to the birth, they were made aware that the baby could possibly have a heart defect. But, the extent of defect was unknown. On February 10, 2007, the Lord blessed Dewey and Heather, as well as their extended families, with a beautiful baby girl – Bailey Elizabeth Hupke.

Unbeknownst to any of us, Bailey would struggle with much more than a heart defect. After two abdominal and open heart surgeries, she continued to fight for her life. On May 8, 2007, the Lord decided that He needed Bailey more than we did. I will never forget my brother's words as he spoke at her funeral, "We were very blessed to have the short three months we did, to love Bailey here with us. Now we continue that love with her in Heaven."

A very appropriate Bible verse that Dewey and Heather chose for Bailey came from 1 Corinthians 9, "*In the race, everyone runs, but only one person gets first prize…run your race to win. Everyone who competes in the games goes into strict training. They do it to get a crown that will not last; but we do it to get a crown that will last forever.*"

I was so blessed to have my niece to hold for the short time I did. I thank God for her every day, and ask that she continues to watch over her family down here on earth.

Prayer: Thank you Lord for life. We never know how many days or years You will give us, but each one is precious. Watch over us and the one's we love this day. Amen.

Amy Hupke Brighton
Teacher and Women's Basketball Official

I went to college with Amy's dad (Leo) and Amy was one of my students at NWC. She and her husband Mark are both fine officials. Amy has worked several years at the National level. She lived with Dot and me one summer while wrapping up some summer school assignments. She remains one of the joys of our life.

May 9

Colossians 3:8; James 3:6-10

Control That Tongue!

Profanity is becoming more and more prevalent it seems. It is insidious, habit-forming, and unnecessary. There used to be rules and laws against it in the media. Unfortunately, these have been relaxed and the radio, movies, and television are filled with it. It shows a lack of vocabulary in my estimation.

But I was guilty too. I heard a lot of swearing as I grew up so I copied some of what I heard. I have never used God's name in vain or used filthy words, but that real hot place down below and those big things that are built in rivers to create lakes got *lots* of usage. I'm ashamed of how often, and with whom, that I swore. It took a great deal of prayer for self-control and discipline, to finally break the habit. I didn't get the habit whipped until my late 20's.

Profanity is another one of those things that other people observe and make judgments about. I can't say I'm proud of the way I spoke now (even when angry or for emphasis), but at least I don't have to be ashamed anymore. Is this something you want to pray about?

Prayer: Thanks for convicting us of what You want improved. And then I thank you for helping us work on things that bring us and You grief. Give us great direction today. Amen.

Dave

May 10

Romans 8:32; Isaiah 58:8-12

Fearsome Passes

A little boy was sent on an errand. About to start, he paused uncertainly at the door and said in a troubled way, "Mother, it's so far, and it's a new road to me. I've never been there before. I'm not 'xactly afraid, but couldn't you go a little way with me?" The mother caught the anxiousness of the child's appeal and said tenderly, "Mother will go <u>all</u> the way with you, son." So, with his little hand in his mother's, he walked the new way unafraid.

Today you are facing a new way. You have never walked it before. Fearsome passes may lie ahead. Perhaps you are facing surgery today, or an interview for a new job, or some difficult assignment. Whatever it is, you are troubled. You are not "'xactly afraid," but you do wish that you did not need to travel the unknown way alone. The assurance of the Bible is that this is not necessary. You may have the presence and help of the eternal God Himself, if only you earnestly so desire. Consult again the passage in Isaiah, *part of which reads as follows: Thou shalt call, and the Lord shall answer; thou shalt cry, and he shall say, "Here I am ... And the Lord shall guide thee continually, and satisfy thy soul in drought ..."*

We have no reason to expect that the road of life will always be smooth and easy. Quite the contrary is true. We may need to fight hard battles against what seem to be insurmountable odds. We may need to face difficult and treacherous passes on life's road. But we must not complain or lose heart.

That is easily said, but not so easily practiced. Even the great servant of God, Martin Luther, fell into periods of fear and discouragement. We are told that upon a certain occasion Luther had again fallen into such a mood. While in that state, he noted that his devoted wife put on mourning garments and assumed an air of grave silence.

When asked by her husband the reason for this change, she replied, "Why, I thought God had died – the way that you have been acting; and so I thought it proper that I go in mourning."

So often we plod upon our pilgrim way as though our loving heavenly Father had died, and as a result we, like orphaned children, must now move through the dark passes of life as best we can, trusting upon our own resources.

We are not orphaned children! God our Father is still ruler of the universe! With Him nothing is impossible! With Him we have adequate resources for every need. That assurance brings peace. Peace has been well defined as "the conscious possession of adequate resources." These we have in Christ Jesus.

Visualize a boat sailing down the great Columbia River. Above it soars an airplane. The captain of the slow moving craft can see no farther ahead than to the next bend in the stream. But the pilot can see beyond that bend, even to distant places into which the river moves. He knows now what the captain must discover a little at a time.

So it is in life. We can see only what lies immediately before our eyes, but God knows the way from beginning to end.

Prayer: Thanks for taking so much of the fear out of so many things we do. Help us to move forward with confidence to accomplish Your will. Amen.

Rev. Henry Eggink

May 11

1 Corinthians 13

Perfect Love

"The Love Chapter" is used so often. It must mean we need to be reminded often of the importance of this agape-type love. Not the love seen on TV, books, and movies. So what should we learn from verses 4-7? Love is patient ... slow to judge but quick to listen; love is kind ... words to be gentle, actions to be thoughtful; love does not envy or boast, it is not proud; loving hearts are humble and see the good in others; love is not self-seeking – speak words that are easy on the ears and on the heart; love is not easily angered and keeps no record of wrongs – forgives others as we have been forgiven; loves does not delight in evil, but rejoices with the truth, standing up for what is right and good; love always protects and always trusts, and is always a refuge for those around us; love always perseveres – hearts continually beat with love for you and for others.

Can't we all glean something from this great chapter to put into use today?

Prayer: Father, forgive our feeble attempts at agape love. Draw us closer to the true love that displays Your honor and glory. Amen.

Dot

May 12

Matthew 11:28; 1 Peter 5:7

Burden Weary

So you have a burden. That is not strange. Rare, indeed, is the traveler who carries no load. That load may not always be apparent, but it is there just the same.

"But my burden is so heavy," you say. "My problems, my cares threaten to overwhelm me. They are more than I can bear alone."

You do not need to bear them alone! That is one of the wonderful Gospel assurances. Read how Jesus put it in Matthew and how Peter described His caring for you. Too often we go staggering along under life's burdens and problems forgetting that there is One who wants to help. We do not go to Him with our burden of sin. We do not go to Him with our anxieties and problems. And as a result He cannot help us and we continue to stagger along.

Frequently this happens, too: When we do finally go to God with our sins, anxieties, and problems, we do not leave them with Him. We speak to Him about them, but when we depart, we carry them away with us once more. We do not really "Let go and let God." We have not mastered what someone has aptly called "the art of relinquishment."

Many years ago, Dr. Mark Pearse was driving along with his horse and carriage. He overtook a woman who was trudging along carrying a heavy basket. Her shoulders were drooping and she gave every evidence of being extremely tired. She gladly accepted his offer to ride. Seating herself in the carriage, she held the heavy basket on her lap.

Dr. Pearse looked at her several times and finally said, "My good woman, your basket will ride just as well on the floor of the carriage as on your lap, and I am sure you will be much more comfortable."

"Thank you, sir," she said, "so it will. I never thought of that."

Dr. Pearse goes on to say, "You know, we often do that very thing. We try to carry our sins, our burdens, our problems alone, forgetting that there is One who offers to relieve us of the load." Simply spoken, we must place our problems in the hand of God and leave them there. That is real trust. That is our Christian privilege. It is so simple, so wonderful. What about that heavy burden you are carrying just now, fellow traveler? Have you tried going to the Savior in humble prayer to tell Him about it? That is your privilege too.

We place our problems in the hand of a loving Heavenly Father and leave them there. Having done that we are in a position to take to the road once more to move steadily and confidently toward the Eternal Home.

Prayer: Heavenly Father we ask you to take our burdens. We know we can't do it without You and our complete trust is in You. Amen.

Rev. Henry Eggink

May 13

Psalm 3:5

When Graduation (Change) Looms Ahead

As the end of the college year loomed, graduating became, what looked like, a daunting task. All the final projects, tests and papers were piled on and had to be finished before the end of the school year. Added on top of the stress of finals week is the stress of the unknown. This is a scary time, not knowing what is next, not knowing where you are going to go or what you are going to do. All the while I was feeling scared, I kept hearing the same advice from those I love and trust. "It will work out; it's in God's hands." It seems so hard to trust in the unknown, but pausing and looking into the future, it's not unknown. God knows. He knows where I am going. He knows what I will be doing and He knows how He will use me wherever He puts me. It's not unknown. That makes graduating less of a daunting task.

Through the week, many verses have risen to my attention on things such as quotes found on the graduation programs, cards from family members, and personal emails from friends. Almost all have one common theme: That God knows my future and He promises to take care of me and all those with faith in Him. My favorite verse of the week that helped calm my nerves was sent in an email from my aunt from the book of Psalms. It said, "Now I can lie down and go to sleep and then awake, for Yahweh has hold of me." (Ps. 3:5) God is telling us to sleep easy; He has hold of us and will forever take care of our needs. It makes graduation not so fearful when the ruler of the universe is looking out for me. In times when uncertainly and change loom before us, the only place to look for comfort is to the One who is the All-knowing and to whom there is no unknown.

Prayer: Thank you God for always having a plan for us. Help us to always follow that plan and to be bold as we follow Your lead. Amen.

Randa Hulstein

Randa is the rare athlete that excelled in two sports at NWC. She helped lead her teams to the National Tournament in both Volleyball and Basketball, winning the Championship in Basketball. She was named All-Tournament and All-American in both! Statistics show that those who excel in co-curricular activities go on to excel in many aspects of life – expect great things from this young woman!

May 14

Deuteronomy 6:10-25; Matthew 4:8-11

God's Way

Jesus' baptism marks the official beginning of His ministry, the work of redemption. Jesus knows that it will be a difficult work. It will mean obediently walking God's way, the way of humiliation, life-long suffering, death on a cross, and burial in a borrowed tomb. But as a reward for His redemptive work, He will be given a kingdom in which "every tongue will confess that Jesus Christ is Lord, to the glory of God the Father." (Philippians 2:11)

However, as always, Satan stands opposed to doing things God's way. In the beginning God created all things for the sake of His glory; but Satan exalted himself over against God in seeking for himself a position of supreme authority. And now Satan tries to frustrate the work of redemption by tempting Jesus to do things his way rather than God's. This is the case in all three temptations, but especially in the third.

"Again, the devil took him to a very high mountain and showed Him all the kingdoms of the world and their splendor." It's as if Satan is turning the globe before Jesus showing him all the kingdoms, all the nations of the world and their glory – their strength, wealth, treasures, resources, military power, cities, and citizenry. Claiming that it belongs to him, Satan says, "All this I will give you, if you will bow down and worship me." What about this claim? In a sense it cannot be denied. As the prince of darkness Satan holds sway over the kingdoms of this world, exercising authority over those in the darkness of sin, paying his price for their service. Ultimately, of course, Satan lies. He rules as a renegade. His claim is the height of presumption, and Jesus will show it for what it really is.

But what does Satan hope to accomplish by this charade? Remember, Jesus is walking God's way to the kingdom, His reign over all things in heaven and on earth. It's a way of suffering and death. It's at this point that Satan intrudes by offering Jesus what seems to be a much easier way. All Jesus has to do is "bow down" – take Satan's way which is easy, instead of God's way which is hard – and Jesus will supposedly receive his promised reward, "all the kingdoms of the world and their splendor." Of course, if Jesus accepts his offer, Satan will have succeeded in his effort to frustrate the redemptive plan and work of God.

However, Jesus rejects Satan's way, saying, "*Away from me Satan.*" Jesus knows that what Satan offers does not belong to him. "*The earth is the Lord's and everything in it, the world, and all who live in it.*" (Psalm 24:1) Jesus knows too, that He does not want what Satan offers. He has not come for the *kingdom* that would pass away, but for the *kingdom that will endure.* Finally, and most importantly, Jesus realizes that to accept Satan's offer is to reject God's way and to become Satan's servant.

Instead, Jesus insists on walking God's way. Quoting from Deut. 6, Jesus recalls Israel's entrance into the kingdom land of Canaan. As they enter the land. Moses warns them. "Fear the Lord your God, serve Him only." Now Jesus comes to claim the kingdom. Rather than submitting to temptation as a servant of Satan, He will serve God only. Choosing the way of obedience – the way of the cross, burial, resurrection, and ascension – He breaks the power of Satan and is given "all authority in heaven and earth." (Matt. 28:18)

Jesus is King! His kingdom has come and is coming!

As King, Jesus calls us, redeemed citizens of His kingdom, to serve Him only, walking in God's way. And surely He will be with us always, "to the very end of the age."

Prayer: Today Lord, we say the prayer you taught us: Our Father in heaven, Hallowed be your name, Your Kingdom Come, Your will be done on earth as it is in heaven. Give us today our daily bread. Forgive us our debts, as we also have forgiven our debtors. And lead us not into temptation, but deliver us from the evil one. For yours is the kingdom and the power and the glory forever. Amen.

Rev. John and Louise Hulst

Rev. John served as the second President of Dordt College (1982-96). He served well and the college grew tremendously. It was our pleasure to have John and Louise as neighbors for many of the years they lived in Sioux Center. He wrote his memoirs "A Doorkeeper in God's Household" and you will find it to be very informative and interesting.

May 15

1 Thessalonians 5:16-18

Alzheimer's and Dementia

It is scary when I think of developing Alzheimer's. I think I could handle Dave with this terrible disease better than Dave taking care of me with it. I pray it doesn't happen with either of us. Then I remember who is in charge – God has the plan in place.

I attended a workshop *Understanding the Person with Alzheimer's* by Jolene Brackey. She has written a book Creating Moments of Joy. That is what we strive for – moments.

It seems the Golden Rule can be applied at so many times. We have to treat others the way we would want to be treated. If you can think of any care givers right now, why not reach out and make their day a little brighter?

Prayer: God, I pray for daily strength, joy, and encouragement for those "caring with love," those with Alzheimer's and Dementia. Amen.

Dot

May 16

Job 36:15

Domestic Abuse

Why did God allow this to happen? What did we ever do to deserve such pain and sorrow? These are the questions I would often ask God as I looked at my baby lying lifeless in the trauma center. This beautiful baby girl did nothing to deserve the abuse waged against her small, innocent body. The horrendous crime of child abuse can send a shockwave through an entire family. The harm that one person can do to another is sometimes unspeakable.

As a Christian, I believe that everything happens for a reason; however, during the time of this family crisis, it was hard to see or find God's reasoning. So I turned to prayer "Please God, show me your purpose, your reasoning for these sufferings." Once the sunshine began to shine in my life again, God's reasoning and purpose became clear. I began a life-long journey to make the rights of victims of violence heard. I built shelters and programs for victims of domestic violence and sexual assault.

Twenty-five years later, I have touched the lives of over 5,000 families affected by violence. During my darkest hour, God had cemented my life's purpose and plan.

Prayer: Dear God, in our time of pain and despair, let us remember to be silent and listen for your purpose to become clear. Amen.

Shari Kastein
Director, Family Crisis Center in Sioux Center

Shari has a great story to tell. We're hoping it may be made into a movie. Always keep the Crisis Center in your thoughts and prayers and support Melissa's Hope Chest.

May 17

Psalm 12:5; Proverbs 29:25

Feet Inside the Circle

Not long after the beginning of the last war between China and Japan, the Japanese bombed a Chinese city in which a mission hospital was located. The planes had come without advance warning, catching the city completely by surprise. The Christian missionary doctor was performing an operation when the planes came over the first time. Bombs dropped everywhere, one near the hospital. A sick woman lay on the operating table with the incision already made. In this dangerous moment her life, humanly speaking, depended upon the wisdom, skill, and devotion to duty of that doctor. He looked at his assistants and said, "That bomb fell close. I must finish the operation. You people are free to go to the basement, if you wish, to find shelter there." Not one person left. The skilled doctor, with the assistance of his staff, successfully completed the difficult surgery. Later, when complimented upon his poise in danger and his devotion to duty, he said, "The only safe place for any of us is the place where our Lord would have us be."

How true these words are! In times of peace or in times of war, in days of youth or das of old age, in prosperity or in adversity, the only safe place for any of us is where the Lord would have us be, doing the thing He would have us do. We must live inside the circle of His will.

Perhaps you have been restless, driven and tossed about by every wind that blows. Your life has not brought deep satisfaction. You have not felt that it was accomplishing the purpose for which it was made. You have longed for something which will steady you, which will give peace, assurance and serenity to your soul. Nothing will do that better than to place your feet within the circle of God's will. And having placed them there, keep them there. Dante, many years ago, stated the truth thus, "In His will is our peace."

The road upon which lies the circle of God's will for your life may not be an easy one. It may not be the one which you had originally planned to take. Traveling it may require laying aside cherished personal plans and ambitions. The road may take you to distant lands and strange places. It may be a thorny, a rocky, a hilly, a difficult road. But, if you have sincerely asked God to place you where He wants you to be, you will travel that road with safety. You will also possess a contentment and a peace which passes all understanding, and your life will realize the purpose for which God made it.

The only safe place for any of us is the place where God wishes us to be. We must live our lives within the circle of God's will. Have you placed your feet there?

Prayer: Thank you Lord for keeping us safe thus far. Many times we may be fearful of what lies ahead or of decisions we must make, at all times keep us "in Your circle." Amen.

Rev. Henry Eggink

May 18

John 14:30; John 16:11; Ephesians 6:12; 1 John 4:4

Just How Powerful Is The Devil?

Pretty powerful I'm afraid, but not nearly as powerful as our God. That's good news. But don't ever underestimate him, or his purpose. He has lots of tools and fellow demons at his disposal. He can, and does, make our life miserable.

Here are some things he is not: Omnipresent, Omniscient, Omnipotent, (Only God has these qualities), Truthful (In fact he's the 'King of Liars'). He does know our weaknesses and will definitely work on them. He's the great tempter, but 1 Corinthians 10:13, lets us know there is an avenue of escape.

It's important to know who you are fighting and where our help lies (Prayer, Fellow Believers, and Bible).

We know what will eventually happen to him (Revelation 20:10), but in the meantime, he's trying to get as many of us as he can. I repeat, never under estimate him, resist him (James 4:7), and we can and will prevail over this evil one. We really do need each other in Christian fellowship.

Prayer: Thank you for helping us to resist the devil. Put a hedge of protection around us and the ones we love. Bind the devil. Amen.

Dave

May 19

Job 1:13-19

Smash Up

So it has happened to you, too. You were breezing along on the road of life with hardly a care in the world. Suddenly, without warning, a black stone wall appeared on the road ahead. Before you could do a thing about it, you had smashed head on into that immovable obstruction. That black wall may have been in the form of a terrible disappointment, a sin, a sorrow, a physical ailment, or any one of many such things. But whatever it was in your case, it is to your mind about the worst tragedy with which one can be confronted. And you hit it and hit it hard. Now you lie broken and beaten. To you, life seems to have fallen apart into a thousand pieces. So far as you can see, the wreckage is beyond repair; it is hopeless.

With all the emphasis we can muster, we say, "That is not true. The Gospel proclaims that no life can be so wrecked and ruined that it is beyond redemption. It tells about a wonderful Savior who has the ability to mend life's broken things.

How a life ruined by sin can be redeemed, how a heart broken by sorrow can be healed, and how other broken things of human life can be mended we may not be able to fully understand. We only know that these things are possible with God through Christ Jesus.

But here is the secret of it all: we must place these broken things in His hands. So long as we keep our broken things in our own hands they remain broken. But place them in His hands and there is restoration.

Years ago in a tiny shop in Europe a marvelously skilled craftsman worked. He specialized in the restoration of hopelessly broken things. With loving, patient care he slowly fitted together the fragments brought to him and by his cunning skill the broken things were made whole again. A patron might bring a ruined vase, or a broken statue, or a shattered glass for which it seemed there was no hope, but, when entrusted to the great craftsman's care, there was marvelous restoration.

The help of God is like that when we place our shattered lives in His hands. Yes, it is more than that, for He not only restores that which was wrecked, He gives to the wreckage placed in His hands a beauty, a glory, a purposefulness and a usefulness it may never have possessed before.

For years a beautiful stained glass window had adorned a village church. One black night a stormy wind blew out this window and it fell to the ground shattered into a thousand pieces. The next morning the village folk with sad hearts gathered up the fragments, placed them in a box and set it in the church basement.

A few years later a stranger passing through heard about the broken window. He asked the church officers if he might have the broken fragments. They consented, realizing that they served no purpose in the dark basement.

Some months later the church officers were invited to visit the studio of a noted artist. There they saw a stained glass window far more beautiful than any they had ever seen before. To their amazement they learned that it had been made from the broken fragments which came from their basement. In the hands of the master artist the once shattered window had not only been restored but had received something new. It had become an object of greater beauty and usefulness than it had ever been before. Restored to its original place in the church, it served with a new power and glory to point the villagers to God.

Thus it is with the shattered things of life. But again, the secret is this – we must place our broken things in the Master's hands. The most broken life will come to its true glory and purpose when it is fully yielded to the Savior's redemptive power.

So your life has suffered a smash-up. Don't just lie there in the wreckage with hopelessness in your heart. Rise up and, with simple faith, place yourself in the hands of Him who can mend all of life's broken things.

Prayer: Dear God, of course we would rather stay away from any smash-ups if possible. But if one comes along we do place it in Your hands. Help us, Jesus. Amen.

Rev. Henry Eggink

May 20

Romans 11:29

What God Can't Do

Do you know there are some things God can't do? No, I'm not talking about that old "Can God make something so heavy, He can't lift it" deal. This is different and the Bible verifies it.

God keeps His promises. He can't break them or change His mind about this.

God can't lie, die, or sin. In Isaiah 43:25 He tells us He can't remember our forgiven sins. Wow! I wish I could do that too.

We worship and serve a fantastic God. The things He CAN do are even better than the things He can't!

Prayer: Thank you Lord for only remembering the good stuff. Help us to forget the bad stuff too. Help us to concentrate on what we can do for You and for others and remember to apply Your Golden Rule. Help us to accentuate the positive. Amen.

Dave

May 21

Jeremiah 29:10-11

After Seventy Years!

Over the years, I don't think there is any text more loved by young people such as those who attend the Christian college where I serve as president, than Jeremiah 29:11. Indeed for any Christian seeking her or his place in God's world these words are filled with stunning comfort. "For I know the plans I have for you, declares the Lord. Plans to prosper you and not to harm you, plans to give you hope and a future."

However, I'm afraid that when most of us quote this text we miss the words that come just before it. It is only "After seventy years are completed ..." that God would bring the deliverance and carry out this good plan that He had in mind for the frustrated Jewish exiles to whom Jeremiah first sent this message.

And that's not something that most college students want to hear. "Maybe after another 70 years, once you're in your 90's I'll show you my good plan." says the Lord. They (and I'm sure all the rest of us as well) would rather have God to make things clear and good right now – or perhaps next week at the latest.

But as Jesus himself reminded His disciples. "Timelines are God's responsibility, not ours:" (Acts I:7) God's plans are clear. They really are good plans and they will bring us eternal blessing. But the day or hour when that plan will be revealed is something for which we need to wait in patience and in hope.

Prayer: So many times we have thanked You because You have a plan for our lives. Forgive us when we show impatience and an unwillingness to listen. Please continue to reveal that plan to us as quickly as we can handle it. Amen.

Dr. Carl E. Zylstra
President of Dordt College

Dr. Carl took over the Presidency in 1996. We became friends several years earlier, when he was a church pastor in Orange City and we were in the Lions Club. It has always been my pleasure to work with him and listen to his ideas. He cares for young people, has a great sense of humor, and follows our Lord's leading.

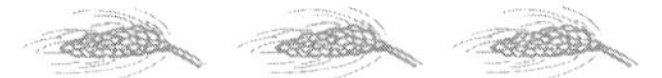 **May 22** 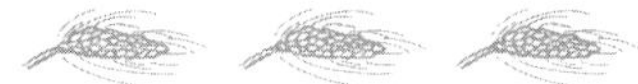

Ephesians 4:26, 27, 32

Words That Hurt – Words That Heal

It was Sunday morning and Lora and I started the day off with words of disagreement over a money issue. We went to church, then out to dinner at some friends, during which time we were smiling and acting like all was well, but the conflict was still brewing. We came home mid--afternoon and it didn't take long before we picked up where the morning had begun. The hurtful words came freely and we each made sure that we "had our say"!

Conflict is a common occurrence in life and we rarely handle it well! You have likely heard that God gave us two ears and one mouth for a reason, and in our case the conflict started to move toward resolution when we actually started listening to one another.

At the root of all conflict there are "heart issues" and when we got to the "heart of the issues" of this conflict our perspectives and words started to focus more on the feelings of our partner rather than ourselves.

As Christians, we ask God to live in our hearts and He wants nothing more than to do just that. When the author of "love" has residence in our hearts, He brings us back to where we need to be and in His Word, He leads us to the words that can heal.

Prayer: Thank you Jesus for your example of love and forgiveness. We praise you for your providence and pray for more love for You and for each other. Amen.

Barry and Lora Brandt
NWC Athletic Director—Registered Nurse

Barry has also done a lot of coaching. He won an Iowa High School State Championship in football before coming back to his alma mater. He has been Head Track Coach and was the Offensive Coordinator in football for a number of very successful years here at NWC. Barry does a lot of lay preaching throughout NW Iowa. He and Lora enjoy a great family life and more and more grandchildren all the time.

May 23

Leviticus 16:8; Joshua 18:10; 1 Samuel 14:42; 1 Chronicles 26:13; Psalms 22:18; Isaiah 34:17; Obadiah 11; Joel 3:3; Jonah 1:7; Nahum 3:10; Matthew 27:35; -John 19:24

Gambling

Whew! This is a tough issue for me. Is it tough for you too? I have studied lots of information about it and I think it's mostly a negative thing, but I like to do it. Crimes are committed, businesses lost, and homes wrecked because of it. It promotes smoking and drinking. These are all big negatives in my book.

This may be rationalization (I'm pretty good at that too), but on the other hand, ponder these. The Bible does not speak of it, except in a positive way (i.e. the "sacred dice" (casting lots) to make decisions). Gambling produces great revenues for many states and other entities. It can be very entertaining for some. It provides a great number of jobs, construction, and opportunities for famous people to perform. You can probably think of other positives and negatives.

So what can be said? Each of us has to evaluate, communicate, and pray about it. I believe that if you think it is wrong, or feel guilt, it is wrong for you. (Romans 14:23) It's one of those things that you have to control, rather than let it control you.

Prayer: There are many things that are difficult to know exactly what Your thinking may be. To me, this is one of them. Please give us wisdom, restraint, and understanding. Thank you for always caring, listening, and advising. Amen.

Dave

May 24

2 Timothy 1:5-7

Grammas and Grampas

What a great institution! We really do love and enjoy our two grandchildren. I think Dot is a fabulous Gramma. She's a very thoughtful person anyway – but she seems to know just when to say the right words – or do the right things. I'm about average. What's my excuse? Maybe it's that I never had any Grampas of my own. Both of my granddads died long before I was born. So did one of my grandmothers. The other one lived until I was a sophomore in college but she spoke mostly Dutch, and I really don't remember ever carrying on a conversation with her.

People live longer today, so most kids have their grandparents for a long time. That's really great. What I'm saying is remember what you love about your grandparents and learn how to become a good one. I'm praying you get the opportunity to be a part of this great institution.

Dot has a different perspective which you'll find interesting.

My Dad's mom was an awesome grandmother. She had a fourth grade education, was divorced, had little money, and later remarried. She never expressed life being unfair. Gramma had a great sense of humor and was fun.

My parents became concerned during the summer polio outbreaks in Sioux City. Therefore, my sister Diana and I spent each summer with my grandparents at their cottage in Northern Minnesota. We still enjoy reminiscing about the wonderful memories. We knew she loved us and we loved and respected her.

Prayer: Thank you Lord for giving us the chance to be grandparents. It is an awesome and fun opportunity. Bless all of the grandchildren that are being prayed for right now. Amen.

Dot and Dave

May 25

Ephesians 4:32

Mom

My mom's upbringing had several hard knocks which caused her to build a shell of protection. You had better not try manipulation with "sweet talk." Mom was very intelligent, talented, hard-working – a model for my sister Diana and me. But she could never let go of the past. It was in her later years of life that she finally shared some of this. What a load of hurt! An unforgiving spirit is poison. That was a lesson for Diana and me as well.

I am so relieved that she received a saving faith in her last years of life so I have the hope and assurance of seeing her again.

"Bernie" was born on this date in 1918. She passed away from an aneurism in 1998 while living in retirement in Florida. We still miss her, one is never quite ready to lose our Mom.

Prayer: Thank you God for giving and modeling the spirit of forgiveness for all of us who ask for it. Keep us mindful of how often we must be forgiven and how many opportunities we have to forgive others. Amen.

Dot

May 26

Matthew 18:5

Kids and Nurturing

Several times, as our daughter Amy was growing up, she called me aside and said, "Now Dad, don't say anything – just listen." She knew me better than I thought. I was used to having students come to me asking for some advice. They wanted me to listen, but they wanted me to say something too. Maybe that's okay for an advisor, but not necessarily so for our own kids. Some people just need you to listen to them. Giving a listening ear, a caring heart, and your time can mean an awful lot.

When it comes to group dynamics and personal communications, listening always comes first. Isn't that also true with God? How much do we consciously listen to Him?

Prayer: Thank you Lord for always hearing us. Thank you for kids. Help us to follow that example as we deal with others. Amen.

Dave

May 27

Jeremiah 29:11-12

A Plan for Each of Us

As I look back on my life so far, it is obvious that the Lord had a plan for me. I didn't realize it when it was happening.

When I graduated from high school in 1952, I had no plan for my life. But God's plan called for me to be drafted into the service in '53. His plan called for me to be sent to England in a small Company made up almost exclusively of college graduates. These friends encouraged me to go to college. His plan called for me to be discharged early, in time to enter college in the Fall of'56. His plan called for me to marry a young lady who encouraged me to go into teaching.

His plan called for me to teach in high school for three years and to get a master's degree in the summers.

His plan called for my favorite college teacher to transfer to another college. He called me and offered me a job teaching with him in the church-affiliated college. His plan called for this teacher to leave before I came the next fall. I was therefore the department head.

His plan has allowed me to teach for forty years surrounded by a dedicated Christian faculty, staff, administration, and student body. They have encouraged my walk of faith every day.

Prayer: May I always be thankful for the many blessings you have given me and the love and encouragement of friends, family, and colleagues. Amen.

Phil Patton
Retired Professor of Bus/Econ at NWC

On July 6, 2010 I lost this dear friend. He was 76 and lung problems were the culprit. Phil was the Head of the Dept. when I came to NWC in the early 80's. What a leader and what a friend! He helped me so much and we had so much fun. Phil did massive amounts for NWC and for his students. He lost his beloved wife Marty 10 years before and that was so tough. His two great kids (Greg and Lynn) stayed very close. He was a very regular member of the DutchMart Coffee Group, a master joke-teller, a very caring and loving person. We all miss him dearly. You will find a couple more devotionals written by Phil in this book.

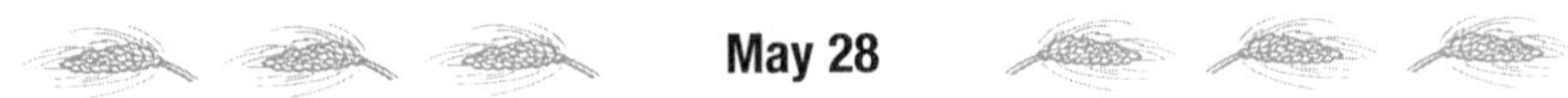

May 28

Romans 12:3

I'm Third

God/Jesus must be first, family second, and then we can start to consider ourselves. Maybe we should put other things ahead of us too. Job, team, education, and you may think of other items. The point is, life can't be about "old # 1." It's not easy to think of others ahead of ourselves. It doesn't seem natural. Does being selfish make one happy? It certainly hasn't worked for me. I hate to admit how many times I have put my job or other things ahead of God and my family. (Remember what the Bible says about idols?) I was particularly guilty when I was coaching. Winning became too important.

What do you spend most of your time, your money, your thoughts on? That can give you a little idea about what may be # 1. It's a real struggle, but never give up.

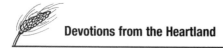

Prayer: Dear Jesus, I'm sorry for the many times I have put other stuff ahead of You. I'm sorry too for the times, I've let my family down. Thank you for forgiveness, both from You and from the ones we love. Help us to do better today. Amen.

Dave

May 29

Proverbs 15:1, 18

Patience is a Virtue

In our twenty years of marriage, we have found out that we can keep learning from each other.

Soon after we moved into our first home we probably found out that differing opinions could challenge us each day. It's not an easy thing in any marriage to decide what to hang on the walls, and when one person is an artist/teacher and the other is an elementary teacher without much training in art, you would probably expect the artist to make most of the decisions. However, the non-artist didn't think so, and could be heard asking questions like, "Doesn't living room art usually match the drapes?" "Don't family portraits fill the empty spaces?" "Is a Goya etching with a war prisoner in chains really your first choice?" Does the Chagall lithograph, with the yellow cross and other orange and purple floating images, really fit above this green chair?"

Obviously, there were disagreements and the temptation to be unkind to each other was present. One of us had to listen and learn quickly that "good art" on our walls was meant to be more than a decorative accessory – and that's still true today!

Which art work to hang probably hasn't been the toughest hurdle for us to cross. So, we've been thankful for the wisdom of Proverbs to guide us daily and we continue to pray for gentle answers and patience so we can continue to keep learning...

Prayer: Thank you Lord, for giving us Your Word to guide us always ... "a lamp unto our feet and light unto our path ... " In your precious name, we pray. Amen.

Bonnie and John Kaericher
Retired Teacher and Art Professor at NWC

Bonnie is a close friend of Dot's and another of our very special babysitters. John is a regular at the DutchMart Coffee Group.

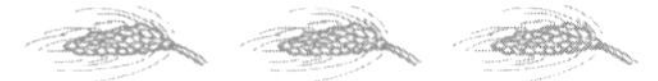

May 30

1 Thessalonians 4:1

Memorial Day

I think there are many advantages in growing up in a small town like Alton, Iowa. So many people influenced my life as I was growing up, but I'm afraid not all of them knew it.

One day last fall, I walked through my hometown cemetery and looked at every headstone. This produced some smiles, some tears, and lots of memories. Many of those men and women played a significant role in my life. I'm sad to say, I'd forgotten some of them. But the more headstones I looked at, the more I realized that bits of me were buried in those plots.

So where am I going with this? Give your flowers to the living, but don't let the good memories of these great people stay in the grave. If you know a wife, son, or daughter of the deceased, give 'em the good word as soon as you possibly can.

Plan a walk today!

Prayer: Heavenly Father, I thank you for those many people that cared enough about me to make a difference. Help us to make a positive difference in the lives that surround us. Thank you especially for those that have passed from this earth and now rest in your arms. We look forward to that same reward. Amen.

Dave

May 31

Matthew 11:30; 1 Corinthians 10:13; James 1:12-14

Easy Yokes and Light Burdens

Easy yokes and light burdens are not what concern us. It's the heavy, difficult stuff ... so much so that we wonder about Jesus' words about EASY yokes and LIGHT burdens in Matthew, and Paul's promise that God won't let us be tempted beyond our strength in 1 Corinthians. We wonder when tragedy strikes, disappointment hurts, or pain (both physical and emotional) won't subside.

Tradition says the oxen yokes Jesus fashioned as a carpenter fit so well the oxen's work was "easy" and the burden seemed "light." The point was Jesus' offer of new life is "suitable," meaning it fits our situation, no matter what. The suffering of a loved one is never easy or light. We can't bear it alone, and we don't have to. Oxen worked in teams, yokes were made for a pair... and Jesus offers to be yoked with us in life, no matter what, with the power of God's grace. God does not ask us to "go it alone" but fits His grace to us ... so together, yoked, we can be all God intends - His children in every situation.

As for "God never gives us more than we can bear," that's not what Paul said or meant in 1 Corinthians. He said, agreeing with James, that God tempts no one, nor permits us to be tested beyond our strength. And what is our strength? We are yoked with Christ who fits God's grace to us and our lives perfectly no matter what.

Prayer: Gracious God, remind us gently who and whose we are. For Jesus' sake and ours, Amen

Rev. Dennis Wilcox
Former Pastor of Central Reformed in Sioux Center,
and presently serving the church in New Jersey

It was my privilege to serve several terms as a Deacon and then an Elder when Pastor Dennis served our church. He was always well-prepared, stuck to the Bible, and had the best Children's Messages I've ever heard. We not only thank him but wish him and his great family all of our Lord's best.

June 1

Proverbs 18:24

Friends

Ron Juffer is one of the nicest people you will ever meet. He is also a great friend to many, and particularly to me.

Ron is a legendary basketball player and coach. He was a 2-year High School All-Stater as a player, and won the State Championship as a coach. He was a great role model to his players and students, and still is.

I could literally write a book about this guy. He is genuinely funny, intentionally and unintentionally. He can laugh at himself and with you. I have never heard him say anything bad about anyone, but I've heard him say countless good things. He's also been voted "Prof of the Year" at NWC and his many students love him (as they should!).

I have learned so many things from this humble man – and that will surprise him when he reads this.

His Christian faith and witness, giving, compassion for the downtrodden, visits with the elderly, competitive spirit, and love of people are exceptional. There's no one like him and he's a treasure as a friend. I wish I could be like him.

It was a privilege being his coaching assistant for 6 years, and lots of fun to be close friends with him and his loving wife of over 50 years. Peg is a perfect partner for Juf. It gives me even greater pleasure to know we're going to share eternity together with our Lord.

Prayer: Dear Lord, I thank you for showing us to be and have friends. You have showed us so many ways to make this life on earth better. We really do need each other. Amen.

Dave

June 2

Ephesians 2:8-9

What Is God's Will For My Life?

Regardless of a person's age, there are very few questions asked more often than this one. Jerry Sittser, a former chaplain at Northwestern and author of the book, "The Will of God as a Way of Life", believes that no matter what career path we choose, we will be doing God's will as long as we accept grace, keep God supreme in our life, and reach out to people around us.

By keeping God #1, Sittser suggests committing our life to being loving, patient, honest, humble, faithful, self-controlled, joyful, kind, and good (fruits of the Spirit). He also recognizes that we will fall short in these areas, so we need to constantly be remindful that eternal life is a gift based on the sacrifice of God's son on the cross. All we have to do is believe.

Prayer: Lord, may we always be mindful of the needs of others. Guide us this day in your means of grace. Amen.

Ron Juffer
Semi-Retired Education Prof at NWC &
Former Head Baseball & Basketball Coach

June 3

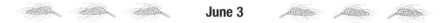

John 14:1-4

Maintaining Control

How often do we see people fail to control their emotions or actions in situations beyond their control? In sports it happens all the time, the baseball player who throws his helmet and bat while cursing the umpire after a strikeout; or a basketball player that slams the ball to the floor in disgust after a foul call. Away from sports and on a bigger scale, it's the mother who becomes an alcoholic after a child's death; the boss who screams at his employees after an honest mistake; or the father who becomes abusive at home because he lost his job and his family faces bankruptcy.

These people usually have one thing in common, the lack of trust in God. Our faith will be tested many times throughout our lives because of adverse situations on many different scales. We can either trust that God has our best intentions at heart or panic and have earthly responses. God does not care if an official makes a bad call or if Team A or B wins, but He does care that athletes/coaches/fans continue to glorify Him in their actions. Disagreeing with someone is not unpleasing to God, not treating people with love and respect because of that disagreement is very unpleasing. God isn't interested in putting us into situations beyond what we can handle; He is interested in giving us help through those difficult times. Trusting God to provide peace and understanding through tough situations is difficult to do, but often times leads to greener pastures. Trust that God does love you and that your faith will be rewarded. This passage in John reassures us that trusting in God will lead us to the Father's house.

The book of Job gives us a wonderful example of how to respect and fear God through a difficult time. We can see how He rewards us for our faith and perseverance. On a smaller scale, and I use this example because it is so rare in American professional sports, Armando Galarraga, a Detroit Tigers pitcher, lost a perfect game opportunity on June 2, 2010 because an umpire missed a safe/out call at first base, for the 27th and final out. Many pitchers in that scenario would have screamed at the umpire, stomped his feet like a two-year-old, and pouted afterwards in the post-game conference. Galarraga, immediately after the miscall, smiled at the umpire and went back to the mound to finish his pitching gem. In the post-game press conference, Galarraga said, "nobody's perfect." The following day he presented the starting lineup to the teary-eyed umpire as a gesture of goodwill and continued to support the umpire a day after he was robbed of the opportunity to have thrown one of only 21 perfect games in Major League Baseball History! Galarraga may have missed his perfect game, but he responded perfectly in the face of adversity and showed millions of people that responding with humility and grace, to a situation beyond one's control, is possible and desirable.

Pray with me: Heavenly Father, please continue to work with me, Your loving follower. Help me understand Your will and Your desires for me in this place. Place in me a trust and calmness that knows You are working in my life during difficult situations. Please continue to remind me to control by emotions and live out Your words in times of struggle. Help me grow in my faith and be a leader in my community through my actions and words. In Jesus name, Amen.

Brian Wede
Head Baseball Coach at NWC

Brian's team won the GPAC Conference Tournament in '10 and proceeded on to the National Tournament. He is a fine leader of young men.

June 4

Acts 5:12-16

You and Your Shadow

So revered was the apostle Peter that when he came to town, people carried their sick friends and relatives out into the street and lay them there on cots and mats, believing that if even Peter's shadow fell on them they would be healed (v. 15). I've read that people did the same thing with Mahatma Ghandi. Ghandi was a small, slender man, and he didn't cast much of a shadow, but what little there was, was precious to people. Imagine that.

The idea that a shadow can heal someone is entirely superstitious, but it is symbolic of something that is entirely true – we do cast a shadow that either heals or hurts, blesses or blights. Your shadow is your influence, the effect you have on other people. You can no more keep from exerting an influence on people than you can keep from casting a shadow on a sunny day.

Most of us make two great mistakes in life. The first mistake: we overrate our importance. You are not nearly as important as you think you are, and you would worry far less about what people thought of you if you realized how seldom they did. No matter how important you think you are, the attendance at your funeral will still be determined by the weather.

The second mistake: we underrate our influence. In an automobile there is forward, reverse, and neutral. But as far as your influence is concerned, there is no neutral.

You are always influencing people. You are either lifting people up, or pulling them down. Helping or hurting. Little do we realize the shadow we cast, the tremendous influence we have. One person, by his or her influence alone, can make or break a committee, a choir, a church, a company. Think about that the next time you look down and see your shadow.

Prayer: Heavenly Father, truly you can and do use us to serve Your will. Help us to be the positive influence You want us to be. In Your precious Son's name we pray, Amen.

Dr. Lou Lotz
Pastoral Leader, Central Reformed Church, Grand Rapids, MI

I got to know Pastor Lou when he served the Morningside Reformed Church in Sioux City and was my cousin Paul's minister. I'll never forget the sermon he preached at Paul's funeral (I kept a copy of it and keep it in my Bible). He always has a key phrase that will stick with you, as I learned when he was a guest speaker in Chapel at NWC many times. I see several in this devotional – don't you? Paul was only 47 when he died and I still shed tears today as I think of him. What did Pastor Lou say at that funeral? "Don't feel sorry for Paul! Yes, grieve for Beach and the kids and for yourself – but don't feel sorry for Paul – he's with our Lord!" Read everything from Pastor Lou that you can get your hands on and listen to him speak whenever you can.

June 5

Hebrews 11 (The "Faith Chapter")

Faith

Faith is an important word to me. There are many, many words about faith in scripture and numerous hymns containing the message of faith. A wonderful definition of faith is found in the Heidelberg catechism – Q. and A. #21

Q. What is true faith?

A. True faith is
Not only a knowledge and conviction
    That everything God reveals in His Word is true;
It is created in me by the Holy Spirit
    Through the gospel
That, out of sheer grace earned for us by Christ.
    Not only others, but I too,
Have had my sins forgiven.

Have been made forever right with God.
And have been granted salvation.

A hymn that has become a favorite of mine in the last few years is entitled "My Faith Has Found a Resting Place." It has many meaningful lines in it that assures me that I do not have to earn my salvation; it is a gift from God by His grace.

My faith has found a resting place – Not in device or creed;
I trust the Ever living One – His wounds for me shall plead.

Chorus:
I need no other argument. I need no other plea;
It is enough that Jesus died, and that He died for me.

Enough for me that Jesus saves – This ends my fear and doubt;
A sinful soul I come to Him – He'll never cast me out.

Chorus:
My heart is leaning on the Word – The written Word of God;
Salvation by my Savior's name – Salvation thru His blood.

Prayer: There are so many ways to worship You and learn of You. Thank you especially for Your Word. Inspire us to pick it up daily and learn more deeply. Amen.

Edie and Howard Lubach

Edie is a lifetime member of Central Reformed and Howard joined back in the '50's. Howie is a retired teacher, coach, and administrator. Howie and Edie have been our friends for many years. They have 4 great kids that were all students of ours and they remain very important to us. They are real servants of the Lord.

June 6

Psalm 23; Micah 6:8; John 8:12

Dear Friends

Here are just a few "things" that I have found helpful in life's journey. I have been a church member for over seventy-one years.

In my teen years we studied the "Westminster Charter Catechism." The first question and answer set the stage. Question: "What is the chief end of man?" Answer: "Man's chief end is to glorify God and enjoy Him forever." Wow, think about it – read His Word, the Holy Bible – Every day. Take the time. You will have favorite verses – sections – chapters – Psalms. It will grow on you. The 23rd Psalm, "*The Lord is my shepherd I shall not want.*" The ever-present God. And God expects from us what is said in the passage in Micah. Take it to heart, it was former President Ronald Reagan's favorite verse.

What you read in John is God's faithful promise to us. Remember, He always keeps His promises.

May God bless you on your journey.

Prayer: Lord, thank you for always being there for us. Thank you for speaking to us so forthrightly in Your Word. Help us to understand and cherish all You say to us. Amen.

Howard and Edie Lubach

Say a prayer for this great couple, their kids, grandkids, and great-grandkids. I did.

June 7

Revelations 3:20

Dad

My dad's church affiliation was very brief – he wanted to play on the church basketball team. So, you could say he was "unchurched." He was known to be honest, hard working, generous, had a good sense of humor and good people-skills. He was so proud of my sister and me, and he wanted the best for us.

As the years went by alcoholism took control of his life. That was the top priority. What a waste of so many years! My mom died very suddenly, so Dad went to an assisted-living complex near my sister's home in Pennsylvania. Due to my sister and her husband, my dad had several good years. During this time, God continued to "knock at the door of his heart." He had not been receptive in the past to my "witnessing." Finally, in his last year of life, he accepted Christ as his Savior. What peace we all experienced at his passing.

So don't give up. Continue to pray and allow God to work in your loved ones' lives. Jesus had to "knock" a long time – but finally Jim opened the door!

On this date in 1917 my dad was born. We "lost" him in 2005, but we'll see him again!

Prayer: God, thank you again and again for never giving up on Your loved ones. Amen.

Dot

June 8

Galatians 6:9-10

Good Works

At times, the desire in doing good works lacks enthusiasm; a sense of self-righteousness takes over; a sense of duty without joy happens. I have experienced all of these. What I found out is God can bless my works even though the proper inspiration may have been lacking on my part. So, I have learned not to follow my feelings. Go ahead and do good works, allowing God to do the blessing in His time schedule.

Many times our efforts may be futile, but God can make something great happen. Let Him use you today.

Prayer: God, thank you for Your daily strength in all that we do. Bless our efforts this day. Amen.

Dot

June 9

Ephesians 1:3-4

Why Me?

Why God? Why me? Why now?

Why did I get to wake up with two of the three kids standing next to me giggling and then jumping in bed with us and laughing? Why did I get to sing in church today with my son as close as he could get, singing his heart out and lifting his hands?

Why did I get to enjoy burgers fresh off the grill that my husband made for me? Why did I get to go for a bike ride in the beautiful sunny weather with the family?

Why did I get the treat of the entire family helping pot and water flowers and make memories? Why did I get to take a 20 minute nap?

Why did I get to watch the kids play out front, and run and laugh and get filthy dirty?

Why did I get to listen to my husband whisper cute nice things to me?

Why did I get to go to a Bible study and fall in love with you more?

Why did I get to kiss my kids goodnight (well, except the big ones!) and tuck them in? Why did I get to snuggle with my daughter and rock her to sleep? and then hold her and cuddle?

Why??? Why did I get blessed? Why me? What did I do to deserve this???? So many times, we doubt when things go wrong Lord. Today, I wanted to ask "why" when everything seemed perfect... Why do we only ask why when it's not what we want?

Prayer: Thank you God for pure enjoyment and blessing. I think I saw a bit of heaven today, and I pray I'll see a bit everyday! I pray You will give me eyes to see the blessings You are surrounding me with and that I could look at the world through the lens of your blessings instead of my focus being on the unanswered prayers. I'm so privileged to know You and Your grace. May I always praise you! Amen.

Jen Sandbulte
Mentoring Coordinator at ATLAS of Sioux Center

Jen helps train, equip, and is a resource to about 70 people who are actively mentoring through ATLAS of Sioux Center. Jen is also a public speaker and is involved in multiple ministries in Northwest Iowa.

June 10

Philippians 4:6-7

Worry!

I don't do it often, but when I let it enter my thoughts I can see how it can become consuming and debilitating. Some worry leads to more worry and obsession on the perceived problem or situation. I'm famous for worrying about travel for our adult children. I have learned that when you not only pray about the situation but truly hand it over to the Lord, only then can you feel peace. It takes practice, but the reward of calmness is overwhelming. He will give you signs that your prayer is being answered. I often hear Him speak to me and remind me that He has taken care of them many times before and what makes me think today will be any different! When you give it all up to the Lord, only then can we have peace that His answer is the perfect answer. Now, go and worry about something you do have control over like what you cooking for dinner!

Prayer: Lord, help me to truly hand my worries over to You and to trust You for the best answer to them. Help me to find peaceful assurance. Amen.

Pam Thornton

Pam and I serve on the Village Northwest Board in Sheldon. The Village is a tremendous place and it is a privilege to serve on the Board with Pam. Pray for and support the Village.

June 11

Philippians 4:4-9

Think on These Things ... Whatever is Worthy of Praise

We all remember "9-11," Hurricane Katrina, the Haiti Earthquake, and the tornado in Parkersburg, IA. These were terrible acts of nature that brought the best out of many of us. We all know people that either sent money, food, other materials, or went to help personally. All of these charitable acts are worthy of praise.

But you know, it doesn't have to be on such a grand scale to be noteworthy. How about that container of soup to a shut-in, or the ride that someone needed, or the kind word, smile, or visit you gave to someone. Can you think of someone that needs a note, phone call (I don't text), or visit today? I bet you can!

Many times we do things that are worthy of praise from our fellow man. But there is someone else that deserves our praise for what He has done for each of us. Let's take care of a few of those items today. Don't put it off until tomorrow because then it won't happen.

Prayer: Again, we come to you Jesus because of thanksgiving for all You have done. Sometimes we need added motivation to reach out and help. Please give us that gentle boost today. Amen.

Dave

June 12

Matthew 7:12

The Golden Rule Again

How does a marriage stay fresh and intimate?

Mary and I just celebrated our 30th wedding anniversary. Milestones such as that tend to cause a person to reflect on what went right and what went wrong so far. In analyzing our marriage it's pretty obvious that the times when things really clicked were when we put each other's lives ahead of our own. When things didn't work as well, it was usually because we felt that our "needs" weren't being met. We were more concerned about ourselves than each other. We had a pity party.

It seems that almost every breakdown in a marriage occurs when people care more about themselves than about each other. The same holds true with families, workplaces, communities, churches, governments ... the list goes on and on, yet it's so simple to avoid.

Jesus taught us how to avoid it in Matt. 7:12 when He said to *treat others the way we want them to treat us*. Paraphrases would be to care for others the way we want them to care for us, love others the way we want them to love us.

When Mary and I practice that wise principle, our marriage is strong. It stays fresh and intimate. Even though we sometimes slip into selfishness, we know what it takes to reconnect, and God blesses our marriage when we do. We wish the same for everyone.

Prayer: There are so many blessings we can thank You for. But now we thank You for those loved ones in our life. Help us to always grow closer to them and to You. Amen.

Bruce and Mary Roetman
Members of Central Reformed

Bruce and Mary have a real heart for the Lord, for kids, and for Missions. That's a great combination. They enjoy a large family because they have adopted some great kids to go with their biological youth. These two are always reaching out to help someone in need.

June 13

John 18:20

Prayer Warriors

This was part of the final prayer Jesus uttered in the garden before he was betrayed. It strikes me how He's praying for those of us who aren't even there. I've come to greatly admire those today who follow that lead. I was the recipient of just such prayers.

I drifted from the faith that was the center of my parent's home, when I was in my teens. I felt somewhat superior when I decided that the Christian faith was based on such shaky facts that it obviously wasn't true. I didn't change that stance until I was in my early 30's, and yet all that time many of those "misguided" believers continued to pray for me. I'll admit that it irritated me when it was brought to my attention. But, it also confused and interested me. Once I allowed myself to actually consider the possibility of a God, He swept in and grabbed a hold of me so completely that I've never been the same.

As I mature in this faith, it becomes more apparent to me that those prayer warriors were keys to my transformation. Because of them I try to look at others the same way. I was not very lovable when I was separated from God, but the prayer warriors loved me anyway.

I know a lot of people in my life that I find unlikable, but I try to see them as one or two prayers away from the moment when the Holy Spirit will sweep in and make them whole. Do you see people that way? If not, try it. There are a lot of lives out there waiting to be transformed!

Prayer: Thank you Lord for those many prayer warriors. Help me to be a better one. Help each of us to spread the message of Your salvation promise. Thank you for being a God that changes lives. Amen.

Bruce Roetman
Valued Maintenance Worker at NWC

What a special Christian Bruce has become. I remember those teen years very well as I was his teacher at SCHS. Bruce, along with Wayne and Bill, are the three I talk about in the sermon of "How Jesus Changes Lives." This is a man you want to get to know and cherish like I do.

June 14

1 Peter 2:17

Flag Day

I had real difficulty finding a verse that mentioned a country's flag; in fact I couldn't find one. But this verse speaks of honoring and showing respect to the people and to the king. We don't have a king on this earth so we'll substitute flag. Honor the flag!

Have you ever seen a more beautiful flag than ours? I haven't. Since I was born in 1939, I can remember the 48-star flag. Of course it went to 50 stars when Alaska and Hawaii were admitted into the Union in the 50's.

Dot and I always have a flag flying in front of our house. Recently we added a flag-like bunting to put under our front windows on holidays.

As an old Boy Scout I learned to fold a flag properly and it really "burned me up" when the U.S. went through those protesting "flag burning years." We are privileged to live in the greatest country in the world, and it brings me great pleasure to see our flag displayed and honored. Just think of how many people sacrificed life and limb to keep her flying. We owe them more than we can ever pay.

May the Pledge always include "Under God" and may we always live that way too. Let's all honor our flag, not only this day, but every day.

God bless you and God bless America again.

Prayer: Dear God, truly You have blessed us in this great country. Thank you and please continue. Amen.

Dave

June 15

Psalm 23:4

Loss

In June of 1999 Marty and I celebrated our forty-second wedding anniversary. We had no indication that we would only have one more.

In February of 2000 both Marty and I had blood panels taken at the College. At the end of the month we were in San Francisco. Our hotel was approximately six blocks from China Town, so we decided to walk there. We had walked about three blocks when Marty stopped and said she could not go any further.

We cut our trip short and flew home the next day. Marty made an appointment to see her doctor. The same afternoon Marty got a call from the College nurse telling her to see a doctor immediately. The diagnosis was colon cancer which had spread to the liver. An operation was done to attempt to remove the mass but it was impossible. Marty tried one treatment of chemo-therapy which almost killed her. Treatment was abandoned and we accepted the terminal diagnoses.

From February until June, Marty was able to be home. Pain was kept at a minimum with morphine.

During the three-and-a-half months, there were many tears but surprisingly many great times of sharing as well. Our children and grandchildren were able to spend quite a lot of time with Marty and to express and show their love. Marty and I grew closer together. I am thankful that I got to be the caregiver for a change. We grew closer together and closer to God. As our minister said, "Marty is blooming, she is taking on an inner glow."

One of the last things Marty said was that she was tired and ready to go and be with God. She said, "I want to feel happy and good again." Those words still bring me some comfort.

Prayer: God, I pray that I will always remember You are the supplier of all good things. You provide the strength I need to meet the challenges of life and that You freely give to all of us who ask. Amen.

Phil Patton

June 16

Proverbs 31:10-30

A Good Wife

I proposed to Dot on our first date (we saw the epic movie "South Pacific"). She said "No." I was serious, but it took her almost 3 more years! Of course I didn't know she would have had to drop out of nurses training as in those days, they didn't allow married women to be in training. That was a dumb rule and I'm glad they got rid of it. Going into my senior year at Morningside College I thought I'd lost her. In fact I thought my whole world was collapsing. On November 5 my dad died suddenly from a heart attack. During Christmas vacation Dot got engaged (but not to me!). Only my career in baseball seemed secure (the Chicago White Sox offered me a minor league contract). For some reason, that didn't seem as important as it had a year or so ago.

In March, Dot broke her engagement! I was back in the picture, and baseball definitely took a back seat (I didn't like that statistic where 80% of professional athletes' marriages broke up). I became a teacher/coach, and we got married on this date in 1962.

This chapter in Proverbs talks about "more precious than rubies," and that really doesn't hit home with me. Rubies don't mean much to me, but nobody has a more precious wife than I do. I think I'll go tell her that again right now. It's impossible to do that too often.

Prayer: I thank you so much for Dot and the many years we have enjoyed together. Please continue to watch over all of us and keep us on Your straight path. Amen.

Dave

June 17

Ephesians 6:10-18

The Attack of Satan—Distraction, Deception, Destruction

The Bible makes it very clear that Satan is real and he is active in trying to mess up our lives and our callings. The Bible also gives us a great outline on how we can resist the devil, using the armor of God. It is so good to know that God has given us weapons to help us in this spiritual battle that we are engaged in.

Through my work at ATLAS, I have noticed that not only does Satan attack us, we sometimes unknowingly cooperate with him by inviting sin or lies into our lives. I have found that there are three main ways that Satan attacks both the redeemed and those who have not yet found their way to Jesus' love and forgiveness. He does so through distracting, deception and destruction.

First of all, he tries to distract us from the "one thing" that David talks about in Psalm 27:4. God wants us to put our identity, our gaze, and our main goals in knowing Him and knowing how He sees us. He does this because if we make Him our "one thing" we will find that thing is constant and more fulfilling than anything this world has to offer. Satan will even resort to using "good" or church activities to keep us distracted from that "one thing."

Second, he uses deception. Many of us have believed lies like, "I'm ugly," or "I'm worthless," or "Nobody could possibly love me" all of our lives, and we assume those lies are true just because they have entered into our thought process. Sometimes, they have even been verbalized by others or us over the years. We must realize that God says that we are His beloved and that we cannot do anything to make Him love us any more or any less. Our worth comes from being His!

Third, because we live in a fallen world and because of our own sin, there is destruction all around us. Destruction can come in many forms…an affair, cancer, the death of a loved one, etc. If there is not something destructive happening in your life right now, there probably will be some day. Destruction comes from the enemy and we must recognize that God will redeem that destruction if you let Him (Philippians 1:6).

Prayer: Lord, help me to fight the battle before me! Equip me with the armor that You promised. Do not allow me to get distracted from that "one thing." Help me to recognize and combat deception. Please redeem all destruction in my life! Amen.

Amy Vanden Bosch-Keahi

June 18

Philippians 4:4-9

Think on These Things ... Whatever is Excellent

Remember I said I like baseball. One time a little left-handed pitcher named Harvey Haddix pitched 12 innings of perfect baseball in the major leagues. He faced 36 batters and got them all out! He was excellent! (Ironically, he gave up a run in the 13th and got beat, so he doesn't even get credit for pitching a no-hitter!) So what he did wasn't excellent? C'mon Man!!

Don Larsen pitched a perfect game in the World Series. (1956) Johnny Vander Meer pitched 2 consecutive: no-hitters. No one else has ever done these things. That's truly excellence.

You know, God declares each of us as excellent when we accept Jesus as our Savior. He looks down and sees the perfect Jesus in us and says "Come here to me!" As an old teacher – I like the way He grades.

Prayer: Thank you God for seeing us as excellent even though we are miserable sinners. Keep us ever mindful of Your great gift and help each of us to help each other. Amen.

Dave

June 19

Exodus 20:12

Honor Your Mother...

What are your thoughts about your mom? Did you ever get to know her, or do you still have her? My mom died in 1995 and she was 88 years old. She was a stay-at-home mom and I loved her dearly. I got the chance to tell her that often. That gives me great comfort now. I know that eventually she became proud of me, but I sure gave her a lot of anxious moments (maybe even hours and days!).

She was a great teacher and she taught me a lot. She also insisted that I go with her to church. I also got the chance to thank her for being a great and loving mom. I pray your relationship is good. If not, and she's still living, is there a way to repair it? Can you adopt a mom? Remember, loneliness is the biggest problem for the elderly.

What kind of mom are you? What qualities and traits do you want your kids to emulate and imitate? I can still picture Mom kneeling beside her bed each night as she prayed for me and others. I know my mom's in Heaven and that I will see her again. (My mom was born on this date in 1907.)

Prayer: Thank you Lord for my mom and for all of the mothers being thought of right now. Help us to be worthy of their praise and even more worthy of Yours. Amen.

Dave

June 20

James 1:13-15

The Way of Escape

Do you ever feel guilty because of your thoughts? I know I do – sometimes even because of my dreams. Remember, when that clever comedian said "The Devil made me do it!" Well, if what we did was bad (or what we thought was bad) it was the Devil that did it. Because tempting is another thing God *can't* do.

Don't ever discount the Devil. He is real and he is powerful. He also has angels working for him.

Notice that being tempted isn't a sin. It's when we give in to the temptation that sin is present. Actually temptation is kind of good, because that means the Devil doesn't feel he has you and is still working on you. Why should he tempt someone he already has in his camp?

Always remember that God in you is much more powerful than the Devil, and He will always show us an avenue for escape.

Prayer: Thank you Lord for helping us control what we do or don't do. Thank you too for showing us ways to avoid temptation and sin. Please put a hedge of protection around us and our families, and keep the Devil's arrows from penetrating. Amen.

Dave

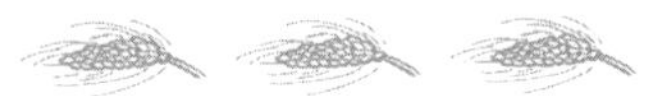 **June 21** 

Acts 17:24-28

When in Doubt, Take a Walk

All one needs to do when they begin to doubt our God is to take a walk. Marvel at this wondrous world He has created. This world is too complex for any mortal to have created!

See the tiny acorns that grow into mighty oaks when the water and nutrients from the soil are available. Look at the bees collecting nectar from the flowers which they will make into honey – all the while pollinating the plants so they can produce seeds to grow new plants. Birds, butterflies, flowers, fish, animals and man – each one has a special place and purpose in God's world.

The Earth is always rotating, always changing, always evolving – day and night, season to season, ocean tides, sun, wind, rain and more. All is necessary to keep this connective web of our world healthy.

God made man the caretaker of His world. We must always treat each integral part of this world, including our fellow man, with tender care. Since this is a heavy burden and also such a privilege, we must continually ask for His guidance so that it may be His will that is done and not ours!

Prayer: You truly are an awesome God. I never cease to be amazed at Your creation. Help us to do everything we can to make it better. Amen.

Diana and Jerry Thompson
Retired Clerk of Courts and Engineer living in Lancaster, PA

Diana is Dot's only sister and we don't get to see them often enough. Dot and Diana keep the phone lines busy and we usually get together at least once a year. They have 3 daughters and a host of grandchildren to love and entertain. Fortunately, all of them live within 20 miles. That's a blessing!

 **June 22** 

2 Corinthians 4:11; Romans 12:9-21

The Christian Pilgrim's Daily Conduct

A Christian's life is read and known by all men. People interpret that life in the light of its profession. As soon as you fail to live up to that profession, you are counted a hypocrite.

As living epistles, all men can read you and can compare you with what you ought to be. As living epistles, you reflect the image of Christ. If you fall short, it reflects on Him. Therefore, we must strive for the mastery.

It is true, we are constantly watched. We cannot come in contact with a single person without having our lives or our deeds leave some mark of which we may not always be conscious. But the mark is there. We need to be asking ourselves: "How has this person been affected by my presence? Have I truly reflected my Savior and Lord or have I left a false and untrue picture of what Jesus can do for a person who claims to love Him?" We can make a difference, for good or for bad.

As Christians we are called to be witnesses and representatives of Jesus, sharing with others the Good News of His love for them and inviting them to receive Him too as their Savior and Lord. For us this is a great privilege but it is also a great responsibility.

There are many around us who perhaps will not see Jesus except by seeing something of Him in us. With lives dedicated to Him, we are called and equipped by the Holy Spirit's power within us to reflect our Savior and to speak words of invitation in His name. Can people see something of Him in us? Are we being good witnesses for Him? In our daily conduct are we representing Him? To help us be better witnesses we must give attention to our daily conduct. Paul, in his letter to the Roman Church, gives us an excellent guide for our daily conduct, especially in our relations to others. Here are some of his helpful instructions:

1. Your love for others must be completely sincere– don't pretend. (v. 9)
2. Abhor evil, cling to the good. (v. 9)
3. Love with brotherly affection. (v. 10)
4. Work hard. Never be lacking in zeal, fervently serving God. (v. 11)
5. Be joyful in hope, patient in affliction, faithful in prayer. (v. 12)
6. Share with the needy, practice hospitality. (v. 13)
7. Bless those who persecute you; do not curse. (v. 14)
8. Rejoice with those who rejoice; mourn with those who mourn. (v. 15)

9. Live in harmony with one another. Do not be proud, conceited. Associate with the humble. (v. 16)
10. Do not repay anyone evil for evil. (v. 17)
11. Conduct yourself in such a way that all can see that you are trying to be honest and fair. (v. 17)
12. If possible, live in peace with everyone. Let it begin with us. (v. 18)
13. Don't seek revenge. Feed your enemy if he is hungry, give him drink if he is thirsty. (v. 19-20)
14. Overcome evil with good. (v. 21)

Try these and note what happens in the area of human relations. Note too, how they make you feel, what you begin to think of yourself.

Prayer: Once again you have given us what is needed to live the life that follows You. Now give us the wisdom and the strength. Amen.

Rev. Henry Eggink

June 23

Proverbs 22:3-4; Proverbs 25:28

Always Under Control

Everybody wants freedom. Everywhere we hear the cry for greater freedom. Most of us are taking up that cry, for we believe in freedom, too. But freedom, to be real freedom, must be bound within limits. If it is not, freedom becomes license and license ultimately results in tragic smash-ups. That is true on the highway. It is true in national life; it is true in personal life; it is true in every area.

Freedom is good, but let us remind ourselves that our greatest need is not more freedom. Our greatest need is a Master! For truly successful living, it is imperative that our lives be completely surrendered to, yielded to, possessed by a Power greater than ourselves. When this is true, our weaknesses and defects will be blotted out and something of the beauty and glory of God will be channeled through us. A life like that will be blessed and will be a blessing.

In 1924 Roland Hayes, the saintly colored singer, was scheduled to give a concert in Berlin. A series of incidents had occurred just before which had stirred within some Germans an ugly spirit of prejudice, hatred, and racism (especially toward people of color). Hayes knew that he was facing a situation charged with dynamite. He was not mistaken. When he walked on the stage, a barrage of hisses full of hatred greeted him.

Hayes took his position in the great curve of the grand piano. He folded his hands before him, closed his eyes, bowed his head, and prayed that Roland Hayes, with his colored body, might be blotted out of the picture, and that the spirit of God flowing through the beauty of song might be channeled through him to the audience. At last the hissing and stamping of feet died down. Softly, almost in a whisper, Hayes began to sing Schubert's "Thou Art My Peace." As the clear notes of that song floated out over that audience, silence fell upon the people. Hayes changed his planned repertoire. He sang a hymn. Another followed. Tears began to flow down many cheeks. At last the concert was over and a mighty, deafening applause broke out. Hayes had allowed himself to be used, to be possessed by a Power greater than himself, and his life had channeled blessings from God. The audience was thrillingly aware that it was so.

Just so can you and I be used. When we allow that to happen, true success, will be ours. When we permit God to have His way in our lives, we shall truly begin to live.

The story is told of the master musician, Mendelsohn, that he was late at a concert in which he was to play. In the meantime a local organist filled up the interval of waiting by playing a selection of Scottish airs. Mendelsohn, when he came, slipped unobserved into his place at the organ and, placing his hands upon the keyboard, carried on without a break, the Scottish strain, adding thereto his own brilliant improvising. At once a thrill went through the audience. They sensed the change and, looking up, saw the explanation. The master organist himself was there.

So Christ Jesus is the great Master in His ability to give meaning to human life. If we will but turn to Him the keyboard of our lives and permit Him to take control, if we will permit Him to sweep over the cords of our lives, He will change our ordinary, humdrum existence into beautiful symphonies. He is the secret of the abundant life.

Our first need in this pilgrimage of life is not more freedom. Our first need is a Master, even Jesus, the Christ.

Prayer: Heavenly Father, teach us self-control and the proper use of the many freedoms we enjoy in this great land. Thank you too for those many men and women who have fought to preserve those freedoms. Amen.

Rev. Henry Eggink

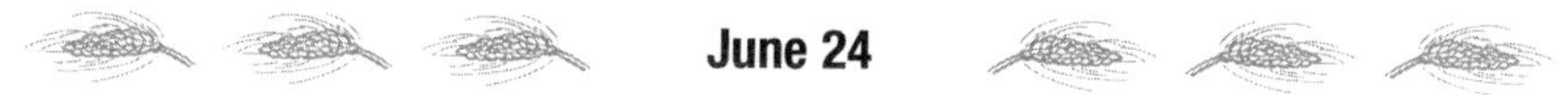

June 24

Luke 11:9

Seek and Ye Shall Find

I walked along the beach today – and as I walked, I noticed in my pathway there lay what seemed to be a fragment of a shell. Upon inspection, I found it to be whole and quite perfect in form. It had been covered, deceivingly, by shifting sand. As I reached for it, I wondered, "How many have passed this way and failed to notice this half-buried treasure?

Indeed, how often have I been too hurried, too lazy, too indifferent, to stoop and find something (or someone) of great value? How often have I ignored God's treasure for my life, simply because I did not dig deeply enough?

Prayer: Lord, help me become a seeker. Help me find those who need my help, encouragement, and love. Thank you for first loving me. Amen.

Di Murphy
Retired Education Professor and Co-President with husband Bruce

What a pleasant lady and great educator. She was a very able assistant to her husband as he served as President of NWC (2001-07). Di loves golf and her dogs. She is a valued friend and I hope and pray their retirement years are plentiful and positively eventful.

June 25

Luke 2:25-32, 36-38 KJV

Depart in Peace

Even though Jesus was a baby, when Simeon saw Him, he knew what it meant to know Him and to have salvation. When he saw Jesus, he could say, "Lord, now lettest thou thy servant depart in peace." Anna too could say the same. Her age was fourscore and four, she departed not from the temple, she served God night and day, and gave thanks unto the Lord. But when she saw Jesus, she could then speak of the Savior "to all of them that looked for redemption."

Today, when we see how Jesus fulfilled all prophecy in the Old Testament, how He did miracles and gave us teachings, how He became a servant and took the wrath that belongs to us, through suffering a cruel death on the cross, we too see a Redeemer.

Through Jesus sacrifice, the price was paid once and for all; and God was satisfied. He no longer looks at us with all our sins, but instead looks at us as He looks at His son whom He loves. Knowing this, we can say, "Lord, now lettest thou thy servant depart in peace." (Note: That's exactly what Kenny did on this date in 2010 at the age of four score)

Prayer: Lord, thank you for your tremendous sacrifice on the cross that cleanses us completely. As much as we love the life you give us on this earth, all the more we look forward to being with You for all eternity. Thank you Jesus, Amen.

Kenny Sandbulte

Kenny and his wife Florence raised 12 kids. Kenny was known for his smile and positive attitude. He loved softball and he loved his Lord. I'll never forget playing ball against him and I'll never forget his smile. God blessed him and us through him.

June 26

1 Thessalonians 5:16-18

Thanks – Prayer – Joy

"Always be joyful. Always keep on praying. No matter what happens, always be thankful, for this is God's will for you who belong to Christ Jesus."

The phone call early that Sunday morning brought bad news. Our sister and family had narrowly escaped a house fire during the night. We left immediately, arriving to find organized chaos. A steady stream of people were coming and going carrying away salvageable items and offering condolences.

By early afternoon, the stream stopped abruptly and only family remained. Just then, their priest arrived and offered a prayer service and communion since no one had been able to attend church. We stood in a tight circle on the front lawn giving thanks and holding hands. Only quiet peace surrounded us and the warmth of the sun touched us for that fifteen minutes.

Miraculously, moments after the last "Amen", cars and people began arriving again. God had blessed and renewed us when we turned our hearts to him in thanks and praise.

Prayer: Lord, help us always to be thankful in all that life gives us. Amen.

Connie and Todd Barry
School Nurse at MOC-FV – Head Basketball Coach at Briar Cliff & former Head Basketball Coach and Athletic Director at NWC.

Todd is an excellent basketball coach and it's hard for me to root against him – but I have to when he plays the Red Raiders. He had great success at NWC and took many teams to the National Tournament. He was also the coach of NWC's present head coach, Kris Korver. Todd won the High School State Title while coaching at MOC-FV. These fine people live in Sioux City now but Connie travels to Orange City each day to perform her duties as the school nurse. We miss 'em – but we're glad they're close. Todd & Connie also serve on the NW Iowa FCA board.

June 27

Proverbs 16:18; Mark 12:28-31

Two Weddings, Tornadoes, and Teammates

Baseball is a wonderful sport. I have either played baseball/softball or watched my offspring participate for over 45 of my 54 years of life. The possibilities of what can occur are endless and every year I have experienced different situations during the games. But this year, my final year of watching/coaching my youngest son during his senior year of college, I experienced something that I hope will stick with me the rest of my life.

During the spring, an average ball club for most of the regular season turned into an outstanding team and advanced to win the conference tournament and finish second in a national tournament qualifier. One major component to their strong finish included encouraging one another and empowering each player to "get hot" at the end, when it counted most. Everyone wanted each player to succeed. During a 50-game season, every baseball player goes through highs and lows, as in life. When "teammates" encourage you when you are down, it is much easier to recover.

During the national tournament games in Oklahoma City, the weather was just what you would expect in late spring in Oklahoma. Our first clue was the baseball size hail that destroyed nearly every car in parking lots the night the team arrived at their hotel. Later in the week, our hotel was invaded by "storm chasers" as we heard of a 90% chance of tornadoes in the city later that evening. During the middle of our night game, sirens went off and the fans and players headed for cover. This was the first of many 2010 "weather" events that would prove extremely memorable.

Fast forward to June 25, 2010 at Omaha, Nebraska. As was consistent with my spontaneity, I decided to call my wife at 4 p.m. and suggest we go to the College World Series game at 8 p.m. We left home at 6:00 and "scalped" tickets by 8:05, sitting about 10 rows behind the 3rd base dugout by 8:15. After watching 8 exciting innings, my phone rang with some serious news. A tornado had just ripped through Little Rock, IA and destroyed buildings housing over 4,000 little pigs that our company managed. An hour later, the same tornado turned into an EF4 and absolutely demolished another managed site near Sibley.

The following afternoon, we had two weddings to attend. On the way to the first, we followed two cars marked "Tornado Chaser" with Oklahoma plates. We knew we were in trouble again. As we left the second wedding, tornado warnings were sounding in neighboring towns. The humidity was 90% and the temperature was about the same. Within an hour, 60-70 mph winds hit our town and trees were destroyed everywhere. I would estimate over 500 trees were either totally uprooted or partially destroyed.

Sometimes it takes God and His power, working through nature, to humble us and make us aware of our need for Him and others around us. I can admit that during the past several years, I had become more focused on me and less aware of my need for my "neighbors" and my "teammates." I had been attributing successes to my abilities, not to the One who had given them to me. How often do we only care about our highs and lows and less about lifting up our neighbors? These storms were a calamitous reminder that we are not in control and that we need those around us. After the tornadoes destroyed those buildings housing thousands of animals, over 200 "neighbors" gathered to corral the animals working until 3 a.m. and all were moved to a safe place. At the other destroyed farm site, nearly the entire town was there to assist in rescuing another family in need of enormous help. In Orange City, my hometown, the day after the 70 mph wind damage, hundreds of "neighbors" were helping to restore conditions to people in need of assistance by removing entire trees that had fallen on roofs, cutting branches and loading them on trailers for disposal.

Situations in baseball and life are similar. The end results are much better when we have "teammates" and "neighbors" to lift us up. Encouragement and assistance in getting us through the rough times gets us "tournament tough."

Please read the Bible passages again. "Pride goes before destruction, and a haughty spirit before a fall." "The second great commandment is this, you shall love your neighbor as yourself."

I have been reminded again by God's word and God's power. We need Him and we need each other.

Prayer: Dear Lord, may we be filled with the Holy Spirit, desiring to serve You and others in Your precious name. Amen.

Dave Bomgaars
Veterinarian and baseball coach, former student and baseball player coached by Dave Mulder

Dave played on a state qualifier in both baseball and golf when I coached him in high school. He was also a member of a state championship football team in high school. He is a member of the NWC Hall of Fame, played on a National Championship football team and often accompanied his lovely wife Anita (then his girl friend) when she babysat our kids

June 28

Daniel 1:4 – Mark 6:34

Education Must Make Good Men & Women & Teach Them to Act Nobly

Education, and the people involved in it, has been my vocational priority since graduation from college. My life has been "about kids" for the most part.

A democracy cannot exist without educated people. Regardless of what I studied, Economics, Baseball, Basketball, Politics, Bible, you name it, the more I learned about something, the more I realized I didn't know. I guess that's good, but it's also very humbling.

As a teacher and learner, I believe we learn better and more when we like the subject, the teacher, and see how what we learn can have a practical application. Learning is fun and it should be. Education must never end.

Education is an investment in kids. Can there be a more important investment?

Prayer: Thank you Lord for kids and the opportunity to work with them. Help us always to make decisions that promote rather than detract. Help us always to show love and concern. Amen.

Dave

June 29

Ephesians 1:4-6

Chosen

My wife and I waited anxiously in the upper lobby of the hotel – at the elevator doors in the remote Chinese city of Nanning. God was adding to our family of four biological children a child of promise from an orphanage there.

That night as I watched our daughter sleep, I began to understand these words of Paul in a new way. Gratitude for my chosen-ness became more complete. Chosen by God, adopted through Christ in accordance with His grace.

Hong Xing had done nothing to become part of our family, but was now an heir and had a new name, Emma. There is no part of me that is righteous, but I now am an heir to eternity and claim the name Christian.

Prayer: Dear Lord, thank you for the many opportunities adoption provides. Thank you too for adopting us into your eternal family. Help us make that family grow. Amen.

Pastor Van Rathbun
Minister, Central Reformed Church

June 30

Matthew 5:13; James 1:27

Your Influence – Salt

As pilgrims we are steadily traveling toward a glorious destination. In route, as followers of Jesus, we are called upon by Him to influence and make an impact for good upon the world and the society in which we travel. We are, in this respect, on a God-given mission. Jesus used various figures of speech in teaching that. We call attention to a couple of them.

1. We are called upon to be <u>The Salt of the Earth</u>.

   A. <u>Purifying Agent</u>

   Sad to say, we have observed a steady lowering of moral and ethical standards. The Christian is troubled by this decline. He resolves "to keep himself unspotted from the world."

B. Preservation Agent

Salt is used to keep food free from becoming spoiled and rotten. Salt prevents corruption and decay. Christians should be an influence like that on human society.

C. Flavoring Agent

Salt gives a flavor to food it touches. We live in a society which is too frequently characterized by depression, sadness, hopelessness, worry, disappointment, etc., etc.; things which take the flavor, the joy, the pleasure, and the sparkle out of life.

Christianity changes that. Through its adherents it brings joy, hope, confidence, pleasure to life. The world needs that. As followers of Jesus, we can allow His love to flow through our lives, into the world around us, thus flavoring our society and making life more joyous and pleasant for many.

Prayer: Jesus, we thank you for changing our life and the lives of many others. Help us to be an instrument of your peace. Amen.

Rev. Henry Eggink

July 1

1 Corinthians 12:28

The Preacher

Reverend Henry Eggink, was a gentleman that impacted my life at two different stages of development. He was the minister at my church in Alton until I finished 8th grade and he moved on to Buena Vista College as a religion professor. I learned many things about the Christian faith from him in those formative years. He always kept track of me as I completed high school and went on to Morningside College. I would get little congratulatory notes and he was always at the baseball games when we played at B.V. He was always an encourager.

Years later, after I had been teaching and living in Sioux Center, Rev. Eggink retired, got married, and returned to his hometown. We got to see a lot more of each other and he asked me to help him with his finances. I was shocked to discover he was a millionaire! Over the next 20 years or so it multiplied about 4 times!

He gave it **ALL** away to colleges, churches, and charities! I learned some great lessons about frugality, patience, compound interest, and giving, from this man. We lost his presence on this earth in 2002, but I know where he lives now.

Rev. Eggink also wrote a book of daily devotionals. I've included several that really spoke to me. Enjoy and learn. He thought of himself as a "Pilgrim" and that is well illustrated in his devotionals.

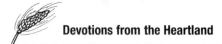

Prayer: Dear God, I thank you for this gentleman's life and influence. Help all of us learn from the many good things he did. He did it all because of You. Amen.

Dave

July 2

Colossians 3:16

A Dwelling Place

When I want to relax, a favorite spot in the house is my big recliner. I take off my shoes, lean back, and in that comfortable, relaxed and safe place, I often find myself in a peaceful sleep. It is a place where I can dwell.

Does the Word find that kind of peaceful, comfortable, and safe place in each of us? Secondly, if we truly desire and make a point to be in the Word; does it become a part of our being? Does it truly "dwell" in us? The Gaither Vocal Band sang a song a few years ago that asked the question, "I hear that you are getting into the Word, but is the Word getting into you'?" May the Word of Christ DWELL in you!

Prayer: Oh Lord, Your Word can assist us with so many concerns, it can heal us, bring us peace, and inspire us to do good things. Help us today to not only think about getting into Your precious Word, but actually do it. Guide our every thought and action. Amen.

Ron and Judy Den Hartog
Director, Inspiration Hills

Ron formerly served as an Administrative Assistant at Central Church. It's amazing the things this man can and does organize. He's a great singer in his own right and continues to direct the Male Choir at Central. Ron also started ATLAS of Sioux Falls. Ron and Judy are a great couple and great workers for the Lord.

July 3

Judges 6:11-12

Fit For Battle

Can you see the headlines of the Ophrah Gazzette-Herald? "Gideon Defeats Midianites with Scant 300 Men." "God Fleeced by Gideon." Gideon, the gritty, gutsy general of Israel was truly a man's man.

We mimic Gideon's faith by throwing out fleece for God to wet when we aren't sure what to do. Yet, when the curtain rises on the First Act of the Gideon story, he is hiding from the Midianites, in a hole in the ground threshing wheat. It's laughable that the angel calls to him, "Mighty Warrior."

We are far from warrior-like when God first calls us, though. Encourage a young Gideon you see today. They aren't perfect. Their intimidation and inexperience is evident. Yet they will be tomorrow's headliner.

Prayer: Dear God, Thank you for Your many avenues of guidance. Help us always to be willing to pursue what it is you want us to do. Amen.

Pastor Van Rathbun
Minister, Central Reformed Church

July 4

2 Chronicles 7:14; Micah 6:8

I'm Proud To Be Patriotic

The United States is the oldest country in the world with the same Constitution and form of Government. That's one of the reasons why I'm such a strong supporter of the two-party system and all of our freedoms. Sometimes I think freedom of speech goes a little too far and that separation of church and state gets misinterpreted as well. But think about it – we're over 235 years old and people still stand in line (and some cheat) just to come to the USA.

Yes, we have some problems, but we have many more positives. Do I agree with everything the President and Congress do? Heavens, no! But then – I don't agree with everything I've done either.

I'm not real big on fireworks either. But we need to celebrate this land of the free and this day. Go out and have some fun. Show your gratitude and your happiness. Be safe and take some quiet time to count your blessings. Tell a freedom-fighter "thank you" and give your loved ones a hug.

Just like I need prayer – so do our leaders and so does all of America. Let's do it!

Prayer: Dear God, I do pray for our President, all of his advisors, and all of the people that lead this great country. Please God, bless America again. Amen.

Dave

July 5

Matthew 5:19-24; 1 Timothy 6:10

Money

Who taught you about the value of a dollar? Our family never really had much as I grew up, but I didn't know it. My Dad was generous with us but not with himself. Mom was a great money manager, and she taught me that "everyone needs some money, but one should never make decisions based mainly on money." Great advice that I've followed throughout my life.

Ray Hildebrand taught me "that you can't out give the Lord." Give it a try.

I've read that if everyone tithed, all of our churches and charities would have ample money to complete all of their programs. That's only 10% of what the Lord gives us! Just think of the great things that could be accomplished.

"*You* can't buy happiness or *friends*." "Money is Power." All kinds of statements are made about money, but what the lord says has to influence us the most. I know I mentioned some of these thoughts before – but it seems so many problems evolve around money, that I think they bear repeating. Forgive me.

Prayer: We are so blessed to live in this great land and be allowed to use so much. Please help us to be good managers and generous with what You allow us to have. Amen.

Dave

July 6

1 Thessalonians 5:16-18

God's Will

It was July 2008 when I was diagnosed with the worst kind of skin cancer, melanoma. An appointment was made to see a cancer specialist to determine the extent of the cancer. Many questions were going through our minds. How far advanced is the cancer? Will surgery be needed? Will I need treatments? Also on our minds was the fact that Pam's dad had just lost his battle with stomach cancer in March.

Pam and I usually do our devotions early in the morning before I go to work. We don't remember the exact day, but the scripture for that morning came from the Thessalonians passage you just read. It talks about being joyful, praying constantly, and giving thanks in ALL circumstances. It says this is God's will for us in Christ Jesus. Wow! Reading those verses that morning could not have come at a better time. Those verses made us realize that no matter the situation, no matter the circumstances that happen, big or small, good or bad, our Heavenly Father is there for us. It was a wakeup call for the both of us. It not only made us realize how important it is to have each other, but how important it is to have our Lord Jesus Christ at the center of our lives.

Prayer: Thank you Lord for allowing us to come before You with whatever problems we have. May we realize that in both good times and bad times, You are there to listen and answer our prayers. In your Holy Name, Amen.

Rob and Pam Van Riessen
Members of Central Reformed, Rob owns Northside Body Shop

This fine couple means a great deal to us. Rob was a great catcher on our State Tournament team in '73 and was a great friend and example to our son Dick. They lived just a couple of doors away. Rob and Pam have this story to tell that is an inspiration and hope for all of us.

July 7

2 Corinthians 4:18

The Daily Planner

I have been working on filling my "Daily Planner" with a schedule – meetings, sporting events, special celebrations, to-do list. I like to pride myself as being a dependable person who doesn't forget or put things off. That's all well and good, but I hate the feeling when I fill my day with the to-do list and forget that my daily devotions are left behind.

John Ortberg's fine book When The Game Is Over, It All Goes Back In The Box says the square date sections in the planner should not dictate. We lose when we choose not to be flexible. God has given us the joy of choices. Someday will be our last day in our earthly planner. Choose to be ready. Paul hits the nail on the head in this passage in Corinthians.

Prayer: God, thank you for all of Your promises. May we be ready. Amen.

Dot

July 8

Matthew 28:19

Witness

The summer of 2010 was marked by several notable events that occupied the national sports' headlines for a significant time. The World Cup, hosted by South Africa, was an international feel-good event that saw dignitaries and spectators from all over the globe descend upon the African nation to observe the world's most popular sport. On the baseball front, while theories abound as to why hitters are easier to retire this season, no one can deny, with the number of perfect games and no-hitters, the balance of power has shifted from the batters' box to the pitcher's mound once again. Making news in south Florida, the Miami Heat evolved as the winner of LeBron James' sweepstakes as NBA franchises put their best foot forward in trying to lure the league's MVP to their team. Particularly striking throughout this process, however, was the noticeable number of Nike commercials featuring James that featured the word *Witness* – certainly an intriguing marketing ploy by Nike.

Christians know that witnessing for God is not a menial task. As believers, we are called to promote God to the un-churched with much more zeal and passion than Nike does for its clients. Before he ascended into heaven, Christ challenged His disciples to reach the corners of the world with the gospel before He returns. As Christians, we have been called to continue this mandate and spread the name of Jesus Christ with whomever we interact. May we strive to proclaim the name of God in our schools, neighborhoods, and places of work superseding far better than a shoe company ever could.

Prayer: Dear Lord, guide and empower us today as we encounter opportunities while interacting with others to further Your kingdom. In Your Son's name we pray. Amen.

Ross Douma
Head Basketball Coach at Dordt College

Ross was a student of mine at NWC and a good basketball player. He went on to a fine coaching and administrative career in High School. Now Ross is developing a fine program at Dordt and living in Sioux Center. It is a great thing to have fine Christian young men leading and teaching our athletes. Ross is a fine family man as well as a sound tactician. Watch out for the Defenders!

July 9

Philippians 4:4-9

Think on These Things ... Whatever is Commendable (Admirable)

Many of you know that I love baseball and the St. Louis Cardinals. Their current star is Albert Pujols. Not only is he a great Christian example but look at what he did in his first 9 years in the majors. He hit over 30 homers, drove in more than 100 runs, and scored over 100 runs in each of those seasons. No one had ever done that before. He has a World Series ring as well. That's Commendable!

Oscar Robertson, ("The Big 0"), at one time in his career with Cincinnati, averaged a "Triple Double" For the season! (That's scoring at least 10 Points, grabbing at least 10 Rebounds, and distributing at least 10 Assists). That's commendable!

Think about the many people Billy Graham has led to Jesus. Think about all the money Bill Gates has given to charity. Think about how Jesus loves us sinners enough to die for us! Now that's beyond commendable! But think about it.

Prayer: Thank you Jesus for seeing us as worthy of Your love and forgiveness. I know we can't do enough to earn our salvation, but we are so thankful for the gift. Amen.

Dave

July 10

Psalm 145:14

Be Humble

Be humble. This is something God told me awhile back. Be Holy, be humble, be helpful. The Holy part is earlier verses of Psalm 145 and now verse 14 is the humble part. It is so hard to be humble. I hear the kids argue over who is to blame for something and no one chooses to just stop the chatter and say sorry. Repentence... forgiveness...prayer. For me, the ultimate expression of humility is prayer. To pray means to yield my thoughts to the Lord, to reveal my inner self and my agenda and my frailty. To pray means to not proudly assume I can handle it, but to willingly say, "God, you handle it. You do a better job." It is in prayer that I can beseech the Holy Spirit to change me, to prune me, to transform me. It is in prayer that I can stop the chatter in my head and say sorry, to repent and be forgiven. I don't know how else to practice being humble. It is not in my nature to be humble so only when I am bowed down am I rightly positioned before God. He can't lift me up or hold me if I am not bowed down. He wants to hold me up when I fall. He promises to hold me up when I am bowed down, on my knees, humbled before his might and power.

God's enemy is Satan and his great separation from the Lord was pride. He wanted to be equal to God. I don't want to share the same great separation from the Lord. I loathe my pride. I loathe it in others, especially my children and family. I will fight pride every time I taste it, and I only know how to do that in prayer. My horizontal words barely scratch the surface of it, but my vertical ones, heard by the Holy, majestic, God and King who is worthy of my praise... God will work it out in me, to be humble.

Prayer: Father God, may be fall on our knees in prayer and humility and be filled with You so that we can be holy, and be humble and then be helpful. Position us to be used by You. Amen.

Niki Kredit
Mentor of ATLAS of Sioux Center

Niki is a mother, a nurturer, a friend, a wife, a prayer warrior, a mentor, and most of all, she is a child of God. She pursues Him with all of her heart, no matter what the cost!

July 11

Mark 12:28-31

Our Help Appreciated

Today would be a good time to start becoming more observant of people around us, noticing especially those who are in need of help. Resist the temptation to pass by, to ignore, to commit the sin of omission. Instead stop and act in their behalf. Follow the example of the Good Samaritan. Even doing little things such as sending a card, making a telephone call, paying a short visit, or sharing a prayer together can make a great difference. Yesterday we talked about those things – today is the day to do them. Who are you thinking about?

If one responds to the need for help by omission of concerned action, ignoring the need, or doing nothing, nothing good will happen. Rather it is likely the need will grow greater and the pain more intense. However, if one responds with positive action, good results begin to come, first in the person in need. Just to know that somebody cares helps so very much. Pain, sorrow, etc. are often relieved. There are benefits and blessings abundant.

Something good also happens to the benefactor: one's own spiritual life is enriched, one begins to feel good about oneself, respects oneself. And best of all, he has reason to believe that Jesus, his Lord, is pleased.

Let this day be that kind of day for you, and it is likely some person whose life you touched will be thanking God for your concern and love.

Prayer: God, show us very clearly the things you want us to DO. It's so easy for us to rationalize and find other avenues. Help us Lord. Amen.

Rev. Henry Eggink

July 12

Hebrews 12:2; 2 Timothy 3:16

Can You Keep A Secret?

So can I. As a magician, sworn to secrecy, I'm often asked after an illusion, "How did you do that?" If I disclosed the secret, the fun and the mystery would be gone.

However, the one secret I'm always glad to reveal is how to experience a rewarding life. Let me share with you how to take the mystery out of finding true happiness.

Growing up as an athlete competing under a variety of coaches in my career, I was impressed that each coach had his own philosophy for success. So as a rookie high school coach I was committed to developing one of my own. Consequently, I studied successful teams, past and present, and discovered the following ingredients common among champions:

1. **The players loved their coach, and the coach loved them.** The team believed in, respected, admired, and followed the coach, and the coach loved the players and was personally interested in their success.
2. **The players were committed to the coach's system.** They won because they faithfully executed every aspect of the coach's game plan – no questions asked.
3. **The players and coaches kept their eyes on the rewards, not on the obstacles.** They chose to make the setbacks their allies, not their enemies. Obstacles became positive vehicles toward their goals.
4. **The players and coaches developed team unity, through an unselfish attitude.** They played to their highest potential, not for personal gain, but for overall team success. They became a close knit family.
5. **Every team member was an ENcourager, not a DIScourager.** They developed a habit of building up one another through uplifting communication. They never dwelled upon the negative.

These same common ingredients visible among successful teams parallel the keys to unlocking the secrets of experiencing a rewarding life. I know this to be true because of an event that changed my life when I was 16. Read about that tomorrow but think on this today.

Prayer: Dear Lord, please continue to reveal yourself to us in a variety of ways. Help us to be great team members and work for mutual success. Amen.

Rick Nielsen
President of Blueprint for Life, and also coordinates programs with the South Dakota FCA

Rick is an outstanding entertainer and speaker. His illusions as a magician and talent as a juggler will keep your complete attention and also keep you laughing. All of this is a setup to present the Lord's message – and he does that in a very good way. I have known Rick since he was the first FCA State Director in Iowa. He has done, and continues to do, many programs for our area youth, adults, and at NWC. His book about prison ministry DOING TIME makes inspiring and interesting reading. He remains a close friend and you can contact him at the FCA office in Sioux Falls.

July 13

1 Peter 5:7; Matthew 20:28; Hebrews 6:10

A Life-Changing Event

1. **I met a loving coach.** We all need a coach to guide and direct our lives. In 1968 I committed my life to Jesus Christ. He became an example for me to follow and pattern my life after ... a coach I respected, admired, believed in, and trusted because I knew He cared about my success (even more than I did!).
2. **I found His system breeds success.** As a Christian, I quickly discovered that God's system for successful living is found in the Bible. I found the answers to the tough decisions of daily living and learned that by faithfully and obediently applying His truth, I would win at the game of life.
3. **I learned to keep my eyes on the reward.** No one is immune to life's hurts. They are inevitable. The difference between winning and losing life's battles is often found in how we choose to handle them. The winning edge depends on our focus. When my wife and I lost our son several days after he was born, we experienced tremendous sorrow, but survived the struggle by focusing on a God whom we trusted to be completely in control of our lives. With the focus on Him, we inherit the reward – a peace and assurance that comes from knowing God loves us and is constantly at work for good, even through life's most difficult moments.
4. **I discovered the joy of serving others.** Jesus said, "It is more blessed to give than to receive," and He certainly knew what He was talking about. Applying this principle in my own life has provided a tremendous source of joy. One of the real measures of success in life is found in how well we use our gifts and abilities to serve others.
5. **I learned the value of encouragement.** A large portion of my work is done in prisons across America. I meet many men and women behind bars who grew up in environments where they were never encouraged, and the results were devastating. They remind me that it becomes difficult to climb the ladder to success without encouragement along the way. Knowing the value of encouragement in my own life, I'm trying to develop a habit of putting others up, not down. Encouragement does make a positive difference!

Now that the secret's out of the bag, you can see there's nothing magical about living a rewarding, fulfilling life. It starts by accepting Jesus as your Lord and Savior and making Him the Master Coach of your life. This relationship then provides the power source you'll need for faithfully and obediently applying God's Word in your daily life, handling your hurts, developing a desire to serve, and becoming a source of encouragement to others.

Prayer: Thank you for being the source of our encouragement in life. Please help us to lead others and put their needs above ours. Amen.

Rick Nielsen

July 14

Psalms 19:14

Blessing Thoughts

A short two-day vacation connecting with friends was a great beginning of the summer. Another "friend" dropped in and joined us for a meal. I must confess that I already had passed judgment on this "friend" as mentally unstable, talkative about her various ailments, probably on medication, and had lost a lot of weight. I was so "righteous" – just listened, but sure wanted her to leave and she did.

The other gals said they noticed I "rolled my eyes" a few times and they were surprised at my lack of compassion. They were right. Even though I controlled my tongue, my thoughts (and I guess, my actions) were not at all pleasing to God. This action started with a negative thought. I regret this happened and continue to strive to seek God's wisdom in the future.

Prayer: Dear God, You are so gracious to forgive and want all of our being to be pleasing to You. Please help us to think, speak, and act that way. Amen.

Dot

July 15

Luke 12:6-7; Matthew 10:29-31

Perilous Passage

There is a beautiful and simple story of a white man who traveled years ago with a native guide in the South American jungles. One day they came to a deep-banked and turbulent stream. The only way across was by means of a native swinging bridge which looked down from a dizzy height to the rushing waters below.

The guide crossed first, as any good guide would do. Then he waved for the white man to follow. Half-way across the swinging bridge the traveler looked down. Far below he saw the tumbling stream, his head began to swim, he became dizzy, he was in grave peril. The guide, sensing the peril, cried, "Down, get down on your knees and look up!" The traveler did just that. He fell to his knees and looked up from the rushing waters to the clear, still sky above, and he was steadied.

So it is with mankind today. So it has ever been. It is inevitable that the traveler on the road of life will come to places of perilous passage. There are times when the world, which confuses and bewilders, threatens to sweep us off our feet and destroy us. We need the upward look. We need to look up to the Eternal One who can steady us. If we keep Him in our daily vision, we shall be saved; we shall be strengthened for every experience of life.

A lonely woman carried a heavy sorrow. She had sought comfort in many places but had not found it. The perilous passage through which she was traveling threatened to destroy her. She was contemplating taking her own life.

One morning she passed the open door of a church. She hesitated, turned, and entered that door. She sat down in the last pew of the silent sanctuary, a forlorn, miserable, desperate heap of life. While she sat there, a sparrow came in at one of the lower open windows. As any bird would do, it flew toward the ceiling. The windows near the top were closed and the poor bird, in seeking to escape, kept flying against one window after another. The woman, watching the bird, said, "How foolish that bird is. Why doesn't it come lower and see the open window over there?" At last the bird, having dashed its little body against window after window dropped to the floor. It was utterly spent, bruised, and beaten. As it lay there gasping for breath, it looked up, and saw the open lower window. After a few moments of rest, it flew out and soared away into the blue.

Then the woman said to herself, "I have been like that. I have been trying to find peace and security from the peril which besets me, but I have been looking in the wrong places, and my condition has only grown worse. But Jesus has an open window, I will fall on my knees and look up and I shall see God's open window of comfort and strength." She did just that and was steadied, strengthened – by looking up.

You and I too, traveling life's road with its perilous places, need to look up and we shall be saved, steadied, strengthened for every experience of life!

Prayer: Heavenly Father we look up to You to steady us and set us straight. Help each of us be a beacon for others as well. Amen.

Rev. Henry Eggink

July 16

Jeremiah 29:11; Luke 11:9

Sometimes He Calms His Child

For 12 months in 2001-02 and 15 months in 2003-05 I took treatment for Hepatitis C. It is a nasty virus that eats up the liver and has an equally nasty treatment. I have some medical background and understood the diagnosis, plan of care, the prognosis (1ittle to no hope of a cure), I understood my lab values and I could give myself the 3-5 shots needed each week. I was able to separate the medical me from the patient me, and the medical me always went to my checkups in Sioux City, except for one time. It was a very discouraging check-up and I was crying as I drove away. I pleaded with God for three things. One, that I would never be crabby; second, that He would not let me let go of His hand; and the third one, I can't remember. Then traffic picked up and I had to suck it up and drive with no tears. The prayers left my mind and I had an uneventful drive home until stopped at the Wal-Mart stop light. A voice said, "I will give you what you ask:" I said, "What?" Again, "I will give you what you ask." I said, "You mean I won't be crabby, or lose your hand, or the other?" He said, "That's right." I said, "Oh, well, what do you say?"

It was a great comfort that the Lord supported me so directly and also through His word. I leaned heavily on the verse from Jeremiah. I am four years after treatment with no sign of the virus, I have an "assumed cure," but whether it comes back or not I know God is holding my hand and will see me through any and all trials.

Luke tells me to ask, so I did, and God promised that through this whole thing, I wouldn't be crabby, that He would help me, sounds good. Well, the insurance company and the pharmacy were fighting about who wasn't coding the drugs correctly so payment could be made. These aren't the kind of drugs you can get at your local friendly Hy-Vee. The payment due the pharmacy was $60,000. and without substantial payment, I would not get my next shipment.

My husband was gone and I planned a pity party. I deserved it. I snuggled in the recliner with a blanket, turned on the TV and prepared to sob. The show that came on was funny. I didn't want to watch a funny show, so I changed the channel. That show was funny too! The third channel also had a funny one. I said, "I don't want to watch funny, I want to cry!" Then that Voice came again, "You said you didn't want to be crabby." I said, "This isn't crabby, it's pity, and I deserve it!" He said, "Same thing, and I promised you that I wouldn't let you be crabby, so all you are going to see is funny – so laugh! So I did laugh, it actually felt better than pity.

It took a lot of effort and help from the HR person, but the problem got straightened out. We can trust God to know (and implement) the plans He has for us. He has plans to prosper us, not to harm us, plans to give us hope and a future, sometimes, we just need to ask.

Prayer: Dear God, help us to remember You are with us through the good, the bad, and the ugly of life. Send us the grace and strength for each moment. Be with us always, we love you Lord. Amen.

Sue Scheffer
A member of Central Reformed

I can't imagine Sue ever being crabby. She's one of the most pleasant people you will ever meet. I like her husband Marlowe as well. He was a fine catcher on the SCHS baseball team and a good guy.

July 17

Matthew 6:3

A Blessed Journey

On a recent trip, my wife Rachel and I stayed overnight in Nashville, Tennessee. As is often the case, I arose early on Sunday morning and went to get a cup of coffee at the convenience store where I had gassed up my vehicle the night before. As I walked into the store, I noticed an older vehicle parked by the front door, and inside the car sat a man and a woman. After getting my coffee and a newspaper, I left the store in a hurry to pick up Rachel and hit the road for home. As I was walking to my vehicle, the lady rolled down her window and politely asked, "Mister, can you help us?" I was more than a little apprehensive, but walked over to their car. The couple was moving from Alabama to northern Tennessee, were out of gas, had no food or money, and the lady was obviously pregnant. They had been sitting in front of the store for several hours, but no one had cared to or dared to offer help. My first thought was what would Jesus do? I filled their car with gas, gave them some money for food, and said a short prayer asking God to guide and protect them on their journey. The lady had tears in her eyes and said she knew a Christian would eventually show up.

Was this couple pulling a fast one on me and laughing all the way to where they were going? I don't think so, but even if they were, God can deal with them. Personally, I felt good all over and was immediately reminded of the passage in Matthew that you read earlier. I'll probably never see those people again on this earth, but I was thankful that I could be God's tool that morning in Nashville. I was the one who received the blessing!

Prayer: Thank you Lord for opportunities to share and be helpful. Continue to use us and please reach out to those that have particular needs. Keep our awareness level keen. Amen.

Terry and Rachel Meekma
The Meekmas are semi-retired – Terry is our New York Life Agent

Terry is a regular at the DutchMart Coffee Group and they are both NWC grads. It's nice when your financial agent is also a close friend.

July 18

Acts 20:35; 1 Corinthians 12:31

The Gift of Giving

I was blessed with wonderful parents. They taught me a great many valuable lessons. But the most important thing they taught me was the Love of Jesus Christ, and the need to accept Him as my Personal Savior. What a joy that has been to me in my life.

Another thing my mother taught me was the importance of giving to others throughout my life. When Mom was in her elder years, and not wanting to wait until her death, she decided to give her most precious possessions to her children and grandchildren. Mom had lots of lovely things: Vases, plates, silverware, and many other items she had collected worldwide and displayed in her china closet. All of these had been purchased in various places and provided many great memories for Mom. As I said, these were very precious to her. But, she decided to give them away so she could also have the joy of giving pleasure to those she loved, while she was still living.

This example showed all of us children and grandchildren how important giving was to her. This happened a long time ago, but I have never forgotten, and I feel this has been a strong motivation in my life. I find great joy in giving.

Prayer: Heavenly Father, You have given us so much. I'm afraid we take much of it for granted and aren't as thankful as we should be. Forgive us for that and help us to give, and then give some more. Amen.

Arnie Ver Hoef

Arnie truly has the gift of giving. In fact, one of the main reasons he is still working (well beyond "retirement age") is so that he has more to give. He sets a great example for all of us in that regard.

July 19

Philippians 4:13; Psalm 91

Only God's Strength

When you are faced with a sudden, life threatening illness, you immediately begin to question God – "Why me? What have I done wrong to deserve this terrible illness – cancer?" We should really ask ourselves – "Why not me?" God has a purpose and a reason for what happens to His people. He has a plan for each and every one of us because He created us! It isn't easy at all for us to remember that we are not in control of our lives – God is!!!!

As people go through life's difficulties, they find themselves lacking faith. They find it very difficult to rely on prayers and scripture to give them strength to face each day. But, when the scripture speaks to them about their certain situation, it can truly give them an inner peace that no one else can give. May God allow scripture to speak to you when you are faced with a situation that you can't understand.

Prayer: Lord, though I feel weak, I know that I am strong as I lean on Your strength rather than my own. May Your Word speak to me in ways no one else can. Please help me to trust in You! Amen.

(Grant was diagnosed with AML (Acute Myeloid Leukemia) on March 19, 2010. These two scripture passages (two of Grant's favorites) were what carried us through the very difficult journey. And, of course, many more scripture passages became very special to him. July 19th, he received news that he is in remission and no more treatments at this time! Praise God from whom all blessings flow!)

Grant and Bonita Vietor

Grant and Bonita are both teachers at SCHS. Grant also coaches a number of sports. Their students and many friends have held prayer vigils, fund raisers, and strong support for one of their favorites. Keep the prayers coming!

July 20

Revelation 3:15-16

Lukewarm

As an old teacher and coach, there's nothing tougher to cope with than someone who doesn't seem to care, and isn't motivated. Give me a student or an athlete that wants to learn and improve and great things can happen. Even if what is being taught causes doubt or questions, complacency slows everything down.

God understands when we get angry or in doubt about bad or sad things that happen to us or people we care about. But if we don't care one way or the other, and never get fired up, He gets upset. So do teachers, coaches, parents, and bosses.

What pushes your "hot" or "cold" button? Who wants to be "spit out"? We just can't fool God.

Today, make up your mind to find something you can get excited about. Get to it!

Prayer: Thank you Lord for diversity. Thanks also that each of us can be attuned to different wants and needs. Help us find something today that "turns us and You on" so we can work together with enthusiasm. Amen.

Dave

July 21

Isaiah 40:41; Luke 22:35-46; Luke 1:46-55; John 13:34-35

Why Wait?

This verse has been a favorite for many, including me. The idea of flying is pretty exciting. We however, can find additional truths here. The words on which we concentrate today are, "*those who wait on the Lord.*"

First, "wait" often means to be quiet, to pray as the disciples were asked to do for our Lord, while He prayed alone on the Mount of Olives. Jesus was teaching His men how powerful faithful prayer support is. (Read the passage in Luke 22)

Another way to wait is to anticipate, sometimes with eagerness and sometimes with dread, something that will happen in the future. Mary waited, knowing with faith and imperfect understanding, that she would bear the Son of God through the power of the Most High. (Read the passage in Luke 1)

The third meaning of the word "wait" is to serve, as one who waits on tables. When we faithfully trust and believe God's Word, we understand that something is expected of us and that is to serve (wait on) the Lord and our neighbors wherever and whoever they are. May God bless you as you wait on Him. (Read the passage in John.)

Prayer: Oh Lord, how we praise You for giving us Your Word so that we may learn and begin to understand Your way for us. We humbly ask that You will guide us today as we wait on Your will. Teach us to pray, to trust, and to serve You and Your children. We pray with love. Amen.

Ardene and Arnie Ver Hoef
Director of Home Management and Owner of Ver Hoef Chevy in Sioux Center, Members of Central Reformed

Arnie and Ardene are also members of our 6-couple Saturday Night Group. We have taken a number of vacations with them and we always have a ball. Isn't it great to have such good friends?

July 22

Psalm 66:1-4

For the Love of Music

Many of you who know me, know that music has always played a vital role in my life. Although I like athletics, competing on teams didn't seem to work so well. Music was another story. I sang in a great quartet, in fine choirs, and also did a lot of solo work.

Many have asked me, "How can you sing at a funeral for someone you knew and loved?" I guess it comes down to prayer, commitment, and concentration. The Lord has to help me. I have to want to do it to honor them, the family, and the person, and I have to devote all of my thoughts to the music.

What a blessing music and people have been to me. It's amazing what God can do when you let Him. It's been great to have the opportunities.

Prayer: Heavenly Father, You have given us so many ways to serve You and Your people. Please continue to bless us and others as we try to serve You. Amen.

Irv Mouw
Retired New York Life Agent

Irv is another longtime member of Central Reformed. This guy can still really sing! He got a standing ovation a few months ago and I think he's about 90 years old! Amazing! Irv has been a longtime friend and it's a pleasure to be in his company.

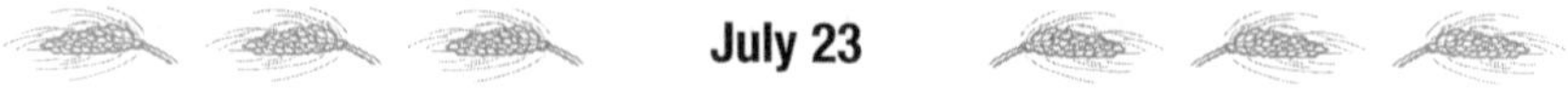

July 23

Philippians 4:4-9

Think on These Things ... Whatever is Honorable (Noble)

For over four years I have received a lot of correspondence to "The Honorable ..." Unfortunately, I can't say I always felt that way. Voting was incredibly tough. Seldom was a law passed that helped everyone. It seemed like it was good for some and not so good for others. What we did seemed to be necessary and sometimes important, but it didn't make me feel worthy of the "Honorable" title.

Don't get me wrong, it was a rare privilege to serve and I cherish those years, but when I think of something (someone) noble or honorable, I think of volunteers that serve: servicemen/women and veterans, people that give of themselves, and I think of Jesus.

Who shall we go out and honor today and tell them "Thanks!"

Prayer: Thank you for the many people You place into our lives that help us succeed. There are so many people we should honor for who they are. Help us find them today and honor them. Amen.

Dave

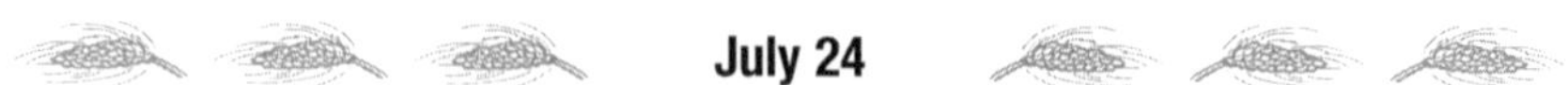

July 24

Matthew 28:19

The Great Commission

Several years ago I was visiting with one of our alums who had returned to campus to be inducted into the Athletic Hall of Fame. I commented to him that I was so impressed that he had made many significant contributions in a number of professional positions during his sterling career. He commented to me in a very humble, yet confident manner, that every place he had been he had attempted to leave "a little of himself" and that his only real professional goal was just to "make a difference."

In this passage in Matthew, Jesus instructed His disciples to go into the world to teach all nations and to baptize them. In essence, I think Jesus was challenging and encouraging them to "make a difference."

I believe God has given each of us an opportunity to make a difference each day. We can make a difference within our vocations by being competent and effective professionals. We can make a difference in our churches and communities by answering the call to service on special projects or standing committees. We can make a difference in people's individual lives in the encouragement we provide to others, or in the kindness we express to our acquaintances, neighbors and friends. Finally, we can make a difference in the world by displaying a Christ-like attitude in all of our daily activities. If we haven't already – let's start today!

Prayer: Dear God, please allow me to be your servant so that I can make a difference each day. Amen.

Dr. Bob Boerigter
Athletic Director, N.W. Missouri State

Bob is a former head basketball coach at NWC and at one time assisted me with the Sioux Center High School baseball team. He has been an outstanding educator and administrator and a great friend.

July 25

Luke 10:30-37

The Jericho Road

All roads do not lead to Jericho. But all roads do have people on them and these people are not too different from the people who walked that Palestinian highway so many years ago. Look a moment at the traffic which moved over that rough road which winds through the hills of that far away land. As you do, also be looking at the people who travel the road you walk today.

First, there was a certain man who traveled with face set toward Jericho, molesting no one, hindering no one. Suddenly a robber band swooped out of the hills and pounced upon that man, taking his possessions, beating him and leaving him half dead. These robbers apparently lived by a philosophy of life which read, "All that you have is ours, and we'll take it." And they did. Is this philosophy of life completely foreign to our twentieth century civilization? Have you not noted that it is an attitude which characterizes so many today?

But back to the story Jesus told. Soon a priest came that way, followed a bit later by a Levite. These men saw the needy person along the road but passed by on the other side. They refused to give of their time and material possessions to help that unfortunate soul. Although they may not have made their feelings vocal, those feelings can perhaps be summed up in these words, "All that we have is ours and we refuse to share it." Is that attitude completely foreign to life as we know it today?

Then a Samaritan came upon that unfortunate human being lying beside the highway. You recall from the story which Jesus told what he did. His philosophy of life can be summarized as follows: "All that I have is yours; with love and concern I stand ready to help."

One does not travel far on the highway of life before he hears the cry of human need. That cry takes so many forms. It may be that of a hungry child, a sorrowing mother, a sick man, a sin-burdened soul. You and I are traveling a road along which lies so much human suffering and want. And, whether we will admit it or not, one of the philosophies characterizing the travelers on that ancient Jericho road is ours.

Be honest with yourself. Where do you fit into this story, which in a sense, is being reenacted every day?

Concerning the good deed of that Samaritan, Jesus said, "*Go thou and do likewise.*" If we call ourselves followers of the Christ, only one course of action is open to us. We will be good Samaritans too.

As you travel today's mile, look for someone who needs you. Make that individual your concern for this day. If you do, today's Jericho road will become for you a glory road.

Prayer: We thank you now for the opportunities that lie before us today. We want to be like the Samaritan. Amen.

Rev. Henry Eggink

July 26

Hebrews 12:16; Ephesians 4:32

Choices

A Bible study leader asked "who are you going to be before God?" This led to the question, "What kind of marriage are we going to create before God?"

Early on, we decided that divorce was never going to be an option for us – never a part of our vocabulary. This meant that we had to choose better ways of settling our differences. Assigning blame or name calling is not a part of our marriage - before God. Yes, at times we agree to disagree.

When we lost two children as infants, each of us grieved in a different way, yet we were able to find ways to support each other – choosing not to become a divorce statistic.

God offers us the choice of accepting the courage of His presence – each day. The Israelites were provided manna in the wilderness – but they had to make the choice to gather it each day. In the same way, we can make the choice to live out our lives/marriages before God each day.

I like the words of this great hymn, "My great Physician heals the sick, The lost He came to save; For me His precious blood He shed, For me His life He gave."

I also like this poem describing: "What is Faith?"

It's seeing a cloudy and threatening sky
And knowing the sun will come out by and by.
It's planting a seed on a bright spring morn
And knowing a flower soon will be born.
It's asking our Father for light for the way
And knowing He'll send grace and strength for the day.
It's reading His word and believing it, too.
And may God in love grant a true faith to you.

Prayer: Heavenly Father, we can only stand in awe of Your grace and love. Thank you. Amen.

Darlene and Marion Mouw
Retired Teacher and Owner of Mouw Motor Co.

Darlene and Marion are very close friends and part of our 6-couple Saturday Night Group. They are both lifetime members of Central Reformed.

July 27

Psalm 118:24

Today Comes Before Tomorrow

People are funny. For example, watch a typical summer tourist. He speeds along today so that by tomorrow he may reach some spot that publicity literature says is beautiful. But when he reaches that spot, he gives it only a hasty glance because already a more distant attraction is on his mind and he proceeds to speed toward it. Constantly he lives in anticipation of tomorrow and the sorry result is that he misses beauties he ought to see today.

Perhaps that is typical of many journeying the road of life. They miss so many riches life can bring today because their thoughts are too much on tomorrow. They are doing one of two things: either worrying about the uncertainty of tomorrow, or anticipating pleasures they hope the new day will bring. And the tragic result is that they miss so much that today offers for the enrichment of life.

This passage in Psalms has the striking words of a traveler on life's road who was not making the mistake to which we have just referred. Today is a gift of God. Today is ours to live. Let us use and enjoy the blessings God gives. Tomorrow may never come for some of us, but if it does, we shall gratefully receive it as God's gift and be glad therein also.

Briefly put, let us not postpone until tomorrow what God intends we shall enjoy today. But so frequently we do! We are like the farmer who stored his apple crop in his cellar. After a time some of the fruit began to rot. So he instructed the members of his family that they were to use the partly rotted apples first. Do you know what happened? That family ate partly rotted apples all winter and never did get to eat a good one because these spoiled about as fast as the rotted ones were consumed!

Years ago I met an elderly lady who had never married. She was an expert with the needle and made many beautiful tablecloths, bedspreads, sheets, pillowcases, and other similar articles. She had drawer after drawer filled with the finest of needlecraft. When visitors came, she found delight in taking out this needlework and showing it to them. After many admiring "oh's" and "ah's" someone might ask, "But, Miss Carey, when are you going to use these beautiful things?"

Sheepishly she would reply, "Oh, I guess I'll use them some day." But her friends knew that she never would. She slept under plain cotton blankets while her drawers were full of beautifully woven spreads. She put off using until tomorrow that which ought to have been used today.

This is the day which the Lord hath made; we will rejoice and be glad in it. Don't hurry through this day. Take time to look up into God's sky where lacy clouds float and song birds fly. Take time to look at God's earth where flowers bloom and children play. Take time to listen, to think, to pray. Take time to enjoy the loved ones in your home. Take time to stand at your neighbor's gate and share his life. Do not postpone until tomorrow what you may enjoy today on this mile of life. Thank God for today.

Prayer: We do thank you, Lord for this day. We can always find something to rejoice about. Help us to always look for those things and for the positives in the people we meet. Amen.

Rev. Henry Eggink

July 28

Proverbs 29:15a; Matthew 18:2-7

"When Making A Decision, First Consider – Is It Good For Kids?" (Bernie Saggau)

Bernie Saggau is the retired Executive Director of the Iowa High School Athletic Association. (Read his devotional tomorrow.) He's a great leader, great speaker, and valued friend. He has influenced me tremendously in so many ways. Many times, as he was addressing coaches, officials, athletic directors, administrators, and parents, I heard him make this statement. And from the many decisions I saw him make, he meant it!

Think about this statement carefully. "If it's good for kids, can it be bad for others? Who? How? Can a decision be good if it's bad for kids? Nope, I don't think so."

So give it a try. It doesn't make any difference as to your age or position. If it's a decision that's going to affect people, particularly young ones, go with the one that's "good for kids."

Thanks again, Bernie!

Prayer: Thank you Lord for great leaders that also put You first in their lives. Please continue to use them and us, to help kids and all those that work with them. Amen

Dave

July 29

Romans 5:3-5

An Olympics Example

It was a beautiful night for the Olympic qualifying track meet in Los Angeles, California. Cliff, a former Ames, Iowa high school athlete, was to qualify in the hurdles. In the previous Olympics (4 years earlier), he had broken the world record in the hurdles, but only won the silver medal, because another runner ran faster and won the gold. Cliff was dedicated and worked tirelessly for four years for <u>this</u> night. He wanted another chance to win a GOLD medal.

Cliff was not known as a fast starter, but this night when the gun sounded, he flew out of the blocks and took an early lead. It looked like a sure victory and even a world record! Then all of a sudden a spike on his shoe hit the top of a hurdle, and he fell and slid down the cinder track. His dream of running in the Olympics was gone in just a split second.

Hundreds of young people in North Dakota signed and sent him a telegram telling him how sorry they were for him. Cliff wrote them back and said "Do not feel sorry for me. Feel sorry for those who have never tried or had a dream. I have in my favor this passage in Romans. I will wash the cinders from my wounds and take one step and then another step. Who knows? I may still achieve my goal!"

I tell you, "Clean up your language, honor your Mother and Father, set goals, and always do your best." We can learn from the Cliff Cushman story that in adversity, we Christians always have HOPE, and we will win the final victory and the gold medal will be Eternal Life!

Prayer: Thank you Father for that eternal hope. Help us to always persevere and fight for what is right. Thank you for great examples for us to follow. Amen.

Bernie Saggau
Retired Executive Director of IHSAA and former basketball and football official

Bernie is retired now and spends a lot of time at the Iowa Great Lakes. He lost his lovely wife Lois a couple of years ago but still can enjoy family and his many friends. Bernie has inspired me many, many times in a very positive way – and I thank him. I have heard no better motivational speaker than Bernie Saggau!

July 30

Philippians 4:4-9

Think on These Things ... Whatever is True

Pilot said "What is truth?" (John 18:38) What do you know that is definitely true? Try these for size –

There is no better country than the one we live in.
Life is precious.
Laughter is the best medicine.
We really do need each other.
Jesus loves me.

We're told to think on these things. I'm sure you know many other positive truths to think about. How can we stay down in the dumps when we fill our minds and hearts with "whatever is true"?

What are the real "truths" in your life?

Prayer: Dear Lord, I don't know if Pilot ever really did find the truth he was seeking, I hope so. Thank you for being truth in our lives and loving us. Help me be more lovable in your sight. Amen.

Dave

July 31

Genesis 2:19-20

Pets

Did you or do you have any pets? I've had a bunch, and presently we have two house cats. Both were rescued and have now been "fixed." They do add a lot to our enjoyment.

As a kid I started with banty roosters, geese, turkeys, turtles, mallard ducks, toads, snakes, dogs, a chameleon, and even an old toothless mink. I have always loved animals and birds. Since marriage I've had pet crows, a cockatoo, a dog, wild turkeys, a lop-eared rabbit, and the cats. I think all kids should have a pet(s). We can learn so much from God's created animals, especially dogs.

Dogs are great on how to greet someone coming home, forgiveness, devotion, and enthusiasm. They aren't great on conscience, but they never remember when we may have neglected or mistreated them. It's better to be treated <u>by</u> a dog as opposed to <u>like</u> a dog.

God placed all of these animals on the earth for a variety of reasons and our pleasure. We can tell a lot about a person by how he/she treats animals. I hope you and your pets feel blessed.

Prayer: Dear God, we thank you for our pets. They become a part of the family. Help us to treasure all of your creation. Some of us learn how to love, show respect, and feel blessed because of our pets. Amen.

Dave

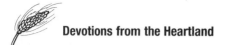

August 1

1 Corinthians 12:28

Pastor Wes Kiel

This man taught about God's love and how to share it with others. "People are more important than things" is what he said and went on to prove to me and to our church.

Pastor Wes taught me about the "humanness" of being a minister. I learned that he struggled with issues, parenting, and frustration, the same as I did. I saw him in some deep "lows" and some great "highs." Regardless, he depended on our Lord and continued to lead.

Pastor Wes and Nell came to Central Reformed at a critical time in her history. We needed to be "brought together" again after a fissure had developed. Wes exuded love and caring – just what we needed. We came together and I cried when they were called to Michigan. (Note: It seems all Reformed and Christian Reformed ministers either "come from" or "go to" Michigan at some time during their ministry. Why is that?)

It is always a pleasure to be with Pastor Wes. May our paths cross often and may God continue to bless him and his family.

Prayer: You use people in so many great ways. Thank you for placing this great man of faith amongst us. Help each of us to move forward and reach out to help others. Amen.

Dave

As this book was being prepared for publication I heard the devastating news that Wes and Nell's grandson was killed while serving for us in Afghanistan. He is Dick and Sue's son. I know this is being read over a year later – but the pain is still there and we need to continue to pray for them. Please do that!

August 2

Revelation 22:21

The Last Word

When I was a child, my father read a chapter of the Bible at the close of at least one meal per day. At the conclusion of the reading, one of my three sisters or I would be asked to repeat the last word of the reading. The purpose of that practice was to monitor whether we were paying attention. I think it worked (although when I was older, I found I could do it without paying conscious attention). The last word of the New Testament is about grace. Is that the Holy Spirit's way of ensuring that we are paying attention to what is most important?

If the basic question the Bible addresses is: "Who is God and how can I be in relationship with God?", then the basic answer is "grace." My favorite paraphrase of grace goes like this:

"Nothing you can do can make God love you more. Nothing you can do can make God love you less."

Let that be the first AND the last word for you today.

"Grace to you, and peace, from God our Father and the Lord Jesus Christ."

Prayer: Lord Jesus, thank you for the bountiful supply of grace you have for each of us. Please enable us to show grace and forgiveness to others and accept it for ourselves. Amen.

Pastor Wes Kiel
Retired Minister, Former Pastor of Central Reformed (1972-79)

You will never see a friendlier smile than the one Wes will flash at you. He is such a "warm" person, and his wife Nell is a perfect mate. I smile every time I think of them. They are always in my prayers – keep them in yours.

August 3

Matthew 25:40; Acts 10:38

The Walking Path

We have air conditioning so no windows are open, both parents working, television and video games, mobility, 3-car garages, lawn services, etc., we don't get to know our neighbors like we used to when I was a kid.

Of course, I grew up in Alton, Iowa where I had a paper route so I knew where everybody lived. Alton didn't even have street names and numbers. Everybody went to the post office a couple times a day to pick up the mail. There were lots of opportunities to visit.

Since the new walking/biking trail goes right through our back yard here in Sioux Center, we've gotten to "know" lots of people (our neighbors) again. It's great – lots of people working in their back yards (the back yard has to be as presentable as the front now!) and lots of people visiting.

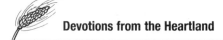

I love it. The art of greeting, welcoming, and visiting has returned. Let's keep it going. How about planning a block party, "burning pit" event, or some kind of gathering in your neighborhood this week?

Neighbors are great! Get to know some more of them.

Prayer: Thank you Jesus for creating us as social beings. We truly do need each other. Enable us to reach out to others and to recognize others reaching out to us. Amen.

Dave

August 4

Isaiah 40

Life's Experiences

This scripture has always been a favorite of mine. The first time I really read it I was in my teens and was singing Handel's *Messiah* for the first time. My high school choir director asked us to read all the scripture passages on which it was based.

As I read, I was struck by all the descriptions of God. He is the Comforter, Sovereign Lord who comes with power, Holy One, Shepherd, Everlasting God, and Creator. As my life experiences have changed, God has shown me all these characteristics of Him in my daily life.

As a teenager I was drawn to verses 30 & 31 and excited to know that God was with me. He was always there and He would help me "soar" like an eagle. As a stay-at-home mom with three kids under foot, I was drawn to verse 29 and relied on His promise that He gives strength to the tired and weary and is my Hope and Strength. As I struggled with family issues of health I was reminded that God carries us close to His heart, (vs. 11) no one or anything compares to Him, (vs. 18) and He is in control. (vs. 10)

Recently I have been drawn to verses 21 and 28 which ask "Do you not know? Have you not heard?" I'm realizing more and more how little I really do know and have heard about Him. So I am trying to get deep into His Word to learn more about this Sovereign and Everlasting Lord.

I don't know the life experiences you've had or are dealing with, but I challenge you to read this chapter again. Identify the times where you have seen this mighty God at work in your life, and then with me, give Him praise.

Prayer: Thank you God for who You are in my life. Give me the desire to know You even more. Amen.

Vicki Franken
Guidance Counselor and long-time friend of ATLAS

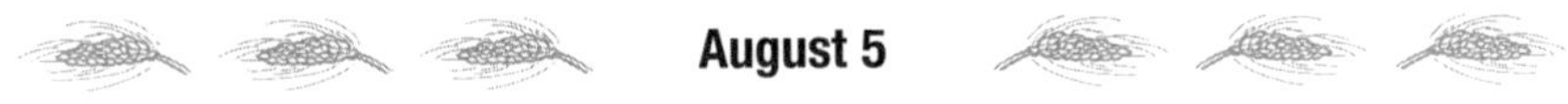

August 5

Matthew 16:2-3

The Weather

As I sit here this morning and look outside, these observations are recorded about one of the most frequently spoken of topics. It's not windy, the sun is shining, and it's partly cloudy.

Here are some facts for N.W. Iowa. For two years in a row (2009-10), we had historically record rainfall in July (the month we traditionally get the least rain). The months we have the lowest wind velocity are February and August – one of our coldest and one of our hottest. (Does that make you a little nervous about wind turbines?)

Professional weather persons will tell you "the further we get past 3-day forecasting, the less credence." Duh! Statistics show those forecasts to be "less than 50% accurate." Most forecasters are about 80% accurate for one day.

I almost never watch the Weather Channel, never complain about heat, and could care less about the wind chill factor. I'm going to try and go this year without using more than a "one-word" answer when someone brings up the weather, never bring it up myself, and change the subject to something positive and uplifting that we can do something about.

Want to join me?

Prayer: Lord, this isn't the only subject that confuses me as You well know. But help each of us to center on You and what we can do to help others. Amen.

Dave

August 6

Nehemiah 5:15b

Go The Second Mile

Every day brings with it the challenge to act this way or that way, the challenge to find out which is the right way. Today will be no exception. For the follower of Jesus the issue is not simply to decide between right and wrong decisions, but to make sure that my actions advance God's Kingdom.

How often have many of us had to look back on a day and deal with regrets? We must conclude that we didn't take the exceptional action that would have caused people to take notice of the love of God that constrains us. Nehemiah took bold action when he decided that, given the extreme *poverty* of the people he was to serve as governor, it would have been preposterous for him or the officials under him to draw on their food allowance. It was an action that clearly set him apart from his predecessors.

Nehemiah's is an amazingly forthright and self-analyzing statement. It singles out his relationship to God as the determining factor for reaching godly decisions and for acting differently from other governors. No, he would not have committed a wrong had he insisted on being paid his official food allowance. Neither would it have become clear to the people that Nehemiah considered his political leadership and office as entrusted to him by God. Therefore, he was accountable to God for his actions.

What we have here is the forerunner of the "second mile principle" that Jesus in His sermon on the mount, sets up as a goal for every one of His followers. It's not what others expect of us or even request of us that should determine our action. Rather, it's what we come to expect of ourselves the closer we grow in our relationship to Christ, even if it means acting differently – -and that often includes giving of ourselves generously – from other dads, teachers, ministers, husbands or wives, managers or senators.

What bold action can you take today that reflects your deep love for the Master who is your Lord and Savior?

Prayer: Dear Lord, again we call on You for guidance and motivation to do good. Help us avail ourselves of opportunities to help others. We know we can't out give You. Amen.

Friedhelm K. Radandt, Ph.D.
Former President of NWC (1979-85)

Friedhelm hired me and brought me to NWC. He and his wife Elizabeth served the college very well and I am very grateful to him.

August 7

Philippians 1:9-11

Family Prayer

And This Is My Prayer:

"That your love may abound more and more in knowledge and depth of insight." We are to be continually learning, not for the sake of knowledge only, but to strive for the insight that the knowledge offers.

"So that you may be able to discern what is best and may be pure and blameless until the day of Christ." God desires our obedience in all ways of our lives so we will be ready for the second coming of Christ.

"Filled with the fruit of righteousness that comes through Jesus Christ." Depending upon Christ's power, we leave our sinful nature and turn to a morally correct manner.

"To the glory and praise of God." Our actions should bring a glow upward and not downward to ourselves.

Prayer: Heavenly Father, may this be our daily prayer in all circumstances. Amen.

Dot

(Today is Dot's birthday (she was born in 1941). Give her a call if you get the chance. Besides a massive gift, I think I'll go give her another hug! ~ Dave)

August 8

James 4:7-8

Persevere

Here's a word of encouragement to those of you who have started, are working on, or are thinking about a project that you feel is a "God Thing."

The more frustrated, disheartened, or maybe even angry you feel, the more important it is to persevere, continue, and finish. It's the devil that is making you miserable and wanting to make you quit. He doesn't like what you are doing and will do everything and anything to make you stop.

So those of you that know somebody working on a "God Thing," help them, encourage them, meet deadlines, and PRAY!

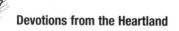

Believe me, this book was like that. You name the "bad" feeling and I had it.

Once again, for those of you doing it, PERSEVERE! It's worth it.

Prayer: Thank you Lord for all those who encouraged, or at least don't discourage. Help us to help others. Amen.

Dave

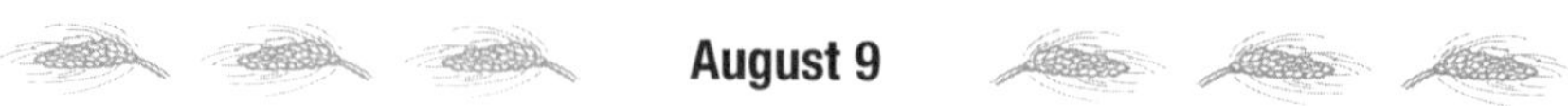

August 9

John 11:35

One Word Answers

"A picture is worth a thousand words." (Fred R. Barnard or Confucius) How many times have you asked a simple question and gotten more of an answer than you wanted or was required? How many times have you done it yourself?

The late Paul Harvey (my favorite newsman) used to say "Now I'm going to tell you more than I know." That always got my attention.

Want to have some fun? As you talk to your friends and family today – ask something like this. "What's a one-word answer for what you like best about ...?" The verse for today is the shortest in the Bible. "*Jesus wept.*" But think about the power of it and what it makes you think about. "Why?" "For whom or what?" "Physical or mental pain cause it?" "When?"

One could go on and on – but remember this about the importance of brevity!

Here are a few examples from my own experience. I asked my granddaughter Sarah upon her return from Haiti, if she could provide just one thing for the Haitians, what would it be? "Jobs!"

I asked nephew Stan what he liked the best about his job. "People." I asked him what he liked the least about his job. "People." I asked Dot what she liked the least about School Nursing. "Paperwork!"

Aren't one-word answers thought-provoking? You can always ask the person "why?" or to elaborate – but isn't it better than talking about the weather?

Here are a few questions for you to use your Bible for. Remember – one-word answers!

What's the last enemy to be defeated?
What are we saved by?
Who did Jesus weep for?
What does Jesus' one Commandment concern?

Prayer: Lord Jesus, You have given each of us great minds to use. Help us use them for the love of others. Amen.

Dave

August 10

John 14:6

The Way

Jesus' words show that the way to eternal life, though unseen, is secure. He has already laid the path to salvation and eternal life, and it is up to us to believe and follow the path. I find that three small words carry such power ... the power to have eternal life. If I don't know Jesus in my life, I am lost. Three simple words can also bring such confusion to many. As I struggle to understand and live the truth, I ask God to keep my heart open to Him and to settle my willingness to believe.

I am the way: He is the road, the path to salvation. His name eases my fear of getting lost because He is my way, therefore, if I have Him I'll never die lost.

I am the truth: He is the King and came to bear witness to the truth ... the reality of God's promises. His name removes my need to keep looking. He **is** the truth.

I am the life: Divine vitality ... giving life to whoever doesn't have it, and creating new life with the knowledge of Jesus Christ. His name reinforces my hope for a home in heaven ... He **is** the life.

I find that "belonging to the way" as Jesus' followers became known in the early days, is a sure way of being united with Him, and feeling secure that Jesus' promise to all who believe in Him **is** the way to eternal life. I thank God for bringing reconciliation where there was alienation, and for the wonderful mediator that has given us peace. As humans, we continue to sin and turn away from Him, and I pray that my heart will not turn away in my darkest moments. I pray that I can always find my way back to the truth and the life. I pray that I can always count on my counselor, my mediator, my defender, and my advocate, so that the Spirit can intercede according to God's will. This is the greatest gift of all ... THANK YOU GOD!

Prayer: Eternal Father, thank you for showing us the Way and for being our defender and redeemer. What a blessing to spend eternity with You. Amen.

Rossana and Bill Barouski
Best friends of son Dick and Kathrine.

Bill interviewed Dick for his job at the Fed. Eventually they and their spouses became best friends and meet together, whenever possible, on Friday evenings. They (along with Paul & Brooke) do many other things together as friends do. It has been our pleasure to be able to spend many pleasant evenings with these fine people as well. As we are welcome in their homes, we would be so happy to welcome them to ours.

August 11

John 15:18-19

Reputation

It's amazing that one can work for years to earn a good reputation, and then have it disappear in a moment because of one indiscretion. I'm sure I don't have to remind you of a number of examples dealing with famous people, and maybe some not so famous.

Here are a couple quotes that I've heard over the years. "Any publicity is good publicity." (I believe that came from the movie industry. Is it true? Even a bad reputation is helpful in this field it seems. Does that give us pause as to how we let movies and television influence us?) How about this one? "If everything I thought about this week was printed in the paper, I'd have to leave town!" I'm afraid this one is true about me. Kind of scary, isn't it? The mind is the most difficult and most important thing for us to control. "Garbage In, Garbage Out." We can't get this control alone.

When one thinks about how easy it is to affect what people think of us, especially in a negative way, we can realize the importance of controlling our thoughts. Very few bad things are done unless they were a conscious thought beforehand.

Prayer: Jesus, please guard my heart and guide my thinking throughout this day and throughout my life. Amen.

Dave

August 12

Matthew 7:3-5

Specks and Planks

How come it seems so easy to see those specks in other people's eyes and ignore those logs in our own? Jesus says that is hypocrisy and it is! But it's not easy to remove those planks is it?

As a teacher these thoughts can enter my mind. "If those were my students, they would be much quieter." "If that was my classroom, those students would know their math facts like the backs of their hands." "If those were my own children, they would have their homework done on time!"

These are some of the thoughts that can run through my mind when I judge others without taking the plank out of my own eye. What are incidents that cause you to look down on others before taking a good look at yourself?

Prayer: Dear Lord, help us all to recognize good things in others and work hard on removing the bad things from ourselves. It's a tough job but You can help us do it. We need You and thank you for loving us in spite of our weaknesses. Amen.

Amy Achterhoff
Elementary (4th) Teacher in Sioux Center and our daughter

Dot and I call her "sweet Am" (pronounced aim) – and she is. She's the mom of Sarah and Ethan, and wife to Kyle. She says "football season" takes on a life of its' own but she loves it. We couldn't be prouder or happier with this very thoughtful and loving young lady. May God continue to bless her real good! By the way, today is her birthday – give her a call.

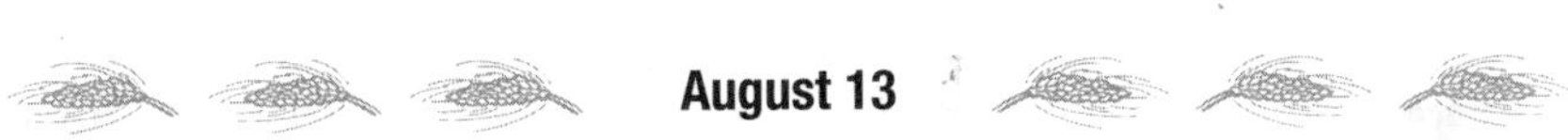

August 13

Proverbs 3:5-6

The Information Age

We live in an information age. Almost instantaneously we are able to gather information about most any topic. Yet, information alone is of little use unless we can understand it. Understanding is of a higher order than information alone.

Understanding information is good, better certainly than just having information, but better still is being able to apply what we know. Being able to apply knowledge

Christianly is called wisdom, and that is in too short supply today for all of us. We've all heard the phrase, "I wish I had the wisdom of Solomon in making this decision." As Christians, we often pray for wisdom – -that God would grant us discernment and the ability to make wise decisions with what we know and understand.

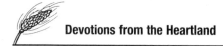

Just imagine what our world would be like if all of us were able to look at information, even knowledge, through a Christian lens that would give us great wisdom in our everyday lives. Ours would be a better world in Christ's name – a taste of God's kingdom here on earth! With God on our side, acting with wisdom should be our mode of operation.

Prayer: Father, we pray for wisdom in all we do. Give us the courage to be your instruments for bringing Your kingdom here on earth. Amen.

Jim and Martie Bultman
President of NWC (1985-99), presently the President of Hope College

Jim and Martie served the college well. He had to be one of the best fund raisers I've ever seen. It was a privilege and a pleasure to work for him. I also greatly enjoyed coaching his son Matt. Matt played #1 on the NWC golf team and it wasn't because he was the President's son! He did it the old fashioned way, he earned it!

August 14

Hebrews 10:23

Hope

As I drove to the hospital that day and entered the ER, I wondered if this would be the last time. At some point, this pattern had to end – either in a miracle of healing – or in death. A young mother I had mentored and grown to love was in trouble again. The scene inside the door was a girl who had obviously not showered in days. An overpowering stench of alcohol seemed to flow from her pores and fill the room. The nurse confirmed that her blood alcohol content was dangerously high, even worse than the last time. My friend voiced sorrow and despair in a way that you knew she meant it. Her words cut deeply, revealing how she really felt about herself. Even the idea of hope seemed to her a cruel joke that only existed in a fantasy world.

She and I had had many conversations about God's love for her and His desire to have a relationship with her. I knew she wanted to believe this, but the very real possibility of losing her husband and little girl clouded any reason to see a brighter future. I silently asked God what I could possibly say this time. I knew there was nothing my words could do to make a difference. That day, and many since, God has reminded me that it's not about *my* ability to speak hope, but it's about *His* ability to encounter someone right in the middle of their deepest pain.

I've often wondered how someone who is hopeless arouses that sense of hope that begins the process of healing. Do someone's eloquent words convince them, or does a dramatic story of victory win them over? In my work at ATLAS, where I try to speak hope into people's lives, one thing has become blatantly obvious: God is the Author of Hope! We may try to love, encourage, entice, or persuade others to put their hope in Jesus, which He often uses in the process; but in the end, it is always His own work in the deepest places of their hearts that really makes a difference.

In the case of this young mom, I have no idea how He did it, but somehow something moved in the heavenlies, and then something moved in her soul. Something was sparked by the One who is faithful, and she saw that tiny glimmer of hope. She made the difficult choice to get help and spent months away from those she loved to learn about her addiction, her potential, and most of all, her identity as a daughter of the King of Kings. Today she is His. Her life is a beautiful example of restoration and reconciliation by the power of the Holy Spirit. Recently, I reentered that same hospital to visit her. This time it was with a pink package in my hands to celebrate the birth of her second baby girl. She and her husband could not be more excited with the miracle God has done in their family. And their baby's middle name could not be more appropriate…it is Hope!

Prayer: Father, you are the real hope-giver and the source of true hope! Thank you for empowering us to be part of the hope offering to a broken world. Help us to do so with humility, truth, and love. Amen.

Melanie Pottebaum
Staff Mentor at ATLAS of Sioux Center

Melanie knows how to bring out the best in the people around her! Those who come in to ATLAS of Sioux Center know that she is wise, loving, and passionate.

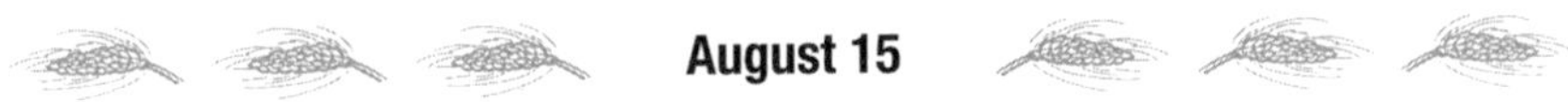

August 15

James 5:16b

God's Gift Of Prayer

Frequently, when I begin to pray, I'm amazed at what an awesome gift our Lord has provided for us. His omnipresence allows us to communicate with him at any time no matter where we are, or what is going on around us. It is almost beyond human understanding to think that our God can hear our individual prayers when there are nearly seven billion people on earth. Even more amazing is the fact that He answers each of our prayers according to our needs and His will.

It is so important for us as Christians to place everything before our Father and to trust Him and His infinite wisdom to provide for our every need. Even though there are times when we are initially disappointed with His answer, we ultimately see that He has chosen the best for us and for our life.

For us to receive God's direction and His blessings for our lives, it is imperative that we bring everything to Him in the form of our prayers. One of my favorite scriptures regarding prayer is the one we read in James, "The prayer of a righteous man (person) has great power in its effect." As Christians, we should all use one of the greatest gifts that God has given to us – the power of prayer.

Prayer: Thank you Lord for always having time for us. We can't fathom how you can know each of us and what we want and need, but we have found that You answer our prayers. We could not go on without You listening, caring, and acting. Amen .

Mel and Carol Tjeerdsma
Head Football Coach at NW Missouri State and
former Head Track and Offensive Coordinator in Football at NWC

What a Coach! He's in the College Football Hall of Fame and really deserves to be. He has won 3 National Titles and taken his team to the finals 9 times! I got to know Mel and Carol when he coached football at Sioux Center. He had two undefeated seasons in-a-row and won the State Championship. He was at Denison for just one year and had a perfect 9-0 record. As the Offensive Coordinator at NWC we won the NAIA National Championship in 1983.

But Mel's not just a coach, and Carol's not just a coach's wife. They are great Christian parents and grandparents, pillars of the church, and positive examples for all with whom they associate. May God continue to bless them and show that nice guys do finish first.

August 16

Job 10:8-9; Isaiah 29:16

Build a Bridge

Many of us can look back over bridges we have crossed – bridges erected by great and thoughtful souls who have preceded us. To them we owe a tremendous debt of gratitude, a debt which can be paid in no better way than to follow their example. Some youth is following us today; will he find a bridge over some sullen stream because we have passed this way?

This whole matter of concern for the well-being of the young is of fundamental importance. A society which lives only for the present, a society which says with that degenerate Louis of France, "After us the deluge," is a dying society.

Look round about at the youth of our day and ask, "Do we really care for their future? Do we care enough to inconvenience ourselves on their behalf, to sacrifice for their well-being, to erect bridges here and there so that they may travel safely? Are we taking thought to open up ways over which youthful feet and aspirations may move through coming generations?" The answers to these questions will reveal in a large measure what the future of our civilization will be.

Children and young people need the concerned interest of their elders in many areas of life, but in no area is this more necessary than in the spiritual. So many of our youth are religiously confused. Nothing is quite so helpful in resolving this confusion as the example of an older person who is following closely and humbly the Savior of Galilee. The gospel of a life like that is far more effective than lectures, books, or scrolls in enabling confused youth to traverse successfully spiritual pitfalls.

A young mother had displayed unusual ability in an amateur sculpturing class in which she was enrolled. A famous sculptor, having looked upon some of her creations, urged her to give full time to the art. She answered by saying, "I feel highly complimented by your kind remarks for me to devote my time working with the clay and marble in your studio. I feel I have a much higher calling." And pointing to her children playing nearby, she added, "There is my clay. I choose to work with that living substance because it is warm and loving. It has a mind and a soul which can and must be turned toward God ..."

Socrates, the wise philosopher of ancient times, said "Could I climb to the highest place in Athens, I would lift up my voice and shout, 'Fellow citizens, who do ye turn and scrape every stone to gather wealth and take so little care of your children to whom one day you must relinquish it all?'"

These words might well be shouted to a materialistically-minded generation of the present century. Our first concern ought surely to be for our children and youth, especially for their spiritual welfare. The material heritage we shall leave them one day will be of minor significance as compared with the spiritual heritage. In fact, that material heritage may prove to be a curse, may prove to be bitter in their mouths, if we have left them no worthy spiritual heritage.

Tomorrow a youth will follow us. Will he find a bridge over the swollen stream because we have lingered to build it? If so, we have made an important investment for eternity, and coming generations shall rise to call us blessed.

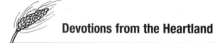

Prayer: Heavenly Father, we do want to build bridges and not burn them. Help us to remember the importance of the example we set. Amen.

Rev. Henry Eggink

August 17

Psalm 147:3; Isaiah 41:10; Isaiah 43:2; 2 Corinthians 1:3-4; 1 Peter 4:12-13

Moodiness

Are you a moody person? I don't think I am, but there are some down times I guess. How do you change your mood or the mood of someone you care about? It goes back to knowing yourself, or the person you care about. I know certain kinds of music can make me more upbeat. Inspirational readings (like Guideposts Magazine), some television programs (M.A.S.H. reruns, "Touched By An Angel), many ballgames (unless the Cards lose), and certain people can help a lot.

What helps you? Ask your spouse, best friends, or kids if they notice different mood swings with you. Do you want to be in a "bad mood?" Nope! Didn't think so. You can get out of them if you want to. Find out what works for you. But first you have to recognize the problem. Pray about that.

I wish you all the best and lots of pleasant times and thoughts.

Prayer: Dear Lord, help us to understand ourselves and those around us. Help us to know what is best for us, and then to do it. Thanks for your love and care. Amen.

Dave

August 18

2 Thessalonians 3:13

Don't Get Discouraged Doing Good

Surely the world is full of needy people, many of whom are reaching out to us. Almost daily we are deluged with appeals. There comes a time when giving and reaching out to help becomes wearisome. After all, the journey of life isn't always easy and we have plenty of problems and anxieties of our own. We are a bit reluctant to get involved in problems of other folks and we think about stopping our efforts. But we know such an attitude is not right.

Try this: start by thanking God for the many blessings He has bestowed upon you – list them, count them. Think of how He has demonstrated His love for you. Think especially of Jesus' agony on the cross, suffering and dying to provide for you full forgiveness, making possible your salvation and redemption. Think of the inheritance awaiting you in glory provided by Him. More immediate, think of the abilities He has given, abilities in helping those seeking your help. Look upon the appeals coming to you not as a burden but as opportunities to show the Savior how much you love Him and are grateful to Him. Then do the good deeds of kindness in His name and to His glory. In doing that, you will likely find yourself blessed even more than the person for whom you reached out in helpfulness.

You noticed how Paul summed up how "we must never tire" in the scripture passage.

Prayer: Dear God, again we call on you for inspiration and assurance. So many times we tend to overlook the needs that are out there. Don't let that happen today. Amen.

Rev. Henry Eggink

August 19

Joshua 1:8; 23:11; 24:15; Romans 12:2

God's Game Plan for Success

Just about everyone I know desires to live a "successful and prosperous" life. Many believe that winning is a matter of what's on the scoreboard at the end of the game, or what size their bonus check is at the end of the year, or how large their house is, what kind of car they drive, or what country club they belong to. While these may be measures of success in the eyes of the world's economy, they are not so in God's.

Joshua was hand-picked by the Lord to follow Moses and lead his people into the Promised Land of Canaan. He had proven himself worthy as Moses' personal aide for 40 years, was one of only two living eyewitnesses to the plagues and resulting exodus from Egypt, and only he and Caleb showed complete confidence that God would help them conquer Canaan when sent in to spy out the territory. But, as brilliant as Joshua was as a military leader and strong spiritual influence, the key to his success was his submission to God. When God spoke, Joshua listened and obeyed. His obedience served as a model that resulted in the people of Israel remaining faithful to God throughout Joshua's lifetime.

The same "Game Plan" that Joshua followed is available to us today. We are to read God's Word, study, discuss, and meditate on it, then "live it out" in our daily lives. Only then can we find true "success and prosperity" in God's eyes.

Prayer: Please open our eyes to see what You see. Help us to strive for success in Your eyes. We know this isn't easy, but we know You are there as an ever present help. Amen.

Dave Turnball
Director of FCA in Iowa

Dave has been a friend ever since he took over the leadership of the FCA many years ago. He lives in Indianola, served with me on the Annual Easter Prayer Breakfast Committee in Des Moines, and is a great leader. He has a love of the Lord and kids. That's a great combination.

August 20

Romans 8:28

This Is A Toughy

I have more names written next to this verse in my Bible than any other. Why is this one selected the most? Unfortunately, this verse gets misquoted quite often. Many tend to remember the first part about "everything working together for good," but leave out the part about "being called according to His purpose." That's a pretty important part.

It's also a mighty tough verse to understand completely. Bad things do happen to good people too. Sometimes it seems nearly impossible to find some good in what has happened. I do think it's imperative that we look for the good in whatever happens.

My best friend Paul died from cancer when he was only 47. That was July 7, 1987 and he left a great family and a host of friends. Even though I know he was saved, it still hurts. What good can I find in this? Because he was taken so early, I try to cherish each day, show extra love to my family, and make my faith grow. I'll keep searching for more "good." It's also good that I don't have to make the extremely difficult decisions that God makes on a moment-by-moment basis.

Prayer: Dear God, You have told us to be thankful in all situations and to find joy. That is so tough to do when a loved one is taken – even when we know they are with You. Help us to understand and to cope. Show us too, how to be patient and find the "good" You intended. Amen.

Dave

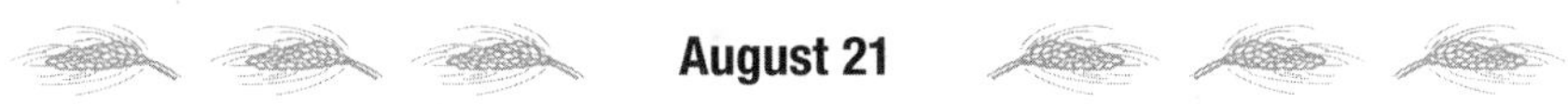

August 21

2 Corinthians 1:9

How's Your Day Looking?

Paul gave up his high status as a Jew to become a Christian. As a Christian missionary Paul was beaten three times with rods, stoned once, received thirty-nine lashes five times and was shipwrecked three times. He was in danger from the elements on his journeys as well as from robbers. He spent many nights and days hungry and thirsty. He had to fight with beasts in Ephesus. He was truly close to death many times.

What difficulty is assailing you today? Is it worse than what Paul went through? Paul is an example to us of what to do in hard times. He did not despair or give up. He used the difficult times to become closer to God. He learned to trust God more in each of these circumstances. We have a choice when bad times come our way. We can try to live through them on our own power or we can trust in God despite what is happening to us.

Pray that God would show you how to trust more in Him.

Prayer: Heavenly Father, we do pray for an increase in our trust and faith in You. Help us to understand what it is that You want us to do. Guide us to the right people and places where we can have complete reliance on You. Amen.

Eric Elder
Economics Professor NWC

Eric and I shared the Economics classes at NWC for many years. I have always appreciated his knowledge, love of students, administrative ability, and friendship.

August 22

Psalm 104:19; Genesis 1:14

School Starts

Many schools and colleges start classes during this week. I know it's the "end of summer," and as an old teacher, it is the beginning of a new year. What an exciting time of the year! It's a new and fresh start for so many.

Every coach of a Fall sport thinks "this may be the year!" Athletes and all co-curricular participants can expect new and great challenges. As fans we can watch the Ryder Cup, Baseball Play-Offs and World Series, and the start of the NFL season.

We get the chance to meet new people, renew friendships, elect new officials, harvest bumper crops, and celebrate Thanksgiving. The only thing I don't like about Fall is that we will have to look forward to two Winters and only one Summer!

What do you like about right now? What are you going to do about it?

Prayer: Thank you God for creating the seasons. Keep us safe and thankful. Amen.

Dave

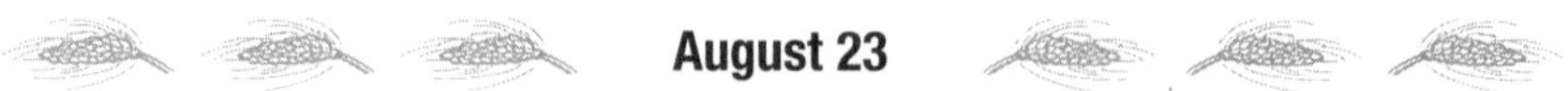

August 23

1 Peter 4:10

Brighten The Corner Where You Are!

Wow, what a challenge that is laid down for each of us as Christians! This verse speaks to me, as this is something that I have been struggling with recently. I have found myself questioning whether I am using the gifts God has given me to the fullest extent. Am I really making a difference in this world in the name of Jesus Christ? My answer: I don't know, so I continue to ask for His guidance and listen for His answer. I have found that this can be a very frustrating time.

A friend reminded me of something very important. Although it is certainly good to be in tune to what God would have us do, we can't lose sight of the opportunities God places before us each and every day. Perhaps there is something more that God has in store for me and my family. In the meantime, I have the opportunity to shine God's light today right where I am. Wow, what a privilege! Let's all take that challenge to heart today and be a bright light for someone else.

Prayer: Dear God, thank you for the privilege of serving You each and every day... right where we are! Amen.

Matt and Becky Ray
Banker and Director of Home Management in Washington

Matt played #1 on my golf team at NWC and he and his family stay very close to us with communication, even though the miles between us are many. We have visited them in Washington and they always make contact on their visits back to Iowa. This is one great Christian family.

August 24

John 14:2-3; Psalm 23

Toward the Setting Sun

Every journey ultimately comes to an end; the journey of life is no exception. Whether we like to think about it or not, it is true that someday we shall begin to travel toward the sunset. That can be a sobering thought, one which immediately confronts us with heart-searching questions, "Am I ready for what awaits me at the journey's end? Do I have older loved ones that don't appear to be ready?"

The late Bishop Moule told about an incident which occurred during WWII. A party was being held in London for soldiers who were soon to cross the channel to France and to the Front. The entertainment had been carefully and thoughtfully planned by several public spirited organizations. The affair had been lively and interesting.

At the close of the party, a young officer rose at the request of his Colonel to express the men's thanks. His words were well chosen, charming, and humorous. Then suddenly the young man paused, and as if in after-thought, in a different tone, he added, "We are soon crossing to France and to the trenches, and very possibly, of course, to death. Will any of our friends here tell us how to die?" There was a long, awkward silence. No one knew what to say. Then one of the entertainers, a singer, made her way quietly to the stage, and began to sing the great Aria from Elijah, "O Rest in the Lord." A breathless quietness hung over the room as the song progressed. When it was completed, there were few, if any, dry eyes in that great hall.

"O Rest in the Lord." Here is what each one of us needs above everything else, if the journey of life is to end successfully. We need to rest ourselves in utter abandonment in the complete, the finished, the all-sufficient sacrifice of Jesus on Calvary's Cross. We, in humble, child-like faith, must surrender fully to Him. We must permit Him to have His way in our lives. We need to place ourselves, as we are, in His nail-pierced hands. We need to yield to the Good Shepherd's guidance and control. We must become His by giving ourselves to Him who gave His all for us. This is the secret.

Having rested ourselves in the Christ, we shall never travel alone again. At our side will be a Companion who will "keep us from falling" and then at journey's end will receive us Home. With these assurances we can travel confidently toward the sunset. Long ago the Psalmist expressed this wonderful truth in words. Later travelers have come to love them and have made them their own.

Prayer: Again we, call upon You for safety, companionship, and assurance. Every path is difficult without You. Amen.

Rev. Henry Eggink

August 25

Proverbs 3:5-6; James 1:2-4; Revelation 3:21-22

Trials – Tribulations – Understanding

"When bad things happen ..." many of us have heard these words. Bad things do happen. The terrible earthquake in Haiti happened. We all watched our television screens show unbelievable misery, and minutes later we saw the unmitigated joy of a rescued family member. As we go through life, we observe terrible pain and sorrow, and we also see and feel abundant joy.

Losing a child is perhaps the greatest pain and sorrow parents can experience. It happened to us, not once, but twice. Our "bright," "athletic," "full-of-life before him," 14-year-old son Lee came home limping one day. Fourteen months later he was gone with a cancer called Ewing Sarcoma. Our daughter Lynn was a happy 8 months old when she died from Sudden Infant Death Syndrome. Our third child, Dan was born with Down syndrome. This opened our eyes and hearts to a new world of caring.

Trying to make sense of life was impossible. Having a boy and a girl – isn't that what we call a "perfect family?" Our "perfect family" was devastated in a matter of months. As Christians, our head told us all the wonderful scripture verses and messages we had heard since our youth. But at that time, the pain in our hearts didn't want to (or wouldn't let us) hear any of those wonderful truths. The old saying is "that time heals all wounds," but the heart remains a broken, although mended, vessel. Life goes on in the same way, but it will always be different. The question we ask now is not where is God? – But, where am I? – Where have we placed God in our life?

Prayer: Thank you God for Your promise that we can and will see our loved ones again. We need that hope just as we need Your love and the love of our family and friends. Please give us the strength and understanding to continue to live for You. Amen.

Marge and Howard Beernink
Both retired now but Marge plays the organ at Central
and Howard is a part of the Praise Team and the Choir

Howard and Marge are good friends that we can, and have, learned a great deal from. In spite of their losses, they exude a joy that only our Lord can give. They are great volunteers and always willing and ready to help – now if I could just get Marge to like Country Music!

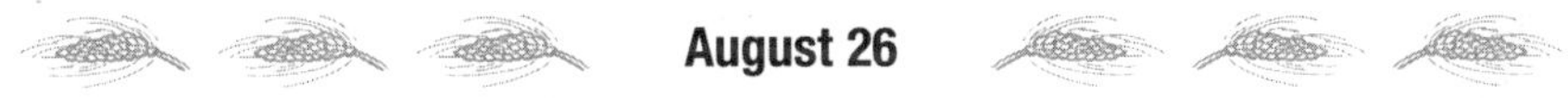

August 26

Psalm 37:7-8;– Galatians 5:22

Patience

Patience is a concept that I continue to struggle with in life. When I try to get my thoughts focused on living patiently, my thoughts are directed to the abundance of patience God has with us. When you recall the Old Testament stories where the Israelites continuously tested the patience of God, He was longsuffering and always gave them a way out or another chance. They did not always respond properly. Sounds like our own lives. How many times have we angered our Lord? Too many for one to count.

If we can apply the example of God's patience with us as sinners to how we could be more patient with others, we would be better servants. I also need to be more patient with God as He works out His plan of salvation. He has been abundantly patient with me. Can I be more patient with Him and others? Lamentations 3:26 says, "It is good to wait quietly for the salvation of the Lord." Let's try to make work of that today.

Prayer: God, grant me the ability and strength to do just that. Please allow me to become more patient with those that I have daily contact with. Thank you Lord for new mercies each day. Amen.

Glen Bouma
Athletic Director, Dordt College

Glen was a fine High School and College basketball player. He then became an excellent Coach. Glen is always a gentleman and he sure appears patient to me! It's great to have good people grow up in a particular geographic area and then stay. That's exactly what Glen and his family have done. That impact is very positive and beneficial to all of us. May our Lord continue to bless all of his efforts.

August 27

Luke 11:1

Teach Us To Pray

Do we pray? Why do we pray? Do we really believe God is able to do "more than we could ever ask or imagine"? Do we really want Him to?

For years I thought of prayer as an appropriate way to prepare to do my work as a Christian. I now believe it is in prayer that the real work is done.

Prayer: Just as your disciples asked You so many years ago Lord, teach us to pray. Amen.

Bruce Murphy
Former President of NWC (2001-07)

Bruce and Di both taught at NWC in the '70's. They knew and loved this college. They also knew how to lead her. I and everyone associated with NWC, benefitted from their great leadership. They are now retired and living on the West Coast, near to children and grandchildren.

August 28

Ecclesiastes 7:24, 8:1, 11:9

"Teach and Coach the Way You Want Your Own Kids to Be Taught and Coached" (Fellowship of Christian Athletes)

FCA is a great organization that does much for kids and coaches. This organization introduced me to a number of great men and women that strongly influenced my life as a Christian (Quite a few of them have submitted devotionals for this book).

When I read this statement in an FCA publication it had great meaning for me. Who doesn't want the absolute best for their kids? That's why this became a strong motivator for me to do my very best at all times. I wanted my kids to be encouraged, challenged, individualized, disciplined in a positive way, and loved. So that's what I tried to do.

Now I used it in teaching and coaching, but I think it's an effective goal to parent the way you wanted to be parented, or lead the way you want to be led. It seems there is a myriad of possibilities to apply this idea.

Give it a try.

Prayer: Dear Lord, continue to motivate us to excellence. Continue to give us ideas that work. Continue to help us share your wisdom and love. Amen.

Dave

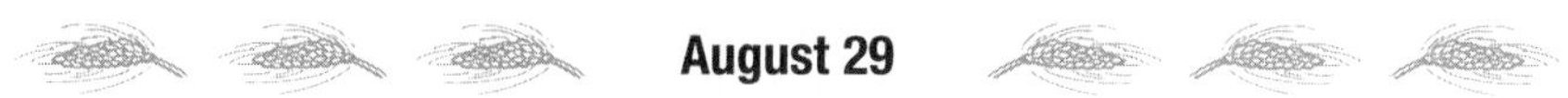

August 29

Psalm 46:1-2, 7

Where is Your Fortress?

The Lord Almighty is with us. The God of Jacob is our fortress.

How often in this life does it feel like the mountains are falling into the sea? How often does life throw us a curveball, especially when it seems like everything is going great? An unstable economy, a job loss, war, sickness, even death. Any number of events can make it seem like there is no hope. A fortress is built to hold fast, even when floods threaten and the earth caves in on itself. God is that fortress, always there for us in times of trouble. When the familiar collapses, we as believers, have refuge.

Isn't it comforting to know that no matter what the situation, we can turn to the Lord, our ever present help in trouble? We can always have confidence in the security of God in the midst of a threatening world.

Prayer: Dear God, thank you for maintaining control, even when we seem to only see darkness. We know You are The Light and we praise you. Amen.

Doug Broek
Radio Announcer for KSOU

Doug is the "Voice of the Red Raiders" as he announces all of the football, volleyball, basketball, and many baseball games. Doug does a great job because even though we know who he is for – his voice inflection remains unbiased. Another fine quality is that he isn't always criticizing the officials or the strategy of the coaches – he just describes the game being played. He's definitely another one of the "good guys."

August 30

Ephesians 2:10

Life's Three Most Frequently Asked Questions

Who are you? Where are you from? What do you do?

In answer to the first question, we usually answer by stating our name, Secondly, where we are from is pretty easy for many of us to answer. For some it takes a little more explaining if we moved a lot as a kid, or experienced the pain of separation or divorce as a child. The third question seems to get most of the attention and requires more of a response from us, at least it has for me, even with my own children.

This happened to me about eight years ago. Our oldest son, Ryan, was seven at the time. We had been in Minneapolis one night for a Twins game. It was late and the van was very quiet as we drove away from the stadium. Our daughter, Maddie, was asleep and I thought it would be a quiet ride to the hotel. But then little Ryan spoke up from the back of the van. He informed us that he wanted to be a major league baseball player when he grew up. I did not want to burst his bubble but also didn't want to crush his dreams. So I said that was great but that not many kids actually make it all the way to the big leagues. I shared with him that I too wanted to be a major leaguer when I was his age. He asked, "'Why didn't you then?" I said, "Ryan, I just wasn't good enough and the Cardinals never called me so that is why I am working at Dakota Wesleyan." At the time, I was the VP for Institutional Advancement there – a title that always made people wonder what I actually did. Ryan thought for a while about my response and then said, "Dad, what do you do anyway?" I said, "You know that Daddy is gone on trips sometimes traveling around the country? I am making friends for DWU and asking them to support the University financially." There was a long pause ... "Dad, I still don't understand what you actually do." I said, "That's okay Ryan, nobody else does either." Another even longer pause ... Dad, – do you?"

I share this story as an example that I know first-hand from my own children that we have to answer this question of what we do. But what I have learned in life is that we really should focus more of our time on who we are and who we are becoming. That is what I love about God – it is not about what we can do for Him but what He can do through us. The passage in Ephesians talks about us being "God's masterpiece ... created to carry out His plan." Two observations – first, God created us with great intentionality we are His masterpiece! And He has great plans for us and things He has planned for us to do.

It is not about us though. It is all about Him and His work in the world. Go and live courageously and faithfully today, following Christ and pursuing His redeeming work in the world.

Prayer: Thank you God for creating us with a purpose in mind. Carry out this purpose today and use us in Your masterful plan. Amen.

Greg Christy
President NWC

Greg and Michelle took over the Presidency in 2008. Although I'm not actually working for the college any longer – I still have close ties. Once again the Board made a wise choice for our leader. Not only does he do good work – but he's a Cardinal fan! The guy knows baseball!

August 31

Philippians 2:5

How Do We Imitate Jesus?

As we live to imitate the one who gave totally of Himself, we must journey through the Bible to become aware of why and how He impacted those He came in contact with. If His life of love, giving, and compassion turned the hearts and souls of those He touched, then we too should follow His example.

In my time as coach and teacher, I came to see the real concept of why the family needs to be the center of this imitation of Jesus. It became very clear to me that Jesus lived as a true servant with a close relationship with His father. For wisdom and understanding, Jesus would pray for extended periods of time, for the answers needed to carry on.

For me, the good news of how Jesus lived His life is why we must prepare and carry out His teachings by starting each Sunday in real worship. It is at this time we can get our attitude right so that our motors will rev and speed up for the real contests of life. Yes, we need to prepare ourselves to imitate our Lord.

Prayer: Lord, I pray for wisdom! Amen.

Larry Korver
Retired Head Football Coach at NWC

"Bubb" is an NWC icon. Of course he is in the Hall of Fame of NWC and the NAIA. He not only was a great player, but a fabulous coach. He won two National Championships (1973 & 1983) and took many teams to conference titles and post-season play. As great as his play was and his teams were – his influence among his athletes is even more impressive. As is true for me, Coach has been blessed with a great and supportive wife. He and Betty are approaching 60 years of married life together and the spark is still there. Bubb is my main golfing partner and a cherished friend. Of course he is also a major part of the DutchMart Coffee Group. The guy stays very active in his church, community, and his workshop – where his woodworking and craftsmanship is in much demand.

September 1

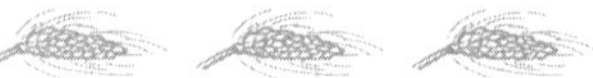

Psalm 37:23

To The Mulders

As God made me
So I am
As He wills
So will I do
As He leads
I will follow
A life yielded
To Jesus Christ

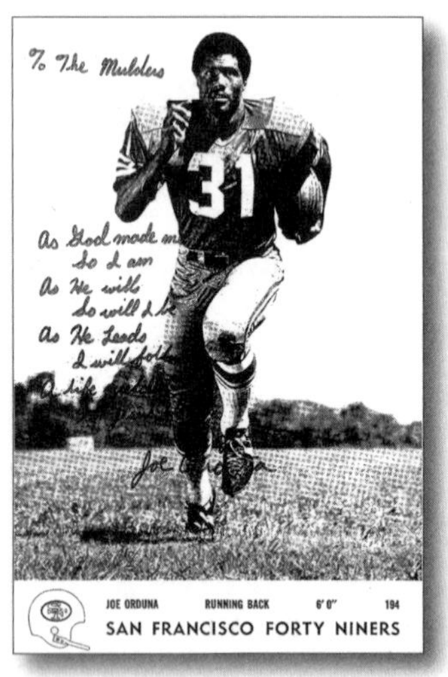

Joe Orduna

Joe got me to read the Bible. I was 31 years old but hadn't really read it because I wanted to. It took the motivation I received from this man of God.

Joe was a fabulous running back for the Nebraska Cornhuskers (and later in the Pros). He was also a Christian that I met at a Fellowship of Christian Athletes camp in Colorado. He gave an outstanding testimony and as a coach, I wanted him to come to Sioux Center and speak to our kids. He agreed to come for the spring athletic banquet.

Oh, did I tell you Joe is a black man and he married a white gal? This was 1969-70 and Sioux Center was an all-white community. Joe and Val stayed at our house for the weekend and it was one I will never forget.

He preached a sermon at the athletic banquet and didn't mention "Big Red" football or any other kind. He met with our FCA group and with our Bible study group. His wife Val was a treasure and great partner. Did they make an impact? Within the next two weeks, 23 kids made confession of their faith in Jesus Christ, in their respective churches.

My wife and I really got into the Bible after that. Our two kids were blessed as well.

Joe, Val, their children and grandchildren, are doing well in California, I'm happy to report. May God continue to bless them!

Prayer: Again, we say thanks for using people in our lives to make us better and draw us closer to you. Help us all to be a blessing to others and to You. Amen.

Dave

September 2

Psalm 139

Seeking And Searching For Those Whom God Loves

You are a treasure to God. He searched for you and when He found you, He spoke words that penetrated your heart and comforted all your hurts and fears. He gave you new life. WHY did he do that? Because He loves YOU!!!!

Do you like the idea/thought that someone loves you enough to search for you until He finds you, and then when He finds you, He gives you a new life?

Many people do not know that God loves them. Maybe they have been hurt by religious experiences, or heard "Christianese" words, but saw no evidence in the life of the one speaking, to make them know that God loves them.

What could another person do to make you know that God loves you? Could they speak a kind word, smile, offer to help, give of their substance, or even tell the truth? – i.e. "God wants you to know that He knows who you are. He knows the desires of your heart. He knows everything about you. He loves you passionately and wants to bless your life and your whole family."

Inviting people to church may be appropriate LATER!! Right now be as Jesus was to people He met. Be approachable, considerate, kind, patient, willing to hear more than to be heard. Speak kindly and encouragingly, but most of all, speak the truth – "God the Father wants to show you that He cares about you and that He wants to bless your life."

If you wonder where to go to search for people, or who to talk to, or what to say, ask the Holy Spirit who dwells in you, who teaches what you need to know, who empowers you to do more than human sufficiency can do, who fills your mouth with the words of life that are needed in that moment, and most of all, who knows the heart of God for the person He sends you to.

Prayer: Father, fill my heart with your love that seeks and searches for those who need to know that you love them. Guide me in all my ways that what I do and say, will be life to those I meet. That Jesus may be glorified, Amen!

Joseph and Val Orduna
Retired Pro-football, presently teaching and coaching in California

One of the side benefits of this book was that Joseph, Val, and I have reconnected. We've had several phone calls and emails and will definitely meet in person again when he comes back to his hometown of Omaha, or we go out to the Golden State. Joe is just as motivated and inspiring and filled with the spirit. Val is a princess. I can't wait to see them again.

September 3

Luke 5:1-11

Go Deep

As a football coach, the thought of going deep means doing something that is of high risk but may result in a high reward. Throw deep and three things can happen, two of which are bad. There can be an incompletion or even worse, an interception. The chance of completing a long pass or getting an interference call can make the difference for a positive outcome of the game. So at the right time we have to go for it.

God expects the same from all of us believers, just like He did with the disciples that night in the boat. Jesus tells them to put out into *deep water* and later He will make them *fishers of men*, taking a risk with the highest of rewards.

So, how is Jesus calling you to "Go Deep"?

Prayer: Dear Jesus, thank you for the great opportunities You give us to serve You and our fellow man. Please help us to do that service the way You want us to. Amen.

Kyle Achterhoff
Head Football Coach at NWC

I'm proud to say Kyle is my son-in-law and the father of our grandchildren. It's never easy for a Dad to give his daughter to another man – but I was happy when this marriage took place in 1989. Kyle is a good man that cares a great deal about his family and his athletes. It's a joy for me to watch him coach and lead the young men. I'm sure there will be many "W's" in his career – but he's a successful coach already. I love him and enjoy being with him.

September 4

Proverbs 3:5-6

A Leap of Faith

Early in our marriage, we chose these words to be our guiding light as we began our journey in life together. In the first years of marriage we bonded together and grew closer to the Lord. We lived and worked in a great community where we built our dream home and where our two children were born. We worshipped and served in a great church. We were surrounded by wonderful friends and family. Glenn loved the people he worked with and his job was very fulfilling. It was easy to praise God and acknowledge Him as Lord of our lives.

Eleven years into our marriage, we began to feel that God was preparing us for something more. God had given us many opportunities for growth and service in our community and church. Was our faith strong enough to leave our comfortable surroundings and go into fulltime Christian service? We surrendered to His leading and took a leap of faith which took us completely out of our comfort zone.

We discovered that God is true to His word. When we trusted Him, leaned on Him, and followed His leading, He took us on an amazing journey. We could never have imagined the people we would meet, the places we would go, the ministries we would work in, the lives we would see changed, or how our circle of friends would expand. Thirty-eight years later we are still praising God for the journey!

Is God nudging you out of your comfort zone in some area of your life? Are you ready to take a leap of faith?

Prayer: Lord Jesus, take our hand as we step into the unknown. Illuminate the path for the journey ahead. In Your name we pray. Amen.

Marilyn and Glenn DeMaster
Former Sioux Center teachers and now semi-retired in California,
They were part of our "supper-club" as we taught together during the '60's

This great couple only spent a few years in Sioux Center but they made a life-long impact on us and many others. After leaving teaching and administration Glenn went to Seminary and became a minister. Eventually they wound up at the Chrystal Cathedral. We look forward to every opportunity we get to be with them. They celebrated 50 years together on this date in 2010. Give them a call.

September 5

Psalm 90:17; Matthew 10:10; Proverbs 27:18, 28:19

Don't Labor Today

This is probably my least favorite holiday. It's kind of the end of summer – most vacations are only a memory now. When I taught at NWC we always still had classes. I was always more pro-management than pro-union, even though we do need unions.

Even though this day doesn't affect me near as much as it used to when I wasn't retired, it is still important to pay tribute to those being recognized. The American labor force is the most productive group of workers in the world. Our workers believe in productivity and earning the pay they receive. Let's honor and promote that philosophy.

Happy Labor Day!

Prayer: I thank you Jesus for people that invent, plan, produce, and work hard for all of us. Keep each one safe, motivated, and productive. Help all of those who have earned this "day off" to be relaxed and well-rested for the morrow. Amen.

Dave

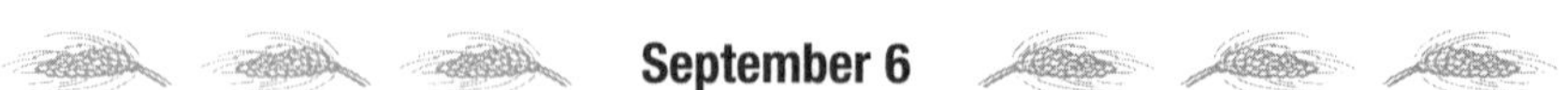

September 6

Ephesians 2:4, 8-10

Grace and Faith

Pray for Grace – Keep the Faith.

That's not easy when life is such a humbling experience. "In the beginning" – After listening to a Billy Graham crusade with my parents, the innocence of youth and the power of God brought me to my knees in the privacy of my bedroom, and I gave myself to Christ. Savoring the blessing of this sheltered childhood in small town Iowa, made sleeping with a Bible and a basketball seem natural! I was saving my soul and our team was winning more games!

"God rested on the seventh day" – I left the comfort and security of our small community to attend the University of Iowa. How does one describe the college experience of the late '60's? We each have our story. I became a skeptic and fell from grace. God was patient and the lessons were yet to come.

Now married with two kids, life seemed good. Then the grieving started. My brother and I suddenly lost our parents in 2001 and 2004. In September of 2007, my wonderful 61-year-old husband kissed me goodnight, went to sleep, and died. In an instant, life changes forever. I had a choice, give up on God, or once again fall to my knees in complete surrender – this time helpless and broken. God's amazing grace has since pulled me along – One Day At A Time.

May we all hold hands, love one another, and be grateful.

Prayer: "Yes, when this flesh and heart shall fail, and mortal life shall cease – I shall possess within the veil, a life of joy and peace!" Thank you Lord, Amen.

Connie Kraai-Smith
Retired and living in Canada.

Because of her brother Bob, Connie has become a dear friend. She was a fabulous basketball player and was an All-Stater as she played for her dad, the legendary Coach Russ Kraai from Holstein, Iowa. We email back and forth but I sure wish she would come back to Iowa to live.

September 7

1 Corinthians 15:55-56

Death

This is something I don't like to think about a lot. But I can't help but think I'm closer to it now than I have ever been. Am I afraid of it? No, not really. I guess "the process, or the actual act of dying" makes me uneasy. But just think about what happens next… Heaven!

Here are some things I've heard people say: "It's getting where I actually have more friends in Heaven than I have here." – "I'm really anxious to see Heaven and Jesus." – "What puzzles me is that I know Heaven is perfect, but I fight to stay here as long as I can!" – "Since experience is supposedly the best teacher, it's the unknown that causes the problem."

Ahhhhh – sweet mysteries of life – and death. What's that other thing that's inevitable?

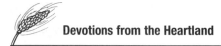

Prayer: Thank you for taking away the "sting of the grave." Please give us peace, comfort, grace, and increased understanding. Amen.

Dave

September 8

Matthew 28:19

Can You Make The Cut?

Jesus' team started with 12 but was cut to 11.

When you set out to develop a team it is necessary that you have team members who are committed and dedicated. As you know, Jesus recruited a team of 12 good, solid, hard-working young men, who did not recognize their potential. It was after His resurrection when one of the 12 left the team. Jesus met with the 11 that remained (the same number as a football team). He challenged and prepared them for the work He came to do.

When you prepare the team for the game you NEED to work on their total development. It is during this time that special attention is also given to the real game – The Game of Life. Each member of the team is challenged in such a way that they deal not only with the physical aspect, but more importantly with the spiritual.

My prayer, my hope and my goal is that in their time, they will recognize and carry out The Great Commission as the 11 did. Yes, a football team is made up with 11 members on the field, but for real success, many more are <u>needed</u>.

Prayer: Dear God, I do pray for team members to recognize where they fit in the game of life. Help each of us as coaches, parents, fans, and supporters to always be an encouragement to these young athletes. Bless each one of them. Amen.

Coach Larry (Bubb) Korver

This devotional centers around what the Coach always strived to do. He tried to create a family with each member knowing his role, purpose, and destiny. No individual is more important than the team. Every player must know that he is important to the coaches and to each team member, because – he is! Is there any confusion as to why he is a great coach?

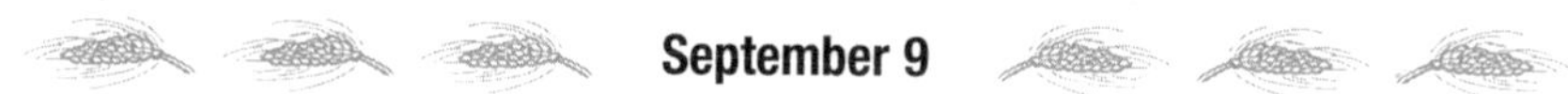

September 9

Jeremiah 29:11

God's Purpose

This verse has been dear to our hearts for a long time. I know I personally think of it every day and take comfort in its message.

Knowing that no matter what is going on in our lives, that the Lord has a plan for us, makes me realize there is a greater power, and He knows what is best.

We should cherish every day and live our lives to glorify God. What a comfort it is to know that He is always there watching over us.

Prayer: Each day we face many different situations and the need to make choices and good decisions. Please help us to make decisions that fit right into the plan You have for us. Help us too so that we want to be a part of Your plan and always accept Your will. Amen.

Scott and Lindsay Speer
Banker and Nurse, living in Sioux Falls

Scott and Lindsay are our grandnephew and niece. They are the proud parents of Ava, and I'm hoping they have a whole bunch more because their grandparents and great grandparents are something else!

September 10

Jeremiah 1:5

From The Womb To The Grave

When we were young and planning our future, we often wondered how things would work out. The military was before us. Bill left for the service five months after we were married. We were apart during his eight weeks of basic training. There was a big possibility of him going overseas. We thought we might not see each other for two years. However, God had other plans. We were together nearly the entire two years.

When it became the time for Bill to be discharged, we wondered what kind of work we would find to do. A farmer, whom we had worked for previously, wrote us about a job opportunity as a hired hand on a farm for his brother. As a result we took that job which included a place for us to live.

We feel God had our lives in His hands and the plans were already in the process before we had time to worry about it. That trust has continued to grow and grow.

Prayer: Thank you Lord for your divine plan and our part in it. Amen.

Lavonne and Bill Riphagen
Retired friends and members of Central Reformed.

Bill and Lavonne are regular members of our Saturday Morning Breakfast Group. They both are active and willing volunteers and proud parents and grandparents. It's always good to be with these friends.

September 11

Ephesians 1:17-18

Enlighten Our Hearts

Both my spouse and I have frequently discussed how blessed we were to each have had the opportunity to spend a considerable amount of alone time with one of our grandparents. Both of us had one of those grandparents that were exceptionally wise in what they perceived, what they said, and how they acted. Each had the ability to look at situations and see them from a spiritual perspective like none other. They would listen to you and not only hear exactly what you said, but they would also hear what you didn't say or maybe hesitated to say. Their touch and mannerisms were firm while still being gentle and loving.

There are numerous scripture passages (Psalm 115, Deuteronomy 4, Jeremiah 10, and others) that all speak of idols which have eyes that cannot see, ears that cannot hear, mouths that cannot speak, and hands that cannot move. I was always told when scripture passages repeated something, we should pay special attention. When one envisions these repeated passages describing an idol, we often think of some type of statue; and the phrase "eyes that cannot see etc." seems somewhat of a "duh." Of course their ears can't hear, they're idols. However, when you read Psalm 115:4-8, it repeats those same phrases and finishes with an additional very important warning. Verse 8 says "Those who make them (idols) *will be like them*, and so will all who trust in them." If we truly desire to be wise like those that have gone before us, we need to consider our own lives to see if we have made any idols or trust in any. If we have, the scriptures tell us, we will be like that worthless idol. Each one of us knows the idols we personally make or trust. Let us remove those idols or our trust in them, and then rely on the Spirit of wisdom to open our eyes.

Prayer: Spirit of wisdom and revelation, help us to know Christ better. We pray You will open the eyes of our hearts and enlighten us. Amen.

Wayne and Diane Westenberg
Math Professor and Assistant Volleyball Coach at NWC, Maintenance at NWC

What a special couple this is. I got to know Diane very soon after arriving in Van Peursem Hall because she was in charge of "maintaining the building." She is a joy to be around and as helpful as anyone can be. She is also a talented speaker. Wayne was a teacher and Head Volleyball Coach at Unity Christian High. He won several State Championships and always had great teams. I was so happy when he chose to come and join us here at the college. He's the kind of man you would want your daughter to play for. He's also an excellent teacher which isn't surprising.

September 12

Proverbs 17:6

Grandparent's Day

Ask any grandparent about their grandchildren and they will love to tell you anything you would like to know (maybe even a little more). Their grandchildren are probably their favorite subject. How exciting it is to hold this new little miracle in your arms for the first time and realize the unconditional love you feel. It's hard to explain until you are a grandparent. They just steal your heart.

Grandmothers are only referenced once in the Bible, (2 Tim. 1:5) but the role of a grandparent is very important. Some memories of my grandparents are sitting at the dinner table while they had devotions; looking for them sitting in their usual spot when we walked into church on Sundays; attending the Sunday School class that my grandmother taught; and having dinner at their house on Sunday afternoons. I realize now that my grandparents were planting a seed of faith into a little girl that God watered and allowed to grow. They knew in all their wisdom that this was what a little child needed to see, but until I became a grandmother, I didn't realize what an important role this is.

It is our job as grandparents to live a life that shows these little gifts from God that we will pray for them and help them understand how faith in God can move mountains. They need to understand that everybody makes mistakes, but with God's help they can learn from their mistakes and pick themselves up and become stronger.

There's so much we as grandparents can teach our grandchildren. It's never too early or too late to start!

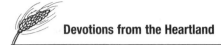

Prayer: Dear Lord, we praise Your name and thank you for opportunities to plant seeds of faith. We ask that You water them and watch over them so they will grow and prosper for Your kingdom. In Jesus name, Amen.

Karen Vander Pol
Athletic Dept. Secretary at NWC

If you ask the coaches (and I have) they will tell you that, besides the athletes, there is one person that is indispensable in the Bultman Center – it's Karen! She seems to know everything and can find anything. And she does it pleasantly, with a smile on her face. We need more people like her! Thanks for all you do Karen, you are a true servant.

September 13

Psalm 46:1; 1 Peter 5:10

The Beauty of Pain

Each day brings new joys and new trials. God's word tells us, "In everything give thanks." How does one accomplish this when one is experiencing pain? Let's take a look at where we would be without pain.

A person without physical pain can be classified as either having leprosy or congenital insensitivity to pain (CIPA). CIPA is life threatening, especially for children. Not being able to feel physical pain is incredibly dangerous. Pain tells us what we should of shouldn't do. Pain informs us when we should stop or move away from harm. Those whom have felt pain, avoid pain, but are only able to do so because they can avoid those things that initially caused the pain. Most people with CIPA do not live past the age of 25. Those with leprosy lose their fingers and toes and other extremities due to the fact that they cannot feel pain and continually damage their body due to inadvertent injury.

Then there is mental pain, where our hearts and spirit feel damaged. How does one give thanks when experiencing this? I have been told that only through suffering do we grow; while this is true, the process is definitely hard and giving thanks for the process is sometimes harder.

In 1987 my mother, then 58, was told she had cancer. If the chemo worked, she would live possibly another year. During this time, I prayed like I had never prayed before. God and I had many conversations and most of the time I was confident He would perform a miracle. Six months later I was called to come home to say goodbye. There didn't seem to be any purpose in her death; after all, wouldn't healing her glorify God more than allowing her death? Nothing made sense to me and I certainly did not feel spiritual growth.

My father, an elder in the church, had spent quality time visiting a hospital patient (I will call him Ted). Dad had been trying to share the gospel of Christ; however, this Ted's heart was hardened and dad simply couldn't seem to break through. The day my mom died, Ted called our home and asked if dad could come visit him. I told dad not to go, that this day was already too hard. Dad simply told me that he felt he needed to go, that Ted would not live much longer. So my dad and another elder from the church went to visit Ted. Ted was as obstinate as ever and not receptive. The other elder then explained to Ted how my mother had passed away and that today was a very hard day for dad. At that point Ted's heart softened, and he said that if dad took the time to see him on the same day that my mother died, well then, his God must really be important and real. That day Ted accepted Christ into his heart. A couple of weeks later Ted died, joining my mother in Heaven. I now saw the bigger picture, how God used one life to save another. I saw a purpose in my mother's death and I realized how pain can be a gift, which allows us to sharpen our focus and draw nearer to God.

Prayer: Father in heaven, I give you thanks. I thank you for pain, even when it really hurts. I thank you for the gift of eternal life. Help us Lord God to see the bigger picture even when the pain is great. Help us to be thankful in all things. Amen.

Tina and Jeff Jansen

Tina works at the computer help desk at NWC. She is an angel that may speak of pain, but she sure reduced a lot of mine. This book wouldn't have been completed without her. She helped me convert all 365 of these devotionals to computer documents for publication. She can make a computer talk – I can start one. This date is the anniversary of her Mom's passing. We're never quite ready to "give up" our Moms – pray for Tina, and all of those in pain, today.

September 14

Isaiah 1:18a

Whiter Than Snow

Sitting here by my window watching the snow fall, I am overwhelmed by the splendor of God's forgiveness. The countryside and the trees are blanketed in the whitest of pure crystal precipitation, and yet, when I go out to the supermarket I begin to see the result of traffic on the snow – it becomes dirty and ugly and slippery – all excellent adjectives for the sin that so easily besets us in life.

For those of us who have no extraordinary conversion experience, it is the gradual pollution of the purity of God's forgiveness that often occurs, without our conscious awareness. We know that confession is good for the soul, but we tend to sponge bathe rather than jump in and soak in the tub awhile, and the vastness of what God's forgiveness really is, evades us.

In Venezuela, the only encounter with snow is usually on the mountain peaks, and so it is in some spiritual lives as well – an occasional experience of retreat or inspirational singing or preaching – and we feel clean again, pure again. I suppose that is why snowfall in the states is so overwhelming for me, because here the snow covers even the banal – like the garbage can and cesspool lid – only to remind me that purity is available every day in the common life we live, and is not limited to the mountaintop experiences. It is in the experience of ordinary forgiveness in the everyday brokenness that we encounter the vastness of the pure, clean, compassion of our Savior's love for us.

Prayer: Lord Jesus, may the splendor of Your forgiving love continue to amaze and attract us to You more and more each and every day, so that we seek to bathe in its beauty until we are together again in the glory of your kingdom. Amen.

Doug Shepler
Former Chaplain at NWC

I enjoyed Doug's sense of humor, dedication, and the fact that he was a "hugger." It took me a while to get used to that, but giving a man a hug is important too. Thanks Doug – I hope our paths cross again soon. May God bless you and your family.

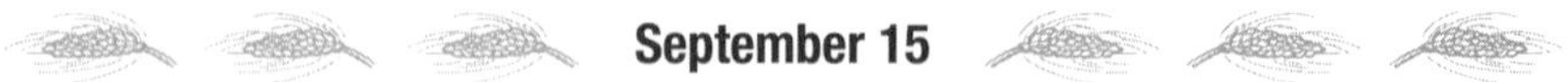

September 15

Psalm 102:1

A Life In Spite of Polio

When I was 24 years old and pregnant, I was diagnosed with polio. In those days, no one knew much about this scary disease, and there was much fear as to how contagious it was. People would visit me through the window, but most didn't dare come into my house. There was not the support that churches give today to hurting families. However, with our church family and community, and our faith and belief in God, we could not have made it through.

Our daughter was born and was fine, the third of four children. But, it has been a lifetime of survival. I would never have thought Francis and I would have to fight this battle for 69 years and still be fighting it. I have learned that you can't survive alone, and God must have thought we could handle it, because we're still here!

Francis and I have learned since that young age that we could not do everything, but made the best of what we could do. Whether life hands you a lifelong disease, an injury, or a financial crisis, just think, "What can I do with what I've got?"

Whether you're 24, 50, or whatever number of years old, life isn't certain, so be prepared in your relationship with God.

Prayer: Thank you that we can find joy and happiness even when things aren't perfect. Thank you for families and spouses that love and care. Guide us through whatever days and years You still have planned for us. Amen.

Jean and Francis Kosters
Lifetime members of Central Reformed - now retired

This great couple always has a smile and a cheerful greeting. I sure wish I could hear Francis croon another of those great old hymns. Today they are celebrating another anniversary! I know it's a bunch of them so give them a call.

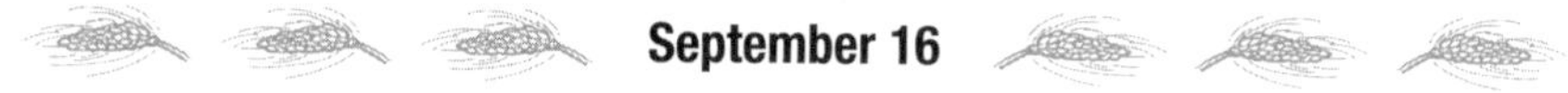

September 16

Philippians 4:4-9

Think on These Things ... Whatever is Pure

"This is pure unadulterated tomato (provide the fruit of your choice) juice." "This bottled water is pure." I could care less about bottled water. I refuse to buy it. It should be "free" like it used to be when I was a kid. I know that's not very sound reasoning, but that's the way I feel on that subject. I don't think about pure much. Ronnie Millsap (A country-singer of course) had a great song out called "Pure love – 99 & 44/100% Pure Love." That's the old Ivory Soap commercial too. Isn't anything completely pure?

I've thought more about pure while writing this devotional than I ever have before. "Pure as the freshly fallen snow, pure gold, without blemish, no additions." Hey! Pure is hard to find – except for one thing – the love of God for us. Now that's something to think about.

Prayer: Thank you God for loving us. None of us are pure, but when we accept Your precious Son as our personal Savior, we thank You for seeing us that way. Amen.

Dave

September 17

Proverbs 4:20-22

What Hand Have You Been Dealt?

"You've got to play the hand you're dealt," was the phrase my mother-in-law spoke as inoperable cancer was spreading throughout her body. I always admired the strength and calmness in her voice at such a turbulent time in her life.

In looking back over my life, I realize that I've been dealt many "winning" hands. I've been blessed with a loving husband and family, wonderful children, good health, etc. We've all been dealt some hands that weren't so great and some people have been dealt hands that are just plain awful.

While life may deal out our hands, God surely helps us play them out. The more difficult the hand, the more God will assist us. God was the strength and calm in my mother-in-law's voice. With God as your partner, there is no hand that you can lose.

Prayer: Dear Lord, thank you for partnering with us each day. It is always safe to trust You. Amen.

Sue and John Steele
Sue Controls the Meal Services at the Bellevue School and John is a Project Manager.

John and Sue are dear friends from Bellevue, Nebraska. I met John, and he helped me a lot, when I was attending Grad. School at Nebraska/Lincoln in 1982-83. We have been good friends ever since and we travel to have a meal with each other every month. They are great friends and have two fine sons, Scott and Craig.

September 18

Joshua 1:8

Success

Someone once said, "Don't let success go to your head, and if you fail, don't let failure go there either."

Thinking back to the fall of 1962, I was newly married, had just moved to Sioux Center, and started a new job as a graduate nurse in the local hospital. A graduate nurse is a nurse waiting to hear if she passed the State Boards. Back then, one had to wait several months to get the test results. I had been sick with fear of failure. While taking the test I didn't have a good feeling. The time always lapsed before I had completed any of the sections. No I hadn't prayed, just worried.

Great News! I passed! I promised God that I would never let any successes go to my head. At that time I didn't realize that God's plan for me included a long, rewarding career in many aspects of nursing. He has a plan for all of us. God is so good!

Prayer: Thank you Lord for the gifts of life and all the things included. Please bless us this day as well. Amen.

Dot

September 19

Philippians 4:11

Vision Glorious

The difference in people is often the difference in their vision. I think I shall never forget the words of one of my instructors at Iowa University, the late Dr. Robbins, when he said "The vision of a man – his outlook toward life – determines pretty much the life he lives. If a man looks at the world through the eyes of a hog, he will live in a hog's world; he will be satisfied with a full stomach and a warm place to sleep. If a man looks at life through the eyes of a criminal, he will live the life of a criminal. If a man looks at life through the eyes of a child of God, he will not be satisfied with merely the physical. What a man's vision is will determine pretty much the life he lives."

We might not state the matter as did Dr. Robbins, yet most of us will agree that there is much truth in what he said. What our vision is determines our life.

The traveler on the road of life usually sees that for which he is looking, whether it be good or bad. Two persons, walking the same road, may see very different things. One may see the sordid, the suggestive, the unclean, that which stirs base emotions. He sees them because they are the very things for which he is looking. The other person may see the lovely, the beautiful, the inspiring, that which lifts his spirit heavenward.

In a world where so much emphasis is placed upon the material, there is grave danger that our eyes become fixed at the downward position. A story is told about a man who one day found a dime lying along as sidewalk. From that moment to his dying day he walked with eyes focused along the path's edge. It is said that he did find a few more coins but he missed beauties and glories around and over him who would have enriched his life far more than did the paltry coins. That man was not a rarity;

there are thousands of travelers on life's road who become so obsessed with the earthly and material that they miss life's best.

The vision of a Christian includes the vertical and the horizontal. He looks upward to God and outward to the glories of God's creation and the needs of God's children. That vision has a transforming effect. No longer is the individual the center of his own life; his attention is no longer focused upon his own petty grievances and disappointments. To live to the glory of God and in the service of God's children becomes the compulsion of life.

When this does occur, almost miraculously a glorious radiance and a thrilling joy possess the pilgrim. Life takes on a new meaning. A deep contentment floods the soul, like unto that spoken of by Paul in Philippians. For the place in which the Christian finds himself, no matter how humble or how restricted it may be (it may even be a hospital bed or a prison cell), becomes a place of vision, a place where the door is open to life's best through the power of Christ Jesus, the Blessed Redeemer.

Wherever you live or wherever you happen to be today in the journey of life is a wonderful place to be. Right there is a place of glorious vision. Do not wait until tomorrow – you can have it now, regardless of the circumstances which surround you. Look up and look out for life at its best.

Prayer: Give us the vision to see the needs of others and our own. Amen.

Rev. Henry Eggink

September 20

Hebrews 9:27-28

Once and For All

Jesus isn't going to get on the cross again. He did it over 2000 years ago "once and for all." Every sin you and I have committed happened after that fact. I used to think as a kid that I hoped I would have a few seconds, just before I died, to quickly ask forgiveness for any last unforgiven sins I may have committed. Well, that isn't necessary because they are all forgiven and forgotten.

When we accept Jesus as our Savior, God sees Him in us and we are pure in His sight. That was hard for me to accept, but these verses say it's true. That's good enough for me.

Believe it!

Prayer: Lord Jesus, we thank you so much for what you did for us. It's hard for our finite minds to understand that kind of sacrifice, but you never lie. It is so comforting to be able to trust You. Amen.

Dave

September 21

Isaiah 64:8-9

Coin Flipping

When I was growing up, my dad would meet friends every morning at a local restaurant for some bad coffee and good conversation. Sometimes he would let me tag along. I would belly up to the table and hear the gathered voices laugh as they told story after story. Then, as if on cue, each man pulled out a silver dollar coin to flip and see who would pay for that morning's cup of conversation.

One morning my dad handed me this coin. "Really?" I said. All the other men nodded with approval. On the count of three I flipped my father's coin. "Heads," I said. I left the table walking tall. I was reminded of whose I was: I was my Father's, and my hands were an extension of His.

I feel the same pride after reading Isaiah. The prophet reminds us of whose we truly are: we belong to God. We are the work of God's hands, created and molded by God our Father. Each week, as we worship together, gather around God's table, telling the family stories, let us remember who we are and whose we are. Let us be thankful for the Father whose hands molded and continues to use our hands to serve His work and will in the world.

Prayer: God, as we gather around a table telling stories we remember, O Lord, You are our Father. Amen.

Rev. Trygve Johnson
Former Chaplain at NWC, Presently Dean of Chapel at Hope College

Tryg was not out of college very long when he became our Chaplain. He had been an integral part of our campus during his under graduate years, and was also an excellent pitcher. He influenced the lives of our students at a much deeper level as the campus minister. He continues to do God's work with college-age youth and faculty. We pray for God's continued blessings on him and his family.

September 22

Proverbs 14:12; 1 John 2:15-17

Economics

It seems like economics enters into every aspect of life. I'm not sure if that's good or bad at times. I taught Economics in high school and college for over 40 years and loved it. Often times I challenged the students to come up with "something that has nothing to do with economics." They challenged me pretty good at times ("whale dung at the bottom of the ocean" was probably the toughest), but the concept is real. Can you come up with something?

It made me mad when someone labeled it as "The Dismal Science," because I think it's exciting and pertinent. Economics can play a big role with religion as well. I don't like it, but sometimes it "pays to be a Christian," or at least to act like it. Do you know some people or businesses that profit from a religious stance they take? Oh, I know that there is a certain amount of hypocrisy in all of us, (there is with me, I'm afraid). But I guess we have to answer the question "Why do we make the decisions or take the actions we do?" Does economics again influence us too much? Each of us has to decide that for ourselves. Think about it.

Prayer: Heavenly Father, we thank you for always being straight with us. Help us this day to take that same position with all those with whom we associate. You have blessed us greatly. Amen.

Dave

September 23

John 15:12-13

Love One Another

No story can be told about the truth of God except the Word of God. It can't be argued, embellished nor televised. You can prove it does exist. The truth of God brings peace instantly. The truth of God is demonstrated daily to us. We get up each morning with thanksgiving in our hearts that He has allowed us to see another beautiful day. We go to bed at night with praise and worship for God leading and keeping us through the day.

Truth is God, and to love one another as He has loved us is a commandment we have to obey and live by daily. So speak truth and you will demonstrate the love of God!

Prayer: Jesus, thank you for showing us how to love each other. Help us keep Your commandment and always follow you in our relationships. Thank you for first loving us. Amen.

Lem and Jacci Barney
All-Pro and Hall of Fame defensive back for the Detroit Lions
Lem and Jacci still live in the Detroit area and are involved in the medical health field.

I met Lem at a celebrity golf outing in Omaha. He saw my FCA hat (as I was getting his autograph) and immediately began talking about Faith issues. We met later and arranged for him and Jacci to come visit us and speak in Chapel at NWC. What a great experience! This great couple knows how to "walk the walk."You will read Jacci's devotional tomorrow.

September 24

Proverbs 10:12

The ABC's of Love

"I **A**ccept you as you are"

"I **B**elieve you are valuable"

"I **C**are when you hurt"

"I **D**o keep my vows"

"I **E**rase all offenses" ...

We could call that the **ABC**'s of Love, and I don't know of anybody who would turn his/her back on such magnetic, encouraging statements.

There is nothing shallow about authentic love. Nor is it a magic wand we whip out and wave over a problem with a whoosh, hoping all the pain will go away. Real love has staying power. Authentic love is tough love. It refuses to look for ways to run away. It always opts for working through. It doesn't cop out because the sea gets stormy and rough. It's fibrous and resilient ... While the world around us gives the opposite counsel. Love Stands Firm. (Charles Swindoll)

Prayer: Dear God of love, guide each one of us on the right path. Help us to follow great examples and also be one. Amen.

Jacci and Lem Barney

Jacci and Lem make a great team. We could readily witness their love for each other, and for God. May our Lord continue to bless them.

September 25

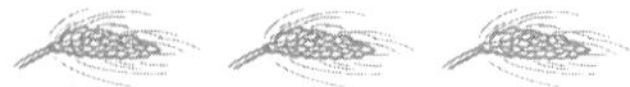

Lamentations 3:24; Jeremiah 29:11

Stuck in a Rut?

Being consistent with my devotions can become a hard task to always stick with. I'm totally in love with the idea, but at other times it becomes a thing that I just check off my "to-do list." When I do my devotions I'm all around happier and nicer. Earlier this year I was really stuck in a rut with devotions. God used one of my friends to draw me closer to Him. All it took was the verse in Lamentations. "*I say to myself, the Lord is my portion; therefore I will wait for Him. The Lord is good to those who hope in Him, to the one who seeks Him.*" After reading this I realized the real reason why it was hard for me to do devotions. I was mad at God, and I wasn't feeling His love. I was mad because He took my cousin away a few months earlier. If God loved me, why would He do this to my family?

The passage in Jeremiah says "*For I know the plans I have for you," declared the Lord, "Plans to prosper you, not to harm you. Plans to give you a hope and a future.*" God doesn't want to hurt His children. I will never know why my loved ones had to leave so soon, but I know that when I walk through those golden gates, they will all be running to meet me. I wouldn't be as close to my Father today if those tragedies didn't occur.

To get through this life "I'm sticking with God (I say it over and over). He is all I have left."

Prayer: Heavenly Father, please continue to be with me and help me stay focused on your love. I know we can't understand everything that happens, but I know You love us. Help us share that love. Amen.

Sarah Achterhoff
#1 Granddaughter!

Sarah starts her senior year in 2010. She is a very high-achiever, both academically and in co-curriculars. One could say "she is driven." This can be very good, but it can also be very stressful. She is a joy to be with but I want her to have more fun and remember "you are only a kid once." She has a big heart for the Lord and for the downtrodden. Missions may well be in her future. We couldn't love her more.

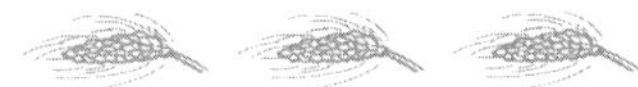 **September 26** 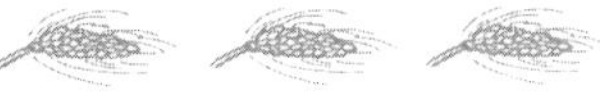

Colossians 1:12-14

Belonging

Because Jesus in love and mercy gave Himself on Calvary's Cross as a sacrifice for our redemption from sin, and we in gratitude and love have opened our hearts to Him, believing in Him, trusting Him, fully committing ourselves to Him, looking to Him as our only hope for time and eternity, we belong to Him. It is written in Colossians and we believe it.

He gave Himself for us – we gave ourselves to Him – a beautiful, new relationship resulted.

One of the great hymns puts it thus:

"I belong to Jesus
Jesus belongs to me.
Not for the years of time alone
But for eternity."

Because this is true, a precious assurance and comfort is ours. The historic Heidelberg Catechism puts it thus:

Question — What is your only comfort in life and in death?

Answer — That I am not my own but belong – body and soul in life and in death to my faithful Savior Jesus Christ. He has fully paid for all my sins with His precious blood and has set me free from the tyranny of the devil. He also watches over me in such a way that not a hair can fall from my head without the will of my Father in heaven. In fact, all things must work together for my salvation because I belong to Him, Christ, by His Holy Spirit assures me of eternal life and makes me whole-heartedly willing and ready from now on to live for Him.

Prayer: Thank you for Your Word. Help us to understand it and be able to interpret for others, especially those we love and work with. Amen.

Rev. Henry Eggink

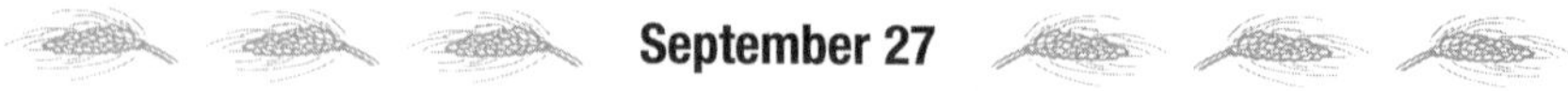

September 27

John 11:1-44

Resuscitation Or Resurrection?

I am the resurrection and the life.

In the wake of the painful loss of their brother, Martha and Mary said the same words to Jesus, as if they had rehearsed them, "Lord, if you had been there, my brother would not have died." Surprisingly, Jesus did not rebuke them. If anything, he demonstrated sympathy, for John tells us that Jesus wept. What the sisters uttered in their grief resonates with all of us. We have spoken or at least thought – similarly. "Lord, if you had been there... my health would not have deteriorated, or my business would not have failed, or my marriage would not have ended, or my child would not have died, or that earthquake would not have happened, killing so many innocents." It is the prayer of anguish that all of us have cried.

In the case of Martha and Mary, the story ended happily. Jesus resuscitated Lazarus, who rejoined his family and friends. But only for a time. That is the problem with miracles. However amazing, they provide only a temporary solution to our problems. In the end suffering and mortality have their way. Lazarus eventually died again. As it turns out, the real miracle of the story was not the resuscitation of Lazarus but the promise of Jesus. "I am the resurrection and the life, he who believes in me, though he die, yet shall he live, and whoever lives and believes in me shall never die." Lazarus enjoyed a few more years of earthly life. But those who believe in Jesus will enjoy so much more – resurrection life.

After making such a grandiose promise, Jesus asked Martha a pointed question. He asks us the same thing. "Do you believe this?"

Prayer: Lord, thank you for this glorious promise. Help us in our losses and sorrows to believe this good news. In Jesus Name, Amen.

Jerry Sittser
Noted author and former Chaplain at NWC
Presently a Professor at Whitworth College in Washington

Jerry is an inspiring speaker and has written some great books. He was an outstanding Chaplain. If you know of anyone that has experienced the death of a family member – Jerry has written from the experience of losing his wife and daughter in a tragic automobile accident. "Google" him. May God bless him – he certainly blessed me.

September 28

Luke 5:8

We Are All Sinners

It's interesting really, to see the false humility displayed by Simon Peter in this recount of Christ's calling to the first disciples. (For context, read verses 1-11). My initial take on this passage is that Simon Peter recognizes that Jesus is a great, wonderful, counselor, and our Savior; but at the same time knows all too well that the life he has led, as he knows it, is over; and Christ's calling is not a onetime thing, but a continuous knock at the door of our heart. Knowing this, Peter, like the fish in the net, struggles against our Lord's persistent calling. And isn't it so, again and again, that Peter struggles against our Lord's persistent calling? He goes so far as to even deny Him three times at the crucifixion. It's really quite easy to imagine ourselves in his place, confidently stating that we would never forsake our Lord.

Upon reflection however, I am forced to account for my own shortcomings. I think of the times I've asked the Lord to choose someone else; the times I've ignored the knock at my heart's door, knowing who was calling. I thank the Lord that He never quits calling us to His love and to His mission.

So the next time your Bible passages take you to the disciples displaying a lack of faith, or Simon Peter denying the Lord, and asking someone else to take his place, take a moment and thank the Lord that he continues to knock on the door of your heart. Even though we deny Him, or plead for Him to find someone else to bear the burden, Christ's continual calling is evidence of His never ending love for us, and His promise of salvation and a place in His house of glory.

Prayer: Thank you Lord for knowing us and still loving us. Help us to be sincere, honest with You and with ourselves. We give You all the honor and praise. Amen.

Dick W. Mulder
Our Son - Senior Examiner for the Federal Reserve, Chicago, Illinois

Dick and his wife Kathrine are a joy to be with. Aside from numerous phone conversations, the special week Dick and I spend at the annual Father/Son Golf Tourney in Myrtle Beach is a time I treasure all year long. 2010 was our 11th straight. There is no greater joy than to know that your children have belief and faith in Jesus.

September 29

Psalms 56:8; Luke 22:62

It's Okay To Cry

This is true regardless of age or gender. It amazes me, but as I have grown older, the tears flow much more easily. I never did cry because of physical pain, and still don't, but happy endings in movies and TV programs, stories, and seeing people I love get emotional, turn them on quickly. So does the pain from the loss of a friend or relative. Sharing someone else's loss also creates the need for hankies and tissues.

I used to be ashamed of those tears flowing so readily, but not anymore. Just the thought of Jesus counting each tear brings understanding. Remember that Jesus wept openly (The shortest verse in the Bible – John 11:35).

Showing love and compassion for the joys or the pain of another is a great human quality. Always carry a hanky and be happy when it's your eyes and not your nose that needs it!

Prayer: Thank you Jesus for caring enough to cry over us and recognize that we need the release that can come with shedding tears. Help us to realize we must shed tears over our transgressions, our fears, and our joys. Amen.

Dave

September 30

1 Peter 2:5

Something Is Being Built

Many years ago, I worked as an electrician for a homebuilder. Neighborhoods in Colorado would emerge as workers followed architects' blueprints.

Today, I am a chaplain at Northwestern College, where students (actually all of us) are being built together by the Holy Spirit, and the model is Christ.

The common denominator – **something is being built**.

Both houses are real. The houses built with lumber receive families and provide warmth and shelter. The houses built with living stones are sent out to point to the kingdom of God, where God's reign is transforming all of creation with the victorious resurrected power of Jesus.

We must admit: One, we are under construction. God is at work in us. We have much to learn. Two, our cornerstone is Christ. He is the author and finisher, the creator and redeemer. Three, the work advances by the mysterious power of the Spirit. Sometimes, we notice a surge in the building. Other times, we cannot see what is being accomplished.

Prayer: O Lord, be gracious to us and bless us as you build us according to your plan, until one day you present us being made like Christ. Amen.

Harlan Van Oort Chaplain, NWC

Harlan continues a great line of Chaplains at NWC. He is an inspiring speaker as well as a great leader and counselor to the students. He is very visible at a multitude of college functions and is very supportive. He lives what he preaches about.

October 1

Proverbs 24:3-5

R. A. Poppen

Mr. Poppen was the Superintendent of the Alton school for all 13 years I attended. He was a very respected man in the school, community, church, and education field,

Here are the specific things I remember about this great man. He gave me a spanking when I was in the 2nd grade (I deserved it!). He taught a variety of classes over the years and was my freshman Science teacher. He kicked me out of a class in high school because he could hear me from an adjacent classroom, (I didn't deserve that one). He didn't realize we were rehearsing a play and I happened to be close to his door. He called me in and apologized. That impressed me. He let me come over to his house every Saturday to watch the major league baseball "Game of the Week." He knew we didn't have a television set and he also knew how much I loved baseball.

Sadly, he decided to "work one more year," even after he had reached retirement age. He never got the chance to retire because he died in that last year. Tears literally are rolling down my cheeks as I write this, because I didn't have the chance, or took the time, to tell him how much he influenced me, and how important he was to me. Please don't let that happen to you – Give your flowers to the living!

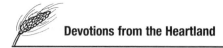

Prayer: Thank you Lord for the "Mr. Poppen's" of this world. Thank you for putting great people into our lives to mold and nurture us. Please help us to return those favors and be blessings and mentors to others. Amen.

Dave

October 2

Romans 12:12

Hope and Joy

My family dynamics are changing. Our two sons are grown and married and have established their own families in a (thankfully) nearby city. We even became grandparents this year, a new and exciting role we love at every imaginable level.

Along with these happy occasions we are also experiencing some concerns and heartaches. Our parents are getting older, dear family members are struggling with serious health issues, and we have lost some close friends to death.

My grandmother always said that growing old was a privilege denied many and her statement is coming to fruition. But is death and loss all that the future holds for us? No! God promises us eternal life if we believe in Him and follow His commandments. Eternal life – now that's something to look forward to! I hope I have more time in this world to enjoy my new granddaughter, and God willing, more grandchildren that might follow. I hope I have more time to spend with my husband, a true man of God whom I adore, and my two dear sons and their families. But more than that, I know that when God calls me home, I will be ready. I have hope for the future and I know that in the hardships of the world, God is right there with me.

I will remain faithful in prayer because God's love overcomes the evils and hurts of this world, and He will lead us to a new home in Heaven with Him.

Prayer: Thank you God for the joys of life and for the hope You give us. May each of our remaining days and years You give us be lived for You. Amen.

Nancy Speer
Elementary Music Teacher and Central Church's Choir Leader

Nancy is my niece and the sister of Steve. I love to listen to her sing. She absolutely loves animals (especially dogs and cats), and she willingly takes care of our cats when we are gone. She's a fabulous musician and a great teacher. Just like her mom (Colleen), whose birthday she shares today! Give them both a call. I did.

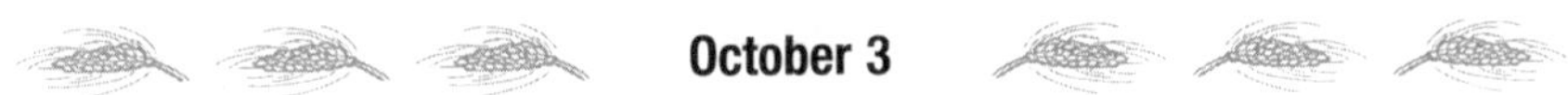

October 3

Exodus 15:21; Isaiah 51:11; Psalms 81:1-2; 2 Samuel 22:1

Music

What kinds of music turn you on or bring you pleasure? I'm fortunate in that I like BOTH kinds of music – Country AND Western! (October is "Country Music Month") I'm sure that information excites many of you. Seriously, music is a very important part of my life. I like to listen to it more than do it. I played a trombone through high school and part of my freshman year in college. I can sing a little bit, but only in large groups and with a very limited range.

Every record, tape, or CD has 10 to 25 songs on it. Nobody likes all of the songs on any single one of them. I've purchased many where I only liked one or two cuts. iTunes and eMusic have made it more convenient to just buy the songs you like. I think I've made about 60 CD's composed of just the special songs I like. They vary from C & W, to the 50's, Elvis, & Gospel. My whole library is on the computer.

There are certain songs that can change my attitude about whatever has or is happening. Give it a try. I'll be happy to make a CD for you of your favorites. (I'm serious) I've done that for many friends. Music truly can "sooth the savage beast" and is the universal language.

Prayer: Thank you God for music and those that deliver it. I know from your Word that You love it too. Help us make a "joyful noise" unto You. Amen.

Dave

October 4

Ephesians 5:19-20

Have You Checked Out The Hymnal Lately?

What kind of a question is that? A hymnal is a hymnal, right? That's what I always thought. But my thoughts changed four years ago when our denomination went through a hymnal change. In order for churches to make the transition easily they sent out a DVD which explained the changes and introduced them to the features of this change.

That DVD opened my eyes and mind to things I had never noticed about a hymnal before. Not only did it contain hymns, old and new, but it also included the church calendar, special services, the Ten Commandments, the Psalms, The Lord's Prayer and all the Creeds. *It contained scripture references for each hymn!* At the bottom of each page, there in the fine print below the credits to the composer, were scripture references.

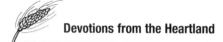

I started looking up some of these references. It was amazing how the scripture was captured in song! Sometimes quoting the verse verbatim and other times telling a Bible story. Why I was surprised by this I don't know. It makes sense since during Biblical times scripture was passed down through recitation or song. Much the same way I learned songs in Sunday School, Vacation Bible School, or church camp.

Sometimes people in church complain about having to learn a new hymn or they don't think that some of the Christian rock songs are any good because they don't come from a hymnal. I now beg to differ with them. I ask them if they have considered the words and if they are scripture-based. I point to the verse above and ask them if God cares how well we carry the tune as long as we carry our praise and glory to Him in our heart.

So, are you going to check your hymnal?

Prayer: Dear Heavenly Father, we thank you for the gift of song. Let us continually sing Your praises not only out loud, but also within the deepest portions of our hearts. In the name of our Lord Jesus Christ, Amen.

Pam Vlieger
NWC Printer Specialist

Pam was one of my student's at NWC and does a great job in the Printing Office. She is a true servant and she does it pleasantly, with a smile (and candy on her counter!). She makes our work easier and more pleasant.

October 5

Proverbs 3:5-6; Isaiah 30:21

The Straight Path

When I was nine years old, I had my tonsils and adenoids removed. After the surgery, I was taken back to my hospital room. My mother and a neighbor lady were in the room as the nurse was taking care of me. All of a sudden she got a horrified look on her face and announced that I was dead! She raced out of the room to seek help. A short time later the nurse returned with several doctors. They checked me out and soon reported that I was breathing again. Later, my mother explained to me that God has a purpose for my life and that is the reason I was still alive.

I did not really know what this purpose was until I was about ready to graduate from high school. I can remember telling my high school coach that someday I was coming back to take his place when he retired.

I joined the Service right out of high school. While in the Army I changed my mind regarding a future profession. I was going to study to become a dentist.

After two years of pre-med courses I felt uneasy about my choice, so I took an aptitude test which indicated teaching/coaching rated higher than dentistry. I still was not convinced until I looked in the Book and came across that passage in Isaiah. That's when I switched to the field of education.

Early in my teaching career I started sending some of my athletes to Fellowship of Christian Athletes' summer camps. They came home each year so FIRED UP FOR THE LORD that I decided I was going to start taking them to FCA camp instead of sending them. This continued for the next 20 years.

When school started in the Fall of 2010, we will have begun our 39th year of FCA at our high school.

Pray for me and our athletes to look to the Lord for direction.

Prayer: Thank you, Father, for setting me on my feet ... Again and Again and Again! Amen.

Bill Lyle
Retired Teacher and Coach in the Sioux City Public Schools, Advisor to the FCA and Northwest Iowa Board Member

Bill is a tireless worker for the FCA and for kids. He is such a great example to follow. I thank the Lord daily for Bill and people like him.

October 6

John 15:12; Ephesians 2:5; John 13:34

Just The Facts

I tend to be a very factual person. Joe Friday, from the old radio and TV program Dragnet (that really dates me), used to say "Just the facts ma'am, only the facts." I liked Joe. In fact (do you like puns?), every Christmas I get two different Almanacs from family members. It's amazing how often these great references are used as we travel, or sit at home reading or watching TV.

Don't you wonder how old that famous actor is? (Kevin Costner was born in 1955 and Harrison Ford in 1942) Where IS Timbuktu? (Mali, West Africa) When WAS the Civil Rights Act passed? (1964) When was it that the Cardinals took the World Series from the Red Sox in seven games? (1967) (We won't mention that the Cubs haven't won since 1908!)

So where was I going with all this factual stuff? It's a fact that our real purpose on this earth is to know and live for Christ. It's a fact that Jesus' only Commandment is "to love each other" (John 15:12). It's also a fact that we can't earn our salvation, because it's free and we are saved by grace (Ephesians 2:5). These are just the facts, ma'am!

Prayer: Thank you God for the fact You love us and save us. Thanks too for sending Your only begotten Son to die for our sins. Be with each of us this day and night. Amen.

Dave

October 7

Psalm 46:10

Be Still

Things are changing in my life, as is true for everyone. I have spent most of my life trying to be the best teammate, husband, father, and friend as well as trying to help others achieve their goals in life. Basically, it comes down to being a little too competitive. Trying my best to help others achieve what they think will make them happy has led me to conclude that I am much more of a control person than I realized.

The other thing I have learned is that people aren't always happy once they have achieved that goal! I have come to understand that God is ultimately in control and He has a plan for all of us. As much as we would like to control our future, especially as I look at the last decade of my employment years, we really don't know how it is all going to work out. We must be faithful, patient, and obedient. We must pray each and every day for direction, wisdom, encouragement, and be grateful for the many blessings we have received.

I find myself worrying about my children, their faith, and their relationships. Now, I'm even worrying about my granddaughter! How can I help her to be happy? It's not my responsibility, and every day I remind myself to "Be still and know that He is God!"

Prayer: Dear God, thank you for caring about each of our needs, and the needs of those we love. Help us to accept Your call and be obedient to it. Amen.

Stan Speer
President of American State Bank

Stan is married to Nancy and is a great banker and friend. I love to play golf with him, but it doesn't happen often enough. He's a great story teller and his entire family plays some incredible practical jokes on each other. I always enjoy being with him.

October 8

John 15:7

Ask What You Wish For

Many times in the wee hours of the morning, I've found myself crying out to my Lord, "What? Where? How?" I so needed His guidance.

I believe children are a blessing from God, but also a responsibility. In trying to give them a firm spiritual foundation, I was being undermined by other factors. In 1 Corinthians 7:15-16 it says, "*A believing man or woman is not bound in such circumstances. God has called us to live in peace.*" This talks about what should be happening, but it wasn't. Because of abuse and other factors, I had to make different choices with several children. Foster children are so vital to my life.

Then came another test, I was laid off at my place of employment, my only source of income. At my lowest point, I walked to church, got on my knees, and came face-to-face with my Redeemer. I wanted to be able to continue to work with kids. This was a great Sunday!

On Monday morning the phone rang and I was offered another job! Did I learn a great lesson? Since then, I have been blessed in so many ways and I know it's only through our Savior.

Prayer: Help us to remember You are with us through the good and the bad and the ugly. Your grace is sufficient. Because I have felt so blessed, I wanted to give a wee bit back. Hence the fostering of children. Thanks for the opportunity to work with those fourteen wonderful creations. Amen.

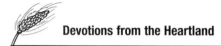

Kathy Van Zee
Foster Parent par excellence!

Kathy is a member of Central Reformed and my Sunday School Class. Her love of deprived and forlorn kids is an inspiration to all of us.

October 9

Luke 13:6-9

What Kind of Fig Tree Are You?

The vision of God, which Jesus offers, illustrates that our Creator does not easily give up on us. The fig tree in Jesus' parable requires a bit of oversight and care. The gardener instinctively knows this care will soon enable the tree to bear fruit, and wisely counsels the man to wait awhile before cutting it down.

In God's eyes, we are much like the fig tree. We are slow to bear fruit, but He knows His continued nurturance and love will eventually enable us to come into full bloom. His patience with us as we grow is but one facet of His wonderful and infinite grace. To be sure, He expects us to do our part, and we owe it to Him to give it our very best.

Surely if God is willing to invest all of eternity in us, we must know it is fitting and proper to be patient with ourselves. We must also remember that God is eternally patient with others. This calls forth from us a willingness to be patient, supportive, and nurturing with those around us. We must never give up on those within our reach as we encourage them to become "fruitful."

The bottom line is this: "Do your best, let God do the rest." We must put forth our best effort in every aspect of our lives. God is God, and by His very nature, He *will* take care of the rest. As He is patient with us, let us also be patient with Him as He carefully tends to what is growing in His remarkable "vineyard."

Prayer: Thank you Lord for allowing us to grow and mature to a productive stage. Thank you too for responsibilities of love You give us. Please give us strength and perseverance to carry on Your work. Amen.

Doug Shull
Retired State Senator, Presently a CPA and County Supervisor in Indianola

Doug served two years with me in the Senate and we became good friends. He has great wisdom in financial and tax matters and is very benevolent. We enjoy his company, golf, baseball, and times we can get together. They don't come any nicer.

October 10

Isaiah 48:17; Proverbs 16:3; 1 Chronicles 22:13; 3 John 2

Do You Have A Price?

Remember now, price isn't always expressed in monetary terms. There have been those that have said, "Everyone has his/her price." Do you believe that? What are your limits?

Concerns about money amounts have never posed a real problem for me. The temptation to steal has never really been considered. But what about position, advancement, reputation, honors? There may be others. Have I struggled with some or all of these as a student, player, coach, teacher, or politician over the years? I'm afraid you know the answer as well as I do. What will you (I) be willing to sacrifice to reach a certain goal? Is that my price?

Any admittance of having a price is a denial of God. Richard Halverson, the late and outstanding Chaplain of the U.S. Senate said, "Having a price is the height of cynicism, degrades God, insults humanity, and is idolatry in its crudest form." Pretty harsh words.

What sacrifices are you willing to make? I can really struggle with this concept. We have to help each other by not putting others in compromising positions or making unjustified demands. Worth thinking about, don't you think?

Prayer: Thank you Jesus for paying the price for each of us. Help us to be willing to take a stand for You and pay whatever price You ask of us. Amen.

Dave

October 11

Genesis 20:3-4; James 1:13-14

Idols

Do we still worship idols like the stories in the Old Testament? Yup, they've just changed. Whatever you think about the most, spend the most dollars on, spend the most time and energy on, may well be your idol.

I know that during the first 22 years of my life it was baseball. I wanted to play pro ball more than anything else. So I read, practiced, dreamt, and devoted tremendous energy to that goal. It worked! I got a pro contract when I graduated from college. But I didn't sign it. My idol had changed. First of all, my Dad died and that changed by perspective. I had also met Dot and I knew I wanted her to be my wife. She wasn't convinced. So all my priorities changed, and once again it worked. June 16, 1962 we were married.

But now coaching and teaching took over my idolatry. I can't tell you exactly when I was able to stop "worshiping idols", but our kids, Bible reading, numerous testimonies, the church, FCA, and my wonderful wife finally won over. Do I still waver? I'm afraid so. But each time I get back to the Truth and try to stay there. I can't do it alone.

Prayer: Thank you God for being the fulfillment of all our dreams. Help us to worship only You. Amen.

Dave

October 12

Matthew 11:27-30; John 6:37; Romans 10:9-10

Invitations and Welcomes

Perhaps there are some among you readers who have never made confession of faith in Christ Jesus as your Savior and Lord, nor have you made a full commitment of yourself to Him. And if it's not you that hasn't made the commitment maybe it's someone you should contact with this Good News. These people may have begun to wonder whether they "belong." Perhaps they are asking whether it is still possible to do the above (confession of faith and commitment), and thus truly belong. Is it too late to do that? The answer is: "No, indeed not." Thanks be to God that the opportunity to do so is still available. Jesus the Savior continues to call, invite, and welcome in words such as what we read in Matthew and John. And don't forget the thief on the cross beside Jesus. You can't wait much longer than that.

Please read again those precious words in Romans and say them. You will be saved.

Prayer: Thank you Jesus for always being ready to welcome us. Now help us prepare the path for others. Amen.

Rev. Henry Eggink

October 13

1 Thessalonians 5:17; Matthew 6:6; Luke 18:1; Colossians 1:9

Where Do You Pray?

Did you look at all these verses and think about your prayer life? Looks to me like there's no place you *can't* pray, "Go into your closet, close the door, pray in secret." Could He mean the "water closet?" Hey, why not? If one can read in there, one can pray. He sees us all the time anyway. He's omnipresent.

Now I'm not trying to be foolish or funny. All of us can probably improve our prayer life. One fella I know glued a coin to the floor of his car. Every time his eye catches it, he prays. Another guy prays at stop lights. Another thing I read and then passed on is about people who, every time they hear a siren, pray for the victims and the many rescuers we have out there protecting us.

It's hard for me to not feel I have to close my eyes. Wrong! That could be dangerous. Hey! Whatever works and gets us to pray more has got to be good. Go for it!

Prayer: Lord, thank you for always being there and always having time for us. Help us to have time for others and to take the time to pray. Amen.

Dave

October 14

Psalm 91

Worry – FAITH – TRUST

When we lived in Montana, our ranch was seven miles from town. This really wasn't a problem since it was an okay trip when the roads were good, and that was most of the time.

Bob and I have four children – two girls and two boys – when they were in high school they all were involved in basketball, football, and volleyball. That in itself is not unusual, but sometimes getting back and forth to practices was not convenient. That situation was nothing compared to getting them home after away games and tournaments. Communities are not very close in Montana. However, when they became 16 and could drive, many travel-time problems were alleviated.

Teenagers driving caused us to face another problem. The vast majority of opponents were in towns at least several hours from Twin Bridges. That meant our children would get home between midnight and 2 A.M. They were all alone, late at night in all kinds of weather. This was before cell phones and there were long stretches of road where there were no homes. Needless to say, I worried about them!

Psalm 91 was my salvation. I trusted God to hear my prayers and He did! I trusted God to keep my children safe and He always did! I quit worrying and relaxed. God saved my children and me!

Prayer: Dear Lord, when we pray, help us to trust you with our requests. We need not worry when you are in control of the situation. We need to let go and let you handle everything because you do a better job than we do. Amen.

Kay and Bob Kraai
Retired Librarian and Veterinarian-Government Meat Inspector

Bob and Kay are two of our very close friends that get together every Saturday night (6 couples). Of course not all 6 couples can make it every time – but those that can, do. Bob and Kay have a lake home in Minnesota and invite us up to fish each year. Bob is a master fisherman and our wives are great cooks. Needless to say, we have a great time. Aren't close friends wonderful?! You'll meet the others as time goes on – if you haven't already. Kay is also in my Adult Sunday School Class.

October 15

Philippians 4:4-9; Romans 1:18-20

Think on These Things ... Whatever is Just (Right)

Who taught you the difference between right and wrong? Was it necessary in all cases? How many times do you really wonder about whether something is right or wrong? God tells us that we are created with an innate inner sense of what is just. "Let your conscience be your guide" is pretty safe to follow.

Another verse in Romans says that "everything that doesn't come from faith is sin" (14:23). So if we don't think it's right, it's wrong. Does that give you and me any comfort? I guess it should, because that means that the ONE who is the most just of all, has confidence in us to do the right thing. So lets' go do it!

Prayer: Heavenly Father we thank you for your guidebook, the Bible. Give us the desire to search it diligently to find what is right for us and You. Make this a good day. Amen.

Dave

October 16

James 1:2-4

The Gift of Adversity

My career has been very rewarding and has open doors to wonderful experiences in my life. It has also been challenging and presented many obstacles that I found very difficult to overcome alone. Every time that I felt that my troubles were too much to bear, God carried me through them.

God doesn't say that He will keep us from pain. He doesn't tell us how to respond **IF** we have troubles but **WHEN** we do. All of our adversity is a part of His plan and purpose for our lives.

Learn from the trials and tribulations that you go through. See them as opportunities for growth. Enduring them faithfully will provide perseverance, character and hope. And putting them in God's hands will ease the pain and strengthen your relationship with Him.

God knows the direction that our lives need to go and exactly how to get us there.

Prayer: Lord, give me strength in the face of adversity. Give me peace and help me to understand Your plan for me. Amen.

Kyle Vanden Bosch
All-Pro Defensive End for the Detroit Lions

Kyle went to West Lyon High School and then played for the Nebraska Cornhuskers. He was first-team All Big 12 and a 3-time Academic All-American. He played Pro ball with Arizona and Tennessee and will now start his 10th pro-season with the Lions in 2010. Kyle is the brother of Amy Keahi, who is the Director of ATLAS of Sioux Center. Every year he comes home to West Lyon and conducts a football camp for the area kids. He believes in "giving back."

October 17

Revelation 3:20

The Knock on the Door

Think for a few minutes about who it is that is knocking at the door of our hearts. It is Jesus Christ, the eternal Son of God, the ruler of the universe, the Savior of lost sinners.

At this point in our meditation is perhaps a good place to admit, to confess that we are sinners – sinners by nature and sinners by conduct. This is a condition which if not dealt with separates us from God as we journey through life and will separate us from God forever if not atoned for.

The Savior stands at the door offering us full forgiveness of our sins and complete salvation. He has made this possible by His sacrificial, vicarious death on Calvary's cross. There He assumed the guilt, the penalty of our sins. He waits for us to seek His forgiveness and pardon. Let us do that now.

Perhaps He had stood at the door before and knocked. But we may have ignored Him, brushed Him aside, or failed to open the door. But He is knocking again. Why? Because He loves us – loves us as no ordinary human can. He cares for and about us. He waits for us to open to seek forgiveness and pardon.

Prayer: Jesus, we open the door to You. Come in, cleanse us, redeem us, and use us. Amen.

Rev. Henry Eggink

October 18

Proverbs 15:1; Colossians 4:6; Philemon

Tact

Lack of, or mistaken communication is a major problem. "I did not say that!"; "You always take it the wrong way!"; "Using the silent treatment filled with hurt." What helps?

Onesimus was a runaway slave from Philemon's household, who may have financed his escape by robbing his master. In God's amazing plan, the fugitive met the apostle Paul; was converted by him; and became Paul's valued helper and companion. Paul could simply order Philemon, a devoted member of the early church, to release Onesimus, because of his need for him. Paul uses the words "my child" and "beloved brother" before Onesimus' name was even mentioned. This letter of Paul to Philemon is a great example for anyone to use when writing a letter of request.

Tact has been called the ability to organize awkward truth attractively. Cultivating tact will help minimize friction and maximize positive communications.

Prayer: God, may our words be spoken in truth and always pleasing to You and the ones we are talking to. Amen.

Dot

October 19

John 3:3-16; Acts 16:30

Believing In Christ

How can we open the door to Jesus Christ? We can do that first of all, and this is of primary importance, by believing in Him, Christ Jesus. Listen to His own words recorded for us in Scripture: "*For God so loved the world that He gave His one and only Son that whoever believes in Him should not perish but have eternal life*" (v. 16). (Study the entire passage carefully)

Believing is trusting; trusting Jesus so much that one rests, body and soul, in His care, trusting Him for salvation, and doing this without reservation, knowing He loves and cares. This is what we are instructed to do.

It is important to notice that this was the teaching of the early Christian Church. Shortly after Jesus' ascension and return to glory Paul and Silas, two of the church's first missionaries were asked by an inquirer from the city of Philippi the question, "What must I do to be saved?" They answered, "*Believe on the Lord Jesus Christ and you will be saved, and your household.*" (Acts)

This has been the teaching of the church ever since and still is in all truly Christian Churches.

"Believe in the Lord Jesus Christ." This surely is the correct response to the knock on your heart's door – it is of first importance.

Closely related (really a result of believing) is another response to the knock at the door: full committal and dedication of life to the Lord.

Prayer: We commit ourselves completely to You. Thank you for fulfilling all of Your promises and saving us. Amen.

Rev. Henry Eggink

October 20

Mark 13:36-37

No One Knows – Not Even Jesus!

I see the movie "2012" came out. Another prediction about the end of the world. It talks about a flood. Whoops! That can't be. God promised He wouldn't do that again, and then put the rainbow in the sky for verification.

These verses say '"no one knows." It also says "Be Ready!" There are lots of signs for the end times, and that's okay. In Matthew 24 it says, "everyone in the world will have the opportunity to hear the Gospel, and then He will come." Is the missionary field and technology good enough for this to take place? Jesus IS coming again, that's exciting, but even He doesn't know when exactly, (V5. 32).

Watch the signs, comfort each other, and be ready. By the time you read this, I may have experienced my "second coming." Praise the Lord!

Prayer: Lord Jesus, we continue to look for Your second coming but we know why You tarry – You want us to prepare as many people as possible so fewer and fewer are lost for eternity. Give us ways, strength, and motivation. Amen.

Dave

October 21

Luke 9:23-26

Comfortable

Comfortable. Isn't that what we all strive to be? We need that bigger house across town for our growing family. We talk to our group of friends instead of introducing ourselves to someone new at a social gathering. The checks we place in the offering plate allow our budget to provide for all the things we think we need to make our lives easier.

We have two sons. Our oldest, as a toddler, would jump in the water on his own and always tries whatever activities we ask him to do behind the boat. Our second son needs a little nudge, sometimes literally, to get him in the water. He never thinks he is able to do what we ask, but within minutes of trying, realizes it isn't as scary as it looks. Yesterday, as I watched the two of them behind the boat, I realized that they are both at the same place. One jumped in full force, and the other needed to get very uncomfortable before getting there.

Sometimes we think that the only way we can serve is by doing something totally comfortable. We believe there are only select people who should be leading, teaching, giving, and reaching out to others. Yes, we all have different gifts and abilities. However, Jesus calls each one of us to deny ourselves, take up our cross daily, and follow Him. You may read that verse and want to jump right in or you may need a little push.

Jesus left His throne in heaven to be born in a stable with animals. Doesn't sound very comfortable, does it? He was rejected by those closest to Him. Jesus was beaten and died on a cross. He did that so we could have life, not a comfortable life on earth, but an eternal life with Him in heaven.

Prayer: Jesus, You have set a great example for each of us. Help us to leave our comfort zones and reach out to Your people. Thank you for showing us how. Amen.

Eric and Stephanie Walhof
ATLAS of Sioux Center Board Member

October 22

1 Corinthians 13

I Love...

Country singer Tom T. Hall (the Old Storyteller) wrote a song "I Love … " and then he enumerates many things he loves from "squirrels to hay" and a bunch of others.

I hope by my telling you the things I love (besides Jesus, my wife and family, etc.) you will give some thought to yourself as well as the compliment this pays to my many special people. (This list is not necessarily in order of preference – just the way they came to mind.)

I Love...
Having coffee at the Dutch Mart (9:00 a.m.) with my friends…
Playing 9 holes of golf with some of those same fellas shortly after coffee…
Dot's cooking…
Our pet cats…
Chocolate…
Birds and wild animals, native to our area…
Small town living…
Kids (especially after about age 2)…
Short, 3- or 4-day vacations…
Coming home from anywhere…
NWC athletics and the athletes and coaches…
Country/Western music (the old stuff and mostly ballads)…
Television (pretty specific programming though)…
My Sunday School class…

Hey, compile your own list! It was kinda fun and also kinda revealing don't you think? Share yours with a loved one and you'll have an interesting conversation – maybe even a gift suggestion.

I hope you love this day.

Prayer: Thank you Lord for love. Not just Yours but the love of many, and the opportunities to share it. Amen.

Dave

October 23

2 Timothy 3:16-17

The Bible

How do you use your Bible? For years as a teacher I told students they didn't have to read the textbook word for word. Was that blasphemy? Nope, I don't think so. Textbooks, for the most part, are reference books. You read about material you *don't* know. Do you look up every word in the dictionary or look at a map every time you go some place? Of course not! You look up the words you don't know. I never read the whole textbook I taught out of (and I changed texts at least every 3 years). I read the "new parts" or "new ideas" in economics, not the old standard supply and demand material I'd known for years.

Doesn't that same thing hold true for the Bible? Yes, I have read the entire Bible through from cover to cover a few times. But it's the most unique book ever published. There are some chapters (particularly in Numbers) that I don't intend to ever read again. But I'm referring to many passages over and over again, on a daily basis.

Enjoy God's Holy Word and let it speak to you today and forever.

Prayer: Thank you God for Your precious Word. Help me plan my day around it. Amen.

Dave

October 24

Deuteronomy 29:29

Reveal Yourself

It was nearly Halloween. Our newly adopted daughters were fascinated by the many scary images that seemed to be everywhere. Shega our oldest, was four years old when her desperately poor Ethiopian mother relinquished her to an orphanage. Her baby sister Megan was sick and dying. Their mother Meseret, desperate to save her baby, placed her in the orphanage as well. She sent Shega along to help care for the baby, asking the orphanage director to keep the girls together.

After about six months, my husband Steve and I traveled to Ethiopia to meet them. Megan had been hospitalized much of the time for treatment and improved nutrition. We traveled to meet Meseret at her home. She blessed our family and asked us to raise her daughters to know Jesus. Through a translator, she told us that she prayed for her daughters and had asked God to go with them. She promised to pray for us as well. She trusted God to provide a Christian family to adopt her precious daughters.

Shega, who had seemingly lost everything, had many fears. It was our habit each night as we tucked her in, to pray for the Lord to ease those fears. Despite, or perhaps because of those fears, she spent lots of time that October looking at scary images in advertising, stores, and on television. Even as we tried to keep her from them, she seemed to seek them out. Each night, she struggled to get to sleep. Oft times I would return to her room attempting to ease those fears, and holding her close until sleep could conquer.

Finally one night I reacted with some exasperation. "Honey! You need to think of all of the blessings in your life. Pray to God, thanking him for all of the good things you can think of." I then showed her how by offering a thanksgiving prayer. I encouraged her to do the same as I got up to leave the room. She stopped me in my tracks when she said, "But Mommy! I can't pray! I don't know God as good as you do!"

Her statement has changed my prayers for her completely. From that moment on, rather than praying for God to comfort her, I have asked for God to reveal Himself to her and to all of those I love. I ask Him to make Himself so real to her that she can feel His presence and know Him.

I know that my prayer for her is exactly the same one that is being prayed on her behalf in Ethiopia.

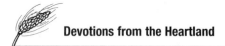

Prayer: Dear God, please reveal yourself to all of us. Thank you for reaching out to little children. Hold them (and us) real close. Amen.

Laura and Steve Heitritter
Professor of Education at NWC and the owner or a Computer Business in Sheldon.

Steve was my #1 golfer for two years at NWC and we still get to play together some today. Laura is an excellent and tireless teacher that really cares for her students and helps them immensely. As you can tell, they have a real heart for kids and doing God's work. Steve sells good computers too – I bought one!

October 25

Ecclesiastes 9:11; 1 Samuel 6:9b; Luke 10:31

What If?

How did a guy from Michigan find true love with a girl from Iowa on the bustling, anonymous streets of New York City?

My wife, Julee Cruise, studied French horn at Drake University in Des Moines. One day she was struggling with a Mozart horn concerto when in sheer frustration she uncharacteristically fled the practice room and went home to her apartment to grab lunch and put the infuriating piece of music out of her mind. She switched on the noon news and started making herself a sandwich, when from the kitchen she heard the most plaintive canine yelping coming from the TV. It was a segment on dogs up for adoption at the ASPCA. The yelping came from the most gorgeous, buff-colored cocker spaniel she'd ever laid eyes on. Julee threw down the sandwich, jumped in her car and within an hour brought Rudy home to her apartment, where they ate the sandwich together.

Rudy became her constant companion, though her dad, Dr. Cruise, a dentist from Creston, had to find her a new apartment near campus that allowed dogs. Eventually Julee worked as an actress in Minneapolis before taking the plunge in the Big Apple. To this day, I still laugh imagining her driving a Ryder truck across the George Washington Bridge, sporting her cowboy hat and a by now very full-grown cocker spaniel sitting in the passenger seat.

Around that time, I too had moved to New York to look for work as a writer. I was walking across W. 72nd wolfing down a bagel one afternoon, when coming towards me was the most stunning, dolled-up blonde with, shall we say, a rotund cocker spaniel tugging on a leash. I wanted to say something nice about the dog but what came out of my mouth, "Gosh, that's the fattest cocker spaniel I've ever seen!"

Not a great conversation starter, and I got a very dirty look and a quickened pace from Julee for my trouble. Rudy, however, decided he had to say hi and used his girth to steer her towards me. Julee's stiletto heels didn't give her much traction to resist and soon Rudy and I were best pals, especially after I shared a bit of bagel. I walked with them around the block trying to make amends for my unfortunate remark. Julee's glam appearance was explained by the fact that she'd just come from a Broadway audition. I'd gone to drama school so we had something in common. By the time I left them at their building, I'd gotten an apparently reluctant Julee to give me her phone number and a vague promise to maybe go for Chinese later in the week. As she tottered towards the elevator she had to pull Rudy along, who wasn't ready to say good bye to me or my bagel.

Usually you get the girl a gift. On the way home I passed a pet store, stopped in, bought a squeaky toy and went back and left it with Julee's doorman, hoping that would soften her heart towards me. What I didn't know was that Julee had gone upstairs, immediately called her mom back in Creston and said, "Mom, I just met the man I am going to marry."

Some might say the whole encounter was random. Yet look at all the what-ifs. What if Julee hadn't found that home concerto so daunting, gone home and saw Rudy on TV? What if I hadn't been walking down the same street as the two of them at the same time years later and made my clumsy remark about Rudy's girth? What if?

Rudy was an abandoned puppy who was only hours away from being euthanized when Julee impulsively rescued him. Rudy, I believe, was ordained to be the agent of our meeting.

Prayer: Lord Father, you reach your divine hand into our lives at the moments when we least expect, setting into motion events we could never foretell. Each and every day I am in grateful awe of your providence. Amen.

Edward Grinnan
Editor, Guideposts Magazine

Guideposts is definitely Dot's and my favorite magazine. We also use their excellent Daily Devotional. When you read Guideposts and the Devotional you begin to feel you know the writers' personally. So when Dot and I went to New York City a few years back we called to schedule a visit at the Guideposts office. We met Edward and he took us on a tour. He loves dogs, his wife, NYC, and the Yankees! I didn't hold that against him but we did become friends and I am excited that he was willing to write this devotional for us. Edward, you showed great wisdom in selecting a wife from Iowa, check out the Cardinals instead, and may our Lord bless you. Creston is just a little over 100 miles from Sioux Center and you are always welcome!

October 26

Joshua 24:15

Choices

We live in a land of choices. That is a mixed blessing for many. Where shall we live? How many kids? Should I change jobs? Is more schooling or training necessary? Should I use credit/debit cards? Shall I choose Jesus?

Think about it. Every day we make lots of choices. Unfortunately, not all of them are right or good.

God created us that way for a reason. He wants us to choose Him and His way. But He gave us a choice. Many times He's in on those choices even when we don't know it. He always keeps His promises, and He said He will help. Which do you choose?

Prayer: Help us this day to make the right choices today Lord. Amen.

Dave

October 27

2 Corinthians 1:4

Cloudy Weather

Recently a mother said concerning her daughter: "I hope she may have just enough clouds so that the sunset of her life may be beautiful." Now most of us dislike cloudy weather. But sooner or later along life's journey we find clouds, shadows, and troubles settling upon us. And we have a tendency to cry out, "Why?"

Meditate for just a moment upon clouds. Clouds are the fabrics out of which beautiful sunsets are woven. That is true not only in the realm of nature; it is true also in the realm of human life. Clouds and shadows, if accepted with humbleness of spirit, may prove to be the very fabrics through which the glory and grace of God shine to make life beautiful and useful in His service. Consider briefly how this is true.

First, clouds and shadows are often instrumental in drawing a person nearer to God. It was only when the Prodigal Son got into serious trouble in the far country and when the clouds gathered thick and heavy that he yearned to go back to his father's house. Sometimes clouds are useful in that they cause us to think more seriously about our Heavenly Father and fill our hearts with yearning to return to Him. When clouds do that, they are surely good.

Secondly, clouds and shadows can be useful in making us more sympathetic and compassionate with our fellow pilgrims. Look at that old grandmother, 70 to 80 years of age. Many clouds and stormy skies have passed over her. But she has allowed them to mellow her, and the setting sun shines through her with a glory. See her as she goes to a young mother to comfort her in the loss of her first baby. This grandmother knows all about the ache in the young mother's heart for she went through the same experience some 60 years ago. See her as she goes to another home where there is grave illness. She knows what that home needs because she has often stood beside sick-beds. See her as she visits a third home, a home which has just received a message from the war dept. stating that a son is lost in action. Her presence is a blessing here; she knows all about such a tragedy, for she and her husband received a message like that years ago. See her as she comforts a neighbor who stands beside the open grave of a husband. A few years ago she passed through the same experience and she knows the pain and then the comforting power of God.

Those who have passed through shadows, and there drew heavily on the comfort and strength which God will give to those who in child-like faith reach up to Him, become the best of comforters. In fact, that is one reason God does comfort us (reread today's passage).

Lastly, clouds and shadows have value in that they remind us that this world is not our home; they help us to remember that we are pilgrims here traveling to a better land. To become too attached to this world in which we journey is dangerous. If shadows and clouds prevent that from happening and cause us to look beyond to that Eternal Home, they are valuable, indeed.

When the clouds of life settle around, look for the sunshine of God's love to shine through. The sunset of such a life will be beautiful.

Prayer: Heavenly Father, truly You do brighten our days. Help us to realize how much our experiences equip us to reach out and help others who travel through similar circumstances. Amen.

Rev. Henry Eggink

October 28

Ephesians 5:21-6:4

You Are (I Am) The Most Important Person in Someone Else's Life

Just think about that. It might be more than one, but it's true for at least one. My wife of nearly 50 years, is definitely #1, and I know she feels the same about me.

It's vital for others to know how important they are, and we should make others feel important. It's also important for you to realize how important you are to others, and especially to that special someone.

We tend to behave differently when importance is involved. We don't want to let anyone important down. Use whatever you can that motivates in a positive way. Realizing that I am important changes my outlook and actions in many situations. This contributes to a better sense of responsibility.

Take today to let "your most important person" know just how special he/she is.

Prayer: Lord, many times we need special motivation to get something done. Give us that motivation today. We want to do something GOOD. Amen.

Dave

October 29

Jeremiah 29:7

Seeing Opportunities

Is it coincidence that God calls and uses almost every major Bible character in a land that is not their own? Just think about all your favorites, Moses (Egypt, Midian), Abraham (Canaan), Jonah (Nineveh), Daniel, Shadrach, Meshach, Abednego (Babylon), Esther (Persia), Joseph (Egypt), apostles (everywhere), and even Jesus found He was more honored away from than in his home town (Mark 6).

Many times God does His greatest work in the lives of His people and in the lives of the people around them when they are away from home, in exile, or just plain out of their comfort zone! This verse in Jeremiah reminds us of what we are to do when we find ourselves "away." Often we long for the comfort and familiarity of home, but the LORD calls us to not only accept where God places us, but to pray for and seek the prosperity of the foreign land, person, or situation.

Having lived in various countries, I found I have missed some of those opportunities to truly "build houses and settle down; plant gardens and eat what they produce." (v 5) Time, energy, and thoughts often drifted to "home" instead of asking the LORD to use me where I was at the time. Reflect on times God has placed you away from "home." Did you take the opportunity to pray for, invest, and build roots where he had placed you? The next time you find yourself being called away from "home" physically, spiritually, or emotionally, remember, it's often where God does His greatest work!

Prayer: Our Heavenly Father, we know that you love us and you are with us wherever we go. Help us to remember that whatever location or situation you have placed us in is an opportunity to do your work. Give us the willing spirit to pray for and work with those around us in a way that glorifies you. In Your Son's name, Amen.

Brandon and Kendara Woudstra
All American (twice) basketball player for NWC (2000-03)

Brandon led the Raiders to a several GPAC conference championships and a National Title. He still holds the scoring record and numerous other records including Scholastic All American. Brandon played pro ball for a number of teams in Iceland and in Europe and had great success. He is a leader and a winner. But he and Kendara are also winners in their personal lives. They are great parents, great church workers, and continue to be fine examples and teachers of our youth. As much fun as it was to watch his prowess on the court, it is even better to have them back home with us. He is in the NWC Hall of Fame.

October 30

Romans 2:20

Basic Travel Tips and Truths Taught by Surprising Teachers

In the late autumn season of every year, those of us who live in northern areas of the U.S.A. are thrilled by the flight of wild geese as they move great distances southward, in the beautiful V formations, to escape the cold winters we normally experience here.

Several years ago a carefully researched article on the flight of geese was written and published in many periodicals. It was also quoted on radio programs. Unfortunately we have never seen or heard who the author of the article was. As a result, we cannot here share his or her name.

More recently a somewhat similar article, which apparently based on the original article, was written and appeared in a church newsletter. It was written by a pastor, a highly respected and precious friend of ours, Dr. Richard Glasgow. We quote his article in the paragraphs below. We share it with you because you as a pilgrim on the long journey of life to a distant destination, and as a member of Christ's flock, with fellow travelers at your side, will appreciate it. The article follows:

Dear Flock,

This fall I have been thinking again about the geese. By flying in the V formation, whole flock adds at least 71% greater flying range than one bird flying alone.

(**Basic Truth #1:** *Christians who share a common direction and give each other uplift in their sense of community together get where they are going quicker and easier. Someone who is always detracting from the flow of things slows down the entire flock.)* When a goose falls out of formation, it suddenly feels the drag and resistance of trying to go it alone. It quickly finds the advantages of the uplifting power of the other birds in the flock.

(**Basic Truth #2:** *We need to stay in close fellowship with other Christians going our same direction. Bucking the wind is not fun!)* When the lead goose gets tired, he rotates with others who can take the lead while he rests.

(**Basic Truth #3:** *Don't think that you are the only one who can take the point; we all need rest and renewal.)* You may have noticed that geese honk from behind to encourage those who are leading.

(**Basic Truth #4:** *Let the noise from the flock be encouragement and not squawking.)* When a goose gets sick or injured and has to stop and recuperate, another goose drops out to stay with the needy one until they are well.

(**Basic Truth #5:** *Let us learn to stand by one another to the end, even when it means personal sacrifice.)*

We are Christ's flock, and we are called to reach out to each other with His love. Honk a little encouragement; be His presence; give an uplift to someone else in His name, and most of all keep flying in formation with the flock. May God give us that inner sense of direction toward His destination for us and may we follow Him as He leads us!

Prayer: You have provided so many teachers for us to learn. Help us apply the good stuff to helping those we love. Amen.

Rev. Henry Eggink

October 31

Ecclesiastes 3:1-8

A Time For Everything

Sometimes life brings us challenges and hardships that are hard to understand. Some are big and some may be not as much. Think on these issues: The death of a loved one; A significant health issue; Tensions in relationships; Wet ground; A lost item; A mess that needs cleaning up. To understand and know that there is a time for everything can be comforting during these hardships. I am amazed at how often when there is mourning due to a death, shortly after, there is rejoicing due to the birth of a precious baby. God has a plan – a perfect plan.

Included in that plan is – a time to die and be born, plant and harvest, cry and laugh, scatter and gather, keep and throw away. In each of these different circumstances, we may know that all of them are in His plan.

We need to trust and appreciate His timing.

Prayer: Dear God, help us to accept Your timing of all circumstances in life. Give us the faith to trust Your plan. Keep us from doubt and resentment. Amen.

Vonda and Steve Post
Professor of Accounting and Chair of the Bus/Econ Dept. at NWC
Steve is also an NWC graduate and farms near Sioux Center

Vonda was one of my advisees as a student and then became a colleague in the dept. She is an excellent teacher, advisor, and mentor to students. Steve and Vonda have been great friends of Dot and mine for many years. We have vacationed together at times and have made some memorable trips to Branson, MO to follow the Red Raiders. They have a great family of four kids that they may well be proud of. Today is Vonda's birthday – give her a call and say a prayer.

 **November 1** 

Philippians 1:21 (Ray's Favorite)

The "Hey Paula" Boy

Ray Hildebrand was a pop singing teen idol. ("Paul and Paula"). In fact, the song "Hey Paula" sold over 3 million copies back in the early '60's. But Ray didn't like that lifestyle, so he left the "Dick Clark Tour" and joined the FCA staff. That's where I met him in 1969. He is a great singer and has written many fabulous songs of faith. I still listen to his music almost daily.

Ray's Christian testimony and life has influenced me and helped me grow. "You can't out give God" is one of his very meaningful messages, that continues to speak to me.

He literally lost everything when he left the secular world of music and entered his present ministry. He was sued for leaving the tour. Since that time he has been continually trying to out give our God. What a guy!

Check out his website at rayhildebrand.com. You'll love him and his music.

Prayer: You give us so much more than we deserve and we thank you. Please make us more and more aware of how we can help others. Make us more generous with Your people. Amen.

Dave

 **November 2** 

John 3:8

Consider the Wind

"Consider the Wind...it blows wherever it wishes...you hear the sound of it...but you don't know where it comes from or where it goes...and so it is with all who are born of the Spirit…Consider the Wind"

I'm past 65 years of age and I have had a very "unboring life." I feel like I have lived three men's lifetimes, following where I thought God was leading me...taking chances, making choices and being obedient as best I knew how ... not always knowing what I was supposed to be or do...except being a "Child of God." I have truly done a lot of things... had different jobs ... lived in different places ... bumping into many people.

Some I question ...did I make the right choices when I did this or that in my past... which led me to where I am today?

It's really wonderful to run upon this passage in John ...after all these years ... and read ..."and so it is with all who are born of the Spirit of God."..Yea! ... it is ok... not to have all the answers about "your profession" or "your life's work." If you keep the main thing, the main thing ...you just might be doing exactly what God wants you to do down here.

Thank you, Holy Spirit, for blowing me around ...it's been a good ride!

Prayer: We do thank you Lord for the many avenues we may follow and be doing Your will. Keep that lantern ahead of us and continue to guide. We will follow. Amen.

Ray Hildebrand.com
The Hey Paula Boy

Ray lives in the Kansas City area and is still entertaining and recording. He and "Paula" do get together for some of those "Music Reunions for the Golden Oldies" – and I bet that is exciting. Ray has a strong faith, and he needs it – not only because of the great lyrics he writes – but because he has known heartache. He lost his wife a few years back and I can't imagine how painful that must be. He was a fine college basketball player, is a great guitar player and entertainer, and the kind of guy you instantly like. Check him out on the internet.

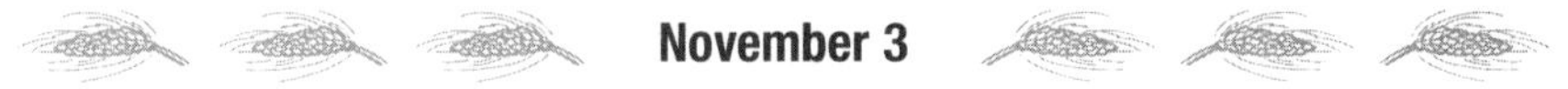

November 3

READY:

Philippians 1:6

What If

SET:

Growing up I watched my brothers play basketball and I wanted to be like them. Then they told me about a man who could spin a ball on all of his fingers and that got me started down a road to where I am today. My basketball spinning, ball handling, and juggling has taken me to every state and over 30 countries around the world to share the love of Christ and to be an encouragement and inspiration to the young and old. God has truly given me a gift, but what if I gave up during all those years of working on new skills and drills?

One of my favorite sayings when I perform is "finish what you start." I am so thankful today for others in our world that finished what they started. What if some people did not finish what they started though? What if the founding fathers of our country did not finish the Declaration of Independence, where would we be today? What if James Naismith did not pick up a peach basket and place it on the wall for his lacrosse players to stay in shape over the winter months? What if Muggsy Bogues gave up playing the game because everyone told him he was too small? There are countless others who could have a "what if" in our world, but each of those individuals finished what they started and changed the course of my life for sure.

As I read God's Word, I also find people who could have had a "what if" that would have changed the course of history. What if David never picked up a small stone when he faced Goliath? What if Esther would have never gone to see the King, her husband, to ask his favor in a crucial matter? What if Jesus Christ did not finish His saving work on the cross for you and me? Where would we be today if these things did not happen? I am not sure either, but one thing I know, I am so thankful that they all finished what they started.

Finishing what we start helps us in so many ways. It gives us a sense of accomplishment, pride in completing a difficult task, and so many occasions it blesses someone else. As I do my basketball shows, I am so blessed when I see the smiles and joy on people's faces as I perform. What if I would have quit years ago? I would have never been able to see how God changed thousands of lives through my ministry. Praise the Lord I have worked hard and never gave up.

Do you know that God has started a work in you that He wants to see finished as well? Maybe it is your homework or housework, it could be your sport or coaching, but whatever you have started, God will give you the strength to finish what you start! Say it out loud "Finish what you start!" When I say it in my shows it tells me to continue God's work until He calls me to do something else for Him each day. I love what I get to do for Him. It brings me great joy to serve the Lord by using the gifts He gave me for His glory.

What is it God is asking you to finish? I know when you put your trust in the Lord He will help you along the way. No matter what the task is, God is there with you all the way. Will you want to quit? ... I am sure you will, but don't do it! I know when you finish what you start it will not only be a blessing to you but countless others in your life. Go for it! Work hard and never give up, and always finish what you start! Don't let your life be filled with a multitude of "what ifs." If you have started your journey of living for Christ daily, the road will get long and the journey will get rough at times, but with God's help, finish what you start with Him! You will be glad you did.

GO:

1. What are some of the "what ifs" in your life you have regretted not finishing yet?
2. Where do you need to let God help you finish what you start by trusting in Him more?
3. Pray right now to ask God to help you finish what you start for His glory!

WORKOUT:

1 Corinthians 10:31

Proverbs 3:5-6

Prayer: Heavenly Father, please don't let me quit doing what You want me to do. I know I can trust You and ask for Your sustaining help. Thank you and Amen.

Tanya Crevier

Tanya is the best handler of a basketball I have ever seen. She is one of the most enthusiastic persons you will ever meet. And what makes her so great, is that she is enthusiastic about all the right things. She wants to serve our Lord and help kids. Never miss an opportunity to see her. Dot and I have had the privilege of knowing Tanya for many years and we first met her through the FCA.

November 4

Proverbs 3:5-6; Hebrews 13:5; Matthew 11:28; John 14:22; Psalm 23; Psalm 27:5; Jeremiah 29:11; Psalm 46:1

I Will Choose To Say Blessed Be Your Name

I have always loved church music; the earliest chants of the ancient church; the works of the masters; to gospel and hymns of faith right up to present day praise songs. They all lift praise and adoration to God our Maker in their own unique way. It is easy to be carried along with a melody or rhythm without real thought about the words and their meaning. One such praise song has spoken to me in a new way. "Blessed Be Your Name" (by Matt Redman) is a popular praise song right now.

"Blessed be your name ... When the sun is shining ...When the world is all it should be ... When the darkness closes in ... You Give and take away ... My heart will choose to say Blessed Be Your Name"

It struck in a most painful way that I had not actually listened or absorbed the words I was singing until about a year ago. It has been the toughest year of our lives. The stark reality of those words came into our lives in a very real and personal way. God has always showered us with blessings in great abundance and has seen us through what were our trials and sadness of that time. Blessed be your name. Then, one of our precious granddaughters, Alex, was taken from us at 19 years of age; suddenly without cause or reason, and with her whole life ahead of her. How could God think this was best? We need her here, she needs us. The words of that song no longer brought thoughts of praise, but rather tears and anger.

After admitting my lack of trust to myself and most importantly to God, He showed me He is still there and in control of our days. He is there to guide and help us through the dark valleys. Time is a healer. Friends and family are the voices; the arms and hands of God on earth to surround and support us – blessed by His name. God's Word instructs and comforts; heals and strengthens and gives guidance at just the right time. Prayer and time alone with God brings a measure of peace over time. I won't ever understand this side of heaven, still I will CHOOSE to say blessed be Your name.

Be sure to read all of the comforting and explanatory Bible passages above. The hole in our hearts will always remain. Tears still come when least expected. The hurt and loss are still so raw. The memories are often painful but always so precious and I thank God for so many good ones. As with all of us who have said goodbye to someone we love – we continue to long to see them again. Through God's saving grace we have the assurance that we will, as well as seeing our Lord and Savior face-to-face. That makes life worth living. Yes, the Lord gives in His great abundance and He walks through the valley of death with us when it comes to us. I may not understand but I will CHOOSE to say blessed by your glorious name.

Some months before Alex's death she chose two verses she wanted to try to live by, her life verses. I think God gave us those verses as well so we can carry on, not on our own understanding, but fully trusting God. I try to think of them as a prayer for each day God gives us.

Prayer: Lord, help me to trust You with all my heart. Help me to not depend on my wisdom and understanding. Help me to listen to Your voice in all I do and wherever I go. Help me to stay close to You and follow the path You have set out for me. Blessed be Your name. Amen. (Proverbs 3:5-6, Alex's verses)

Marty and Bruce Ver Hoef
Members of Central Reformed and my Sunday School Class
Both are semi-retired and doing extensive volunteer work

Bruce and Marty are also great friends and we all hurt with them in the loss of their precious granddaughter. One never gets over that kind of loss completely. I don't know how non-believers can stand it. We Christians know we will see them again in Glory. We'll see these two too.

November 5

Exodus 20:12

Honor Your Father...

What are your thoughts about your dad? Did you get to know him? Is he still living? (I lost my Dad on this date in 1960)

My thoughts about my dad are much more troubling. And may I say that my sister, who is 6½ years older than I, has much different recollections of Dad. Other than funerals, I can only remember my dad going to church on one occasion. I know he read his Bible, but he never talked to me about his faith. I lost him when I was a senior in college and he was only 56. There were still many things I wanted to tell him. Many times I've said that I wish he would have lived long enough for me to have gained some sense.

Dad was generous, a big tease, a hard worker (he was a painter and wallpaper hanger) and well-liked by many. But he never once gave me a compliment. I've had others, including Mom, tell me that he spoke of his love and being proud, but he never said it. I still have a note he sent me when I was a kid at Boy Scout camp. He signed it "Love, Dad." That was nearly 60 years ago and I still have it. Do you think it's important to tell your kids of your love? Talk about important things with those you love. I can't stand the thought of not seeing him in Heaven, but I don't know if I will. That makes me very sad.

Don't ever let your loved ones wonder about your relationship with the Lord.

Prayer: Heavenly Father, You know how many times I've prayed for my dad. I pray for myself as a dad and for all the dads out there. Please give us mercy, wisdom, and love. Amen.

Dave

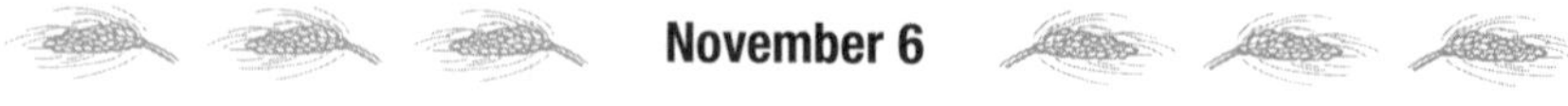

November 6

1 Peter 4:10-11

Use Your Gifts to Serve Others

Each one should use whatever gift he has received to serve others, faithfully administering God's grace in its various forms. To Him be the glory and the power forever and ever. Amen.

I have the opportunity to coach women's basketball at a Christian college. Each year I am blessed by the women who are a part of the team. We are regularly reminded that God has truly gifted us; it is our goal to honor Him in the way we prepare, the way we play, and the way we interact with others.

I have been taught by these young women what it looks like to "use your gifts to serve others." It is truly a matter of the heart – for out of our hearts comes the wellspring of life.

May you find true joy today as you consider the gifts that God has given you. May God use you in a mighty way as you use those gifts to serve others through the strength that He provides. May Christ Jesus truly be praised!

Prayer: Heavenly Father, may you be glorified as Your servants seek to honor You as we seek to love and serve others. In Jesus name, Amen.

Earl and Karen Woudstra
Head Women's Basketball Coach, Ass't A.D., Prof. of Kinesiology at NWC, City Council Member

Both Karen and Earl are NWC grads and both played college basketball. Earl has taken his teams to 8 National tournaments and won the National Championship 3 times. He and Karen, who works for NW Realty, have 4 children (Brandon, Jaime, Brady and Jenna). Karen is a former Alumni Director at NWC.

November 7

Matthew 10:33

The World Judges Our Actions

This important verse from scripture is one I consider often as it relates to my personal life and my life as a public servant. It isn't just about denying faith in Jesus Christ, but also how I demonstrate it daily in words and deeds.

It is our actions by which the world examines us to judge the validity of our faith. Time after time in scripture, there are examples of men and women of faith who demonstrated both the power and the love of God through their actions rather than their words.

St. Francis of Assisi once said, "preach the gospel at all times, and when necessary, use words." He understood we are giving a testimony of our faith whenever we are awake. In our homes it is demonstrated by how we treat our husbands and wives, parents and children. And from the moment we walk out into the world our testimony is on display for all to see.

When the world looks at our testimony in action will they find us denying Christ, or acknowledging His Lordship in our lives? On the day Jesus was crucified, after insisting he wouldn't, Peter verbally denied the Savior three times before the rooster crowed. But, surely hundreds more denied Him that day with their actions.

So, my challenge to you today is the same as the one I give myself on a regular basis. Always acknowledge Jesus with your words and more importantly, with your actions. If we make this our goal, rather than being denied before the Father, we will hear the words, "Well done, my good and faithful servant."

Prayer: Thank you Jesus for showing us what to do and how to be a good example. It is not easy and we can't do it alone. We need you, and we need each other. Amen.

Senator Chuck Grassley
United States Senator

Chuck has been Iowa's Republican Senator since 1980. He also served in the House and before that in the Iowa Legislature. He's held many important Committee Chairs and is very accessible to his constituents. It's nice to have a man of faith representing us in Washington.

November 8

Hebrews 13:17 – Daniel 5:21– 1 Kings 1:35 – Colossians 1:16 – 1 Timothy 2:1 — Romans 13:1

Who Is Your President?

Do you only pray for people you voted for, or is in your party? I sure hope not. Please take a look at the above verses. All of our leaders, (authorities), were put in place by God (Rom. 13:1). President Obama is my President whether I voted for him or not. He and all of his advisors need our regular and fervent prayers. When our leaders fail, we fail with them.

I still can't imagine why anyone would want to be President. But thank the Lord there are some that do. There is no country better than this one and we want to keep it that way.

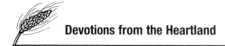

We are a nation "Under God", so let's keep seeking His love and help.

It's so easy to be judgmental of our leaders. I'm old enough to remember a President with the initials H.S.T. that had the lowest approval ratings on record while he was President. He said "The Buck Stops Here" and he meant it. Today he is one of the most revered Presidents in our history. Keep Praying!

Prayer: Heavenly Father, we do pray for leaders and all who advise them. Keep them safe, inspired, humble, encouraged, and caring. Amen.

Dave

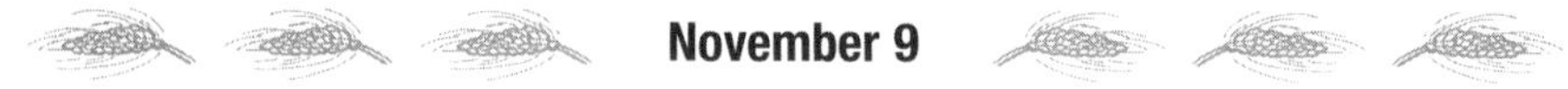

November 9

Matthew 6:25-34

Why Concern Yourself?

In this day and age of hustle and bustle and the stress that comes along with normal everyday living, I have found a credo that I can truly live by – "sweat only those things over which you have control." The rest will be taken care of by the Almighty and He will help with the ramifications of those decisions. We may not understand some of the decisions that are made. We may be upset, happy, or not really concerned. We may agree, disagree, or remain neutral. Some decisions affect us directly and some take a more indirect route.

After my re-election bid failed for the State Senate, I found myself wondering what I could have done to make the outcome positive. After the narrow defeat I was feeling pretty low. That faded into obscurity when confronted with the scary news that my bride of 37 years was diagnosed with breast cancer. All that election business seemed pretty frivolous at that point. Here I had been concerned with an election that was lost by a mere 300+ votes, and now we had to face news that was life-threatening.

I look back at those days and feel that God knew something more than I did. He knew I had to have the time to be at my wife's side throughout the next months of treatment. I would have been anyway, but I wouldn't have been able to take her to all of the radiation treatments, doctors' appointments, and countless hours of consoling and nurturing.

Time has passed and the reports continue to be encouraging and very positive. But I still wonder if she is really "out of the woods" with this deadly disease. I used to sweat all those little things at work, and still do a little, but I put those back into perspective when it comes to what really counts in my life.

Prayer: Dear God, thanks for the recovery that is so evident with Peggy. Please continue her complete healing. Thank you for helping us to keep things in perspective. Amen.

Frank Wood
Associate Principal and Activities Director, North Scott High School, Eldridge, Iowa

Frank was my best friend the 4 years we served in the Senate. Of course we didn't agree on everything, but we could talk, listen, reason together, and agree to disagree. But most of the time we agreed on Education issues and were able to complete some legislation. Frank is a very intelligent, practical and reasonable man. I wish he was back in the Senate and I surely hope he was elected as Supervisor for Scott County. We need men like Frank Wood making decisions that help us. I pray every day for Peggy, and of course include Frank and the rest of his fine family. Won't you too?

November 10

Psalm 40:1-5

Patience and Faithfulness

Waiting can be so hard, especially when you know what you want, or at least you think you do. So often our timing and God's are not the same. I've learned that waiting on God and trusting His promises are always for the best.

After 17 years of a childless marriage, through many tears and broken hopes, God answered our prayers. He gave us the tremendous gift of a son. Now, 14 years later, we have seen over and over again how God's faithfulness and His timing were perfect. We have been blessed with a wonderful son who shows us every day how great and good our God is.

Prayer: Dear God, thank you so much for Your faithfulness. Help us to trust completely in You and Your promises. Amen.

Lora Jeltema
Official Scorer for Women's Basketball at NWC

It's a pleasure to work and visit with Lora while we Score and Announce Women's Basketball at NWC. Her husband Randy is a well-known official in the area.

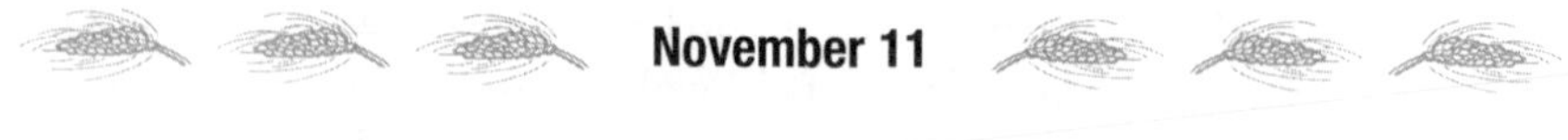

November 11

1 Peter 2:17

Veteran's Day

The wars that occurred in my youth did not directly involve any of my family members. My dad worked for the Chicago Northwestern Railroad, and therefore was exempt. My only concern was for the U.S. to "win the war." There was never any discussion if we should or shouldn't be involved in the war. Then, in the late '60's, during the Vietnam War, Dave's first cousin Randy Schutt was killed. The family grief was so painful and very evident. In addition, the returning vets that would even talk about it, told some real horror stories. What an impact for me!

It is not a matter if we should or shouldn't go to war, but to respect and honor those who now choose to serve. Let's give a heartfelt "Thanks" to every service person we know. It's so important that we pray frequently for all of them. Let's do it now.

Prayer: God, I continue to pray for our country's service people. May they return safe and with emotional healing as well. May there be peace. Amen.

Dot

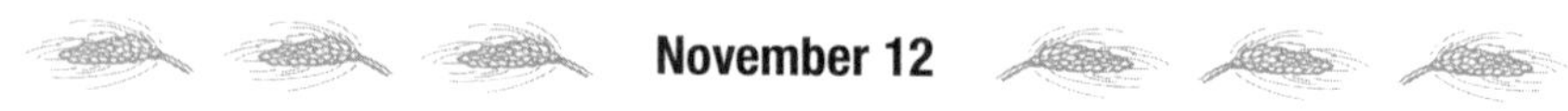

November 12

Acts 4:36

Be A Barnabas

Barnabas was the encourager. Do you realize how important encouragement is for all of us? Think about this true story.

A number of years ago I traveled with some men to Colorado to attend a Promise Keepers event. It was great, very inspiring, and I learned a lot. Tremendous world-renowned speakers made outstanding presentations. Not the least of which was the noted author/speaker Chuck Swindoll.

Chuck delivered a heart-touching message and left the stage. Shortly after, the PK leader Bill McCartney appeared to introduce the next speaker. But first he said this, "Chuck delivered a great message and had to rush away to another commitment, but I wanted to say a thankful word and just barely caught him in the waiting taxi. I complimented him on how our Lord had used him in a great way." Tears came to Chuck Swindoll's eyes! Even *he* needed to hear encouraging words! What does that say to you?

Who are you going to encourage today?

Prayer: Dear Lord, thanks for our ability to encourage others and thanks too for the encouragement we receive. Amen.

Dave

November 13

1 Chronicles 4:10

Good Old Jabez

Several years ago, I gave up nursing to go into sales. I was about to have my first evaluation and everyone in my pod was waiting with bated breath to see if I passed, because rumors were running rampant that our department would be closing.

I passed and got a raise! Everyone rejoiced. The rumors must be just that – rumors! Management wouldn't give me a raise and then close our department, right?

Wrong! Two hours later, a meeting was called and my whole department was laid off!

One of my co-workers gave me the book, The Prayer of Jabez, as a farewell gift. I read it and started praying the prayer daily. I didn't ask God for a new job or lots of money, or even peace about not having a job. I just asked Him to bless me and left it up to Him to choose a blessing for me.

The first thing that happened was that my company HR department called to tell me that through the Trade Adjustment Agreement, I could have two years of school, along with unemployment pay, and mileage to go to school.

I was 50 years old. I had quit nursing. I didn't have any desire to go back to school. Could this possibly be the blessing I had been asking for?

Reluctantly, I went back to school – in nursing. Many times as I drove to school, after I had prayed the prayer of Jabez, I would add, "Now Lord, I have a microbiology test today. I believe this was your idea, so I really need your help."

We made it through school, even graduated with honors. "That HAD to be a God thing!"

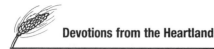

Prayer: Thank you Lord for always having a plan, even when it is so hard for us to see it. Thanks too for helping us complete that plan. Thanks for never letting us down. Amen.

Greta and Marv Siebersma
Members of Central Reformed and my Sunday School Class

It is a joy to spend time with this couple. They always have something constructive to do and say. You will read another of their devotionals tomorrow.

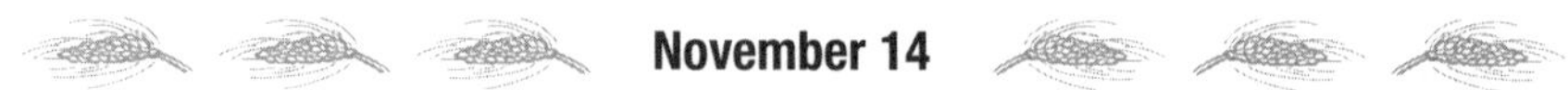

November 14

Romans 5:8

Forgiveness

The chaplain couldn't be there that day so I was to facilitate the group on the topic of forgiveness. (In our outpatient therapy department, we feel that forgiving others is so important to one's mental health that we dedicate one session a week to that topic).

I came armed with a wonderful handout. We talked a little about how difficult it can be to forgive. Then a middle-aged woman asked if she could share her story.

She had been raised in an abusive home and her brother had raped her. No one defended her and she suffered a great deal. Her self-esteem was attacked, and as soon as she could, she left home. After much therapy, she said she had decided to forgive her brother.

One day she was driving down the highway and saw a man with a backpack, hitch-hiking. He looked like her brother. She stopped and offered him a ride. It was indeed the brother who had raped her. He had recently been released from prison after serving time for raping someone else. He was shocked that the person who picked him up was his sister. He was silent for a while, and then haltingly said, "I know you remember what I did, and I know there is nothing I can do to change that, but I want you to know that I am really sorry."

She didn't yell at him, telling him what a worthless person he was or how he had messed up her life. She didn't say, "Oh, that's OK." She simply replied. "I forgave you a long time ago."

I quietly tucked my "wonderful handout" away.

She had said it all much better than the handout or I could ever say it.

Forgiveness is not a feeling. It is a conscious decision not to let the behavior of the one who wronged me, control my behavior.

Isn't that exactly what Jesus did? He didn't wait for me to say "I'm sorry." He decided to love me anyway ... so much that He gave His life for me.

Apologies benefit the one who was wronged but are even more beneficial to the wrongdoer.

Only when I acknowledge my sin, can I receive the gift of forgiveness that Jesus is offering me, and enjoy the restoration of my relationship with Him.

Prayer: Dear Lord, thanks for forgiving me even before I was born. Your dying on that cross enables me to forgive myself and all others. Thanks too for forgetting all of my transgressions. Amen.

Greta Siebersma

I think you can see why Greta is such a helpful and caring person.

November 15

Daniel 5:21b

The Senate

As most of you know, Dot and I served 4 years in the Iowa Senate (2005-08). As I write this in the summer of 2010 there hasn't been a week pass that someone hasn't said something like, "I bet you're glad you're out of politics!" or "How did you like the political world?"

My answers were consistent in that we liked 85-90% of it, but the 10% or so we didn't like, we really didn't like. Even so, we're very glad to have had the opportunity and it's a tremendous honor. We really liked the people down there. Of course, we really like the people up here too.

I truly believe that every one of the 50 Senators, when elected, wants to do what is best for the people and expect to do just that.

What I really disliked was the partisanship. I actually thought we would work together to try to make each bill the best we could for Iowa. Party politics get in the way of that.

Every day I prayed that Jesus would be my partner and lead me. He doesn't make mistakes, but I sure did.

So what's the purpose of this devotional? Two-fold. One, we need to pray for our politicians at all levels, regularly. It's a tough job and they need it. Second, each of us must stay involved in the process. Vote – Pay Attention – Correspond – Run For Office. If I were younger, I'd still be there.

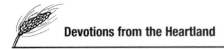

Prayer: I know that You position each leader and that is a comfort. Please be with all of our elected officials and help them make decisions that help our state and our country. Amen.

Dave

November 16

Psalms 19:14

Christians Aren't Perfect – Just Forgiven

I had plans to meet the gals for coffee and time was short. Why do I always get behind an old duffer, not going the speed limit, straddling the lane so I can't pass? Sure enough, he turns (very slowly) without signaling. All of the preceding are unspoken thoughts and no shaking fist to show my irritation. Then I realize scripture memorization doesn't help one bit if I don't internalize it. That passage in Psalms talks about "words and thoughts being pleasing to our Lord." My thoughts weren't too pleasing I'm sure. Besides, I'm fast approaching the "old duffer" age myself. I know the gals will understand if I'm just a tad late anyway. Aren't good friends (and old duffers) great!

Prayer: God, may I gain wisdom and knowledge to live a more kind and compassionate walk with you and all those around me. Amen.

Dot

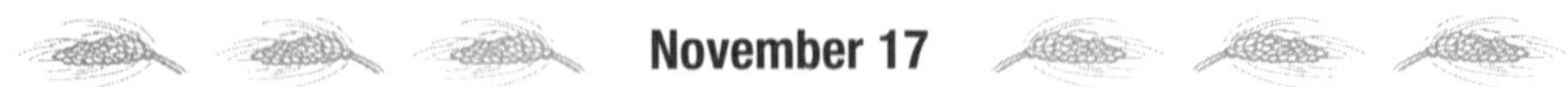

November 17

Philippians 3:12

Keep Going

The Christian life is a journey to be traveled, a race to be run, a battle to be fought. But regardless of which metaphor we use, the Christian life is often rugged and before long, we grow tired and are inclined to slow down or perhaps even to stop altogether our progress. We must not do that. To do so would be sad.

It is imperative that we press on. To put it in the words of the Apostle Paul: *Press on to take hold of that for which Christ Jesus took hold of me.*

The great goal and prize toward which we move is eternal life, the race itself should be actual growth in Christ likeness, holiness.

The spiritual blessings we enjoy here by way of God's grace are surely greatly appreciated. They are life enriching. But compared to the good things prepared for us in the wonderful life beyond, they are small. The peace we find on earth in Christ is precious but it's only a reflection of the peace we shall have in Him in heaven. Our present joy is only a preview of the glory awaiting us. Life will be even better farther along. Keep this in mind when you, in life's journey, tend to grow weary and tired and you consider slowing down or stopping in your efforts. Press on!

Prayer: Heavenly Father, it is easy for us to reach a plateau and just not move forward. Sometimes it seems there are peaks and valleys in our Christian life. Help us to stay on top and motivate others to do the same. Amen.

Rev. Henry Eggink

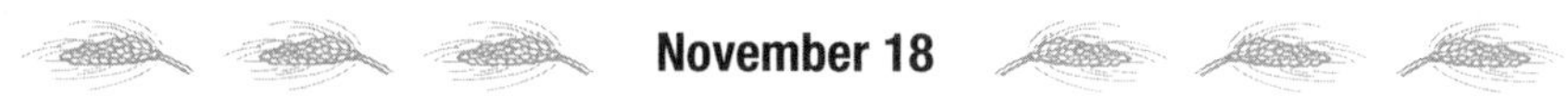

November 18

Matthew 5:31-32

Divorce

I've found that writing and collecting a book of devotionals made me think of lots of topics. Some I didn't want to think about much. This is one of them.

After 48 years and counting, Dot and I have never considered divorce as an option. (Dot says she did consider murder upon occasion). I do think divorce has been made too easy since the laws were changed back in the '60's. Stats show that the success rate for 2nd, 3rd, or ... marriages is even lower than the first nuptials. I certainly don't think "living together" is the answer either. I also know that when your kids hurt, you hurt.

So what's the answer? Jesus! Stats also show that when both members place Jesus as the head of the house the success rate multiplies exponentially. Jesus is the answer for lots of problems, isn't he?

Prayer: Thank you Jesus for helping us to grow old together and for blessing new starts even after something You denounce. Amen.

Dave

November 19

1 John 4:4; 1 Peter 1:21; Hebrews 11:1-3; Jeremiah 29:11-13

Who's In Control?

Have you ever been in a situation and felt that you were in total control of the happenings around you? Or maybe a time when you felt that you had no control over what was happening? I am one of those people who likes to be in charge or in control of the things around me. Our twins, Mitchell and Madison had just turned 18 (April 21, 2010). When they were about three months old we could tell that Maddy was not developing as a normal baby should. Through a series of tests we discovered that she was mentally disabled.

I soon realized that God was in control of that birth, the doctors that we had to deal with, and the many things that we were going to encounter in the future. God had plans for her life and ours. Believe me, they were not "normal." We learned a lot, changed much, and grew tremendously through the whole, continuous process. We are not in control of the things around us – God is. We may think we are and want to be, but the quicker we realize that a higher being is in control of all things, we can grow, mature, and develop as the Christian people God wants us to be. I believe it's good to be proactive and do as much as we can to control the things around us. That's all well and good. When it comes down to who has the final say, it's our Father in Heaven who is watching over us and dictates the final outcome (good or bad) of any and all situations.

God knows exactly how much stress or how big a challenge we need. He also knows when to give us whatever He gives us. I thank God daily for giving us Maddy, even though the challenges have been great. He is in control and I am very thankful for that as well.

Prayer: Thank you God for knowing us so well that we can trust You completely and always. Please continue to shower Your love on our loved ones. Help those that can't help themselves, and help each of us to be willing to reach out in assistance. Amen.

Paul and Sheila Janssen
NCAA Basketball Official and New York Life Agent

Paul and Sheila are good friends and Paul is part of the DutchMart Coffee Group. He was an excellent football player at NWC and has helped coach at the high school and college levels here in Orange City. If you watch major college basketball on TV you can pick out Paul as he works the games. He is a regular in being selected for the March Madness and it won't be long and he will be working the Final Four.

November 20

1 John 5:13

Words of Comfort

This is my absolute favorite verse. I'm a very fact-loving person. That's why I receive a new Almanac each Christmas. I want to know what the numbers say or who did whatever it is we are talking about and when. When this verse says, "you may KNOW," it puts the icing on the cake. We can never be good enough, know enough, or even do enough good and kind works, but because God is love and all we have to do is believe and confess, we can know NOW where we will spend eternity. Everyone faces eternity; it's just where will we spend it? For us believers, it will be in Heaven!

What do you say we all meet in the Northwest corner when we all get there!

Prayer: Lord Jesus, I know it sounds strange to talk about where we will be in Heaven, just the fact that we will be there is tremendous. Thank you for showing us the way. Help us guide as many as possible to join us. Amen.

Dave

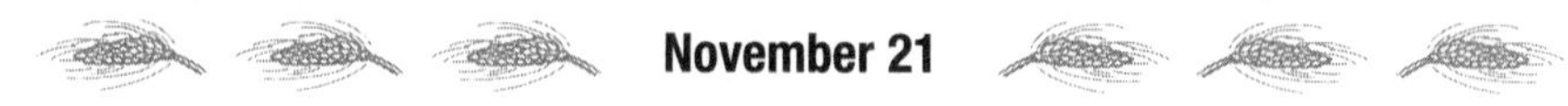

November 21

1 John 5:13

It's Great To Know...

Since this is my absolute favorite verse (Bill Wegman's too), I decided to write two devotionals on it. I have mentioned before that I don't think of myself as a very "original" person. I mean that the vast majority of things that influence me have come from others. Ecclesiastes 1:9 rings pretty true " ...there is nothing new under the sun." Oh, I guess there have been a few original thoughts in my 71 years but here's an example of what I mean.

Back in the early '60's I became aware of the Fellowship of Christian Athletes organization. They published a little magazine ("The Christian Athlete" – now called "Sharing the Victory") and there was this quote, (sorry, I don't know who first said it) "Coach your athletes the way you would want your son or daughter to be coached." What a great idea! (It's been one of my credos for living). So that's what I tried to do during my career. But the phrase changed a bit as time went on. The first part changed to "Teach your students ...Advise your students ...Parent your kids ...Legislate your constituents," and you might add some others. Remember to always end it with "the way you want your kids (or loved ones) ....

So how about "Husband" or "Wife?" "Be the kind of husband you would want your daughter(s) to marry." "Be the kind of wife you would want your son(s) to marry." Go ahead – you be original with the phrase and then give it some action as God blesses you. It's never too late to make improvements.

I also kinda like to know what's coming up – so that's why the verse above is my favorite. What's your favorite? See you there!

Prayer: Again we thank you for your promises and the way you keep them. Help us to do the same. Amen.

Dave

November 22

Mark 10:17 -27

Questions? – Questions?

If you were to have a face-to-face encounter with Jesus, what would you ask Him? For me, it would be hard to nail it down to just one, there are so many I would want to ask. Some might appear trivial in the scheme of God's kingdom; in fact, maybe most of them would – because every vital and important question about life is answered on the pages of His Word.

There was a rich young ruler who had the opportunity to ask Jesus a question. He picked one of the most important questions anyone could ever ask, "good teacher...what must I do to inherit eternal life?" What a question! This is no trivial question.

Jesus answers the ruler with a question and statement, "Why do you call me good ...no one is good, except God alone." In this answer, Jesus states a fact that will help interpret the rest of His answer. Christ understands that the young ruler is asking for a set of commandments to keep, in order to merit salvation. This ruler wants a works-based pass to enter into eternal life.

As a result, Jesus tells him to obey the second table of the law: do not murder, steal, lie, or commit adultery, and honor your parents. The ruler gives an amazing response, "all of these I have kept since I was a boy." There he stands facing the Son of God, confronted with his own sin by the Lord, and he flatly denies that he has sinned! So Jesus presses further with, "go sell every-thing you have, give it to the poor and you will have treasure in heaven. Then follow me."

Again, it seems funny that Jesus gives the ruler another works-based requirement to inherit eternal life. Look deeper at Jesus' interaction with this ruler. First He tells him to obey the first commandment ("Have no other gods"). He does not tell him to obey the commandment directly, instead, He tells him to do an act that indicates that the ruler serves no other gods. This young man stood condemned because he placed his money (a god) over the one eternal God.

Jesus is NOT giving a universal command to every person to give away all that one owns. He is simply pointing out that the rich young ruler was a sinner! This ruler wanted to know what he could do to EARN eternal life. Look at his original question, "What must I DO to inherit eternal life?" Jesus, through a series of questions, in essence, tells the young ruler he is unable to DO anything *on his own* to inherit eternal life.

What is our reaction to the commandments of the Bible? I know I often like to think very highly of my own works. Yet, the Bible says that even our best efforts, are "filthy rags" before God. It is at scary thing to be exposed as a sinner before a righteous God! The truth is that the rich young ruler is no different than we are. We are miserable, condemned sinners, unable to save ourselves.

I'm glad this Bible story doesn't end with our condemnation. The disciples ask Jesus, "who, then can be saved?" The disciples understood their own sin and when Jesus tells them what true righteousness means, they simply throw up their hands and tell Jesus that no one can keep the law perfectly. The disciples understand that if keeping the law perfectly is the only way, then we have no chance.

Fortunately, Jesus says later in the chapter "with man this is impossible, but not with God, with God all things are possible." The requirement of obedience to the law has not changed. We still need to be perfect to inherit salvation. Only God is righteous. The "Good News" is that Christ's perfection becomes our perfection. By faith, when we someday stand in judgment, God will not judge us as our sins deserve. Instead, we will be covered by the white, unblemished robe of Christ!

Prayer: Thank you Lord for dying for us so that we may live eternally. Amen.

Nick Scholten
All-American football player for NWC, Member of the NWC Hall of Fame, and New York Life Agent in Orange City

Nick was a great offensive lineman and a great student (Scholastic All-American). He is an equally fine person. Nick is my substitute announcer for NWC games and works at the scorer's bench during many basketball games.

November 23

Genesis 5:24; Luke 12:47-48

Are There Stations in Heaven and Hell?

Not that it makes much difference – but I think so. What else can be concluded when the Bible says, "some will be whipped with few stripes?" That means some others must get more. We aren't supposed to judge but compare Ghandi to Hitler. Neither were professing Christians but who would you whip the most?

Well, I'm not really worried about hell 'cause I'm not going there.

The same rationale holds true for Heaven doesn't it? There's no way I measure up to Paul, Enoch, John (either of 'em), Billy Graham, and a host of others. This just names a few. Common sense says they are at a different "station" than I am, or ever will be. Do I care? Not really. In Heaven we are in the presence of God Almighty, that's what counts. You and I could attend the concert of a major country-western singer. We'd both enjoy it tremendously but I might get a *little* more out of it because it's my favorite genre. The point is, we both got a lot out of being there.

This isn't a salvation issue, but it's interesting to think about. Our job is to take as many with us as we can. That's all we can take with us, family and friends.

Prayer: Dear Lord, thanks for giving us minds to think and reason. Help us understand what You want us to know, and accept the rest on Faith. Amen.

Dave

November 24

Colossians 3:12-17

Anniversary Thoughts

We chose this scripture for our wedding passage 25 years ago. We believed we were God's chosen people and that we were dearly loved. However, we were certainly not as holy, kind, humble, compassionate, gentle and patient as would be needed to have the kind of marriage we dreamed about. Yes, marriage takes work, but the peace of Christ is even more important. Lots of hard work without the assurance of God's love through the person of Jesus Christ still leaves a void.

As we've discovered the peace of Christ, we understand even more how much we are dearly loved and what it means to be chosen.

Prayer: Father in Heaven, thank you for your love. Thank you for the peace of Christ that shows us how to treat those we love and live with every day. Amen.

Mark and Lori Bloemendaal
Retired Baseball and Men's Golf Coach, Presently the Alumni Director at NWC

Mark succeeded me as golf coach and has been a long time Admissions Counselor. Mark and Lori are NWC grads and are devoted to making their kids and the college the best they can be. In the summer of 2010 Mark became the Alumni Director.

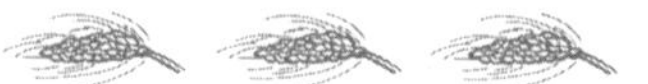

November 25

Follow each Scripture Reference and Note the Promise:

1. *The Lord is near to all who call on Him, to all who call on Him in truth.* (Psalm 145:18)
2. *God is our refuge and strength, a very present help in trouble.* (Psalm 46:1)
3. *The Lord will watch over your coming and going, both now and forever more.* (Ps. 121:8)
4. *Ask and it will be given you, seek and you will find, knock and the door will be opened to you. For everyone who asks- receives, everyone who seeks- finds, and to him who knocks- the door will be opened.* (Matthew 7:7-8)
5. *For God so loved the world that He gave His one and only Son that whosoever believes in Him shall not perish but have eternal life.* (John 3:16)
6. *I am the vine, you are the branches. If a man remains in me and I in him, he will bear much fruit; apart from me you can do nothing.* (John 15:5)
7. *If you remain in me, and my words remain in you, ask whatever you wish, and will be given you.* (John 15:7)
8. *And if I go and prepare a place for you, I will come back and take you to be with me that you also may be where I am.* (John 14:3)
9. *And we know that in all things God works for the good of those who love Him, who have been called according to His purpose.* (Romans 8:28)

10. *Because God has said: 'Never will I leave you, nor will I forsake you, so we say with confidence, the Lord is my helper; I will not be afraid. What can man do to me?* (Hebrews 13:5-6)
11. *The Lord will rescue me from every evil attack and will bring me safely to His heavenly kingdom. To Him be glory forever and ever.* (2 Timothy 4:18)
12. *He will wipe away every tear from their eyes. There will be no more death or mourning or crying or pain, for the old order of things has passed away.* (Revelation 21:4)

Prayer: Thank you God for each of these promises. Thank you too for the fact that You always keep Your promises. Help us do the same. Amen.

Rev. Henry Eggink

November 26

Luke 18:1– Colossians 1:9

My Prayer

Remember that great song by the Platters? They had a bunch of great ones, but that is my favorite. When is prayer inappropriate? Paul, Luke, and Jesus indicated it's always the right thing to do. God *always* answers prayer. "Yes!", "No!", and "Wait" are His answers.

Why don't you keep track of your prayers. Just write down what you prayed for, for about a week. Follow what happens in each case. There's nothing like proof and sometimes we have to "keep track" to get that proof.

I think I'm going to start record-keeping again. I haven't done that for a while. How about you?

There's no time like the present!

Prayer: Thank you God for always keeping Your promises and answering our prayers. You always know what is best. Help us to be accepting and faithful. Amen.

Dave

November 27

Mark 4:41

The Calm Center

We first encounter God in the Bible as creator and sustainer of all creation. God is not just a manager but is the owner and operator of all that is. The One who created order out of chaos, who hovered over the abyss, and who mastered that which was formless and void, is our God. And only our God can command chaos to become order. So, when the disciples ask the question, "Who is this man that even the wind and the waves obey him?" they also know that only God has command over the wind and waves. Only God controls the abyss, and only God creates order where once chaos reigned.

Jesus is in the process of gradually, sometimes subtly revealing himself to the disciples. He is letting them in on the mind-blowing secret that he is the Son of God. That he is the one who has come to tame the chaos they experience in the world. Jesus offers himself to them, and us, as the calm center of a world often spinning madly.

Allowing Jesus to be the calm center means that we don't participate in the chaos that surrounds us. This happens to us at least once a year as we drive to Michigan to visit family and friends. We're cruising along on Interstate 80 and all of a sudden traffic comes to a halt. We creep forward slowly and move about 3 miles in an hour and a half. Finally we get up to what's causing the problem and we find that there's an accident on the other side of the road. People are gawking and looking across the median. They're interested in the chaos and they want to see what's going on. But in the process they are adding to the chaos! Sometimes this happens with people, too. Something happens between two individuals and gradually many others become involved. People are repeating portions of conversations that they weren't meant to have heard. New "facts" get added while other very important parts of the story get left out. The chaos that was once between two people spreads and others begin to participate and add to the chaos.

Allowing Jesus to be the calm center means refusing to participate in the chaos. The storm might be raging outside of your boat, but when it starts to rage inside your boat (as it does with the disciples) you have real problems.

Prayer: God, help me to be someone who cooperates with you by refusing to participate in any chaos. I want to be a calm center like Jesus. Amen.

Pastor Tanner Smith

Tanner is one of the pastors of First Reformed Church in Sioux Center. He and his wife Kristin have a love for both of the states they have lived in (Iowa and Michigan), but Tanner does not have mixed alliances when it comes to rooting for the Hawkeyes over all Michigan teams!

November 28

Hebrews 4:12 – Matthew 21:22 – Jeremiah 33:3

Start Each Day with Bible Reading and Prayer

I was about 31-years-old before I started reading the Bible because I wanted to. I know that's a sad commentary and it makes me feel guilty. Oh, I read the Bible upon occasion, but only because I had to for some assignment, task, or from guilt. Joe Orduna, a man I wrote about for the September 1 devotional, provided the motivation for me to start daily devotions. I started in Matthew. When I got to chapter 24 it really scared me. I thought I could never "measure up" and wouldn't be ready to meet Jesus when my time came. This precipitated individual studies on Christ's Second Coming; the "Therefores" in the Bible; the Existence of Hell; and some others that increased my hunger to read the Bible over and over. Daily Guideposts, Words of Hope, and numerous others have helped to establish this habit of daily devotions.

Find out what time of the day or night that works best for you. For me, it's the first thing in the morning. (I always fell asleep prematurely at night). If you miss a day or whatever, just start up again. Don't feel guilty or anything, just start up again. The Devil will try to help you find all kinds of excuses to quit or miss. Find stuff you like to read that motivates you, and then talk to God. Then listen to Him. He will never let you down. You will never form or perpetuate a better habit.

If you're struggling with materials or something give me a call (cell 712-441-5669), and I'll try to help you with it. Also call me if you find something great that I can use.

Prayer: It is amazing all of the material You help us with. Please enable us to grow, reach out, and form good habits with Your Word. Amen.

Dave

November 29

John 1:37-39 – Mark 8:36-37

Priorities

One day as Jesus walked here upon earth in His ministry He noticed two fishermen following Him. He turned and asked them, "What are you seeking?" (We can assume, can we not, what they needed and wanted most of all – their highest priority). They responded by asking, "Rabbi, Teacher, where dwellest thou?" He said unto them "Come and see." They came and saw where He dwelt and abode with Him that day.

What a great day that had been for these men. It is likely that they spent more days with Jesus where He dwelt. Later they accompanied Him in His ministry through the country side. They became members of Jesus' inner circle, The Apostolic Group. They had found what they needed, and want most of all – their Savior and Lord, together with a new mission for life – their highest priorities.

Suppose that we take into the streets of our contemporary cities this question Jesus asked so long ago: "What are you seeking?" Or in other words, "What are your highest priorities?" If we ask a dozen people there these questions. It is likely we will receive answers somewhat like the following: "I am seeking a better job – a job with higher pay." Or, "My highest priority is my vocation, profession, business – I am seeking their perfection, hoping they will be financially rewarding." That is their highest priority.

Others may tell us that their skills, talents, abilities, (perhaps in the arts, music, drama, sports, etc.) are their highest priorities. They are seeking perfection in them with the hope of public favor and reception, resulting in honors, awards, trophies, and a good financial income.

Another individual tells us that he is preparing a sound and safe financial investment program which will bring an adequate income for himself and his family until he reaches retirement age. Upon his decease this will provide care for his loved ones and support for charitable causes he will have named.

Another citizen says that he had become a regular reader of the Wall Street Journal. He follows the market faithfully. He is reviewing his stock and bond portfolio. He is constantly on the alert looking for real estate which promises large increase in value. Accumulation of more wealth has become his aim. These are his highest priorities.

Thus we could go on. But we can't help but notice that the emphasis is on the material, physical, and temporal with no mention of the spiritual and eternal. They are conspicuous by their absence.

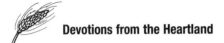

This is a sad, dangerous, cause for concern.

Jesus asks, "*For what shall it profit a man if he shall gain the whole world, and lose his own soul, or what shall a man give in exchange for his soul?*"

The priorities we have mentioned thus far have value but there are priorities of greater importance. What are your top priorities?

Prayer: Help us to make You our constant highest priority. We know it isn't easy, but it is the most important reason You put us here. Amen.

Rev. Henry Eggink

November 30

Exodus 14:13-15

Turn It All Over

Have you ever been in a group where everything that is talked about is bad news? I was recently in several conversations like this. The topics ranged from who had recently lost their job, who was in the hospital, who had just been diagnosed with cancer, which families were having marriage problems, and more.

Sometimes we forget what God can do if we will let Him. He wants us to bring each piece of bad news to Him. "*Do not be afraid. Stand firm and see the deliverance the Lord will bring you today.*" The Israelites had every reason to be discouraged but they also had a powerful God to give them hope and a future. We too must turn our problems over to God, let Him work for us, and then move on.

Prayer: Lord, help us to turn our whole life over to You. Calm our spirit as we watch You work. Move us on to the life You want us to live. Amen.

Stan and Marietta Vandersall
Stan is a retired Minister and Marietta retired from her clerical job at NWC.

Stan is part of the DutchMart Coffee Group and is also in the Lion's Club with me. Marietta is one of the sweetest ladies you will ever meet. These are just good friends.

December 1

Proverbs 14:26

The Lord Provides A Place

"May you trust God that you are exactly where you are meant to be." St. Therese

For the past 21 years, I have been riding the "coaching carousel." A position opens up, the challenge is intriguing and the ride begins. I have had the opportunity to work at the Division II level as an assistant coach, the Division II level as a head coach, the Division I level as a head coach in a mid-major conference and a BCS (Bowl Championship Series) conference. I have had teams with great success and teams that have experienced much adversity.

On or off the court, there are times that you need to turn to that "special play"; otherwise known as your "Faith."

Five years ago, when my wife was diagnosed with cancer, we both relied heavily on our family, friends, and our faith. If she ever allowed herself to question God on why she was chosen to have this terrible disease, she would recite her favorite Catholic prayer from St. Therese:

May today there be peace within
May you trust God that you are exactly where you are meant to be
May you not forget the infinite possibilities that are born of faith.
May you use those gifts that you have received, and pass on the love that has been given to you.
May you be content knowing you are a child of God.
Let this presence settle into your bones,
And allow your soul the freedom to sing, dance, praise and love.
It is there for each and every one of us.

This prayer is so powerful! Too often we question God when things are not going exactly as we planned. This simple little prayer can provide comfort knowing that "*you are exactly where you are meant to be.*"

Prayer: Thank you Jesus for inspiring those around us to pray. Thank you too for always providing for our needs. You truly have a place for each of us. Amen.

Greg and Theresa McDermott
Head Basketball Coach, Creighton University

Greg and I became friends when he was coaching basketball and golf at Wayne State and I was coaching golf at NWC. At many meets the coaches get to play some holes as well. That's how we "connected" and have stayed friends for all the years as Greg moved on to North Dakota State, UNI, Iowa State University, and now makes the move to Creighton. He is the kind of man you want your son to play for. We're so happy that the reports for Theresa are good, keep praying for them, and we also hope the team is unbeatable.

December 2

Ephesians 2:8-10

Bloom Where You Are Planted

Spring Break 2010, the Northwestern Volleyball Team took a mission trip down to the Dominican Republic. It was an experience where God moved in our team's lives in unique and amazing ways. Our mission down there was to teach middle school and high school-aged girls how to play the game of volleyball. We didn't speak the same language, but both groups had two things in common – the love for Christ – and the love of volleyball.

During the day with these girls, we would set aside about ten minutes where one of our girls or I expressed what God's love is like in our own lives, or what God has been teaching us. It was amazing how the Lord brought the team and the girls of the Dominican Republic together so quickly because of the one bond of being open about our relationship with Christ.

Our intention going to the Dominican Republic was to talk about Christ and to spread His word to the people that we came in contact with down there. We wanted to share our experiences and just show love to these kids. What ended up happening was by being real with these girls about our past experiences, and by telling them what God means to us, they ended up giving back to us in so many ways. Our relationship became very real and very strong so quickly because of the bond of Christ. We came back so "on fire" for Christ because we could see Him working between us and those girls.

The challenge now comes each day to make an intentional conversation about what God is doing in our life with someone around us. We are all people of habits and routine. We all probably know exactly what the schedule of our day is going to be like, down to the hour. So today, set aside ten minutes to talk to someone or ask someone a question about Christ. It can start out as simple as talking to someone about this past week's sermon, or it can start out a little deeper as to say "where have you seen God working today?"

Be bold and bloom where you are planted. God put us where we are today for a reason. As Eph. 2:10 says, "*For we are God's workmanship, created in Christ Jesus to do good works, which God prepared in advance for us to do.*" The first step to "blooming" is to start a real conversation.

Prayer: Lord, give us boldness today to step out of our comfort zone to have a real conversation about You. Take away any insecurities and fears about talking about you Lord. Make it clear Lord, who each of us should visit with today about You. We love you Lord, and we want to be Your workers today. Amen.

Kyle Van Den Bosch
Head Volleyball Coach at NWC

Kyle has had great success with his teams, resulting in many Conference Championships and National Tournament appearances. It is a pleasure to watch him coach and relate to his athletes, excellent assistant coaches, and even the officials. He had a great model to emulate. His Dad, Tom, is the long time volleyball coach at Hull Western and Dordt College. (You read his parents' devotional back on April 3). I wonder what it's like to coach against your Dad.

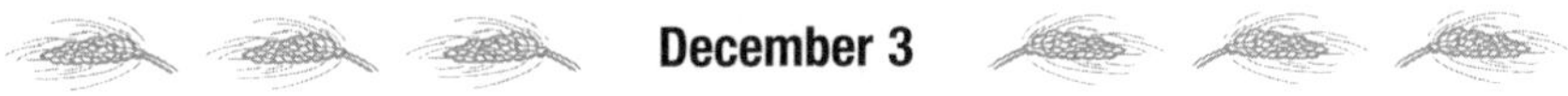

December 3

2 Chronicles 20:20

Faithful Changes

It was December, 1992; my husband Arlin tells me that he has a job opportunity in Sioux Center, about 90 miles from where we were living. Not exactly what I wanted to hear. When you have three children involved with friends and school activities, the thought of pulling them away, was not what I had in mind.

We aren't always receptive to change and to what will happen in a different place. But God has a plan for all of us; we just have to have faith. That sounds easier than it is. Now, 12 + years later, I know it was the right move. God puts you where you need to be.

Prayer: Dear God, help us in times of change. Keep us strong so our faith will help us through difficult decisions. Amen

Laura and Arlin Roskam
Central Church members and leaders

Laura and Arlin live in our neighborhood and wrote this for our younger church members as they were on a weekend retreat. It was the writing of these devotionals that was the inspiration for this book. See, I told you I don't have many original ideas!

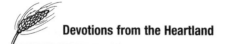

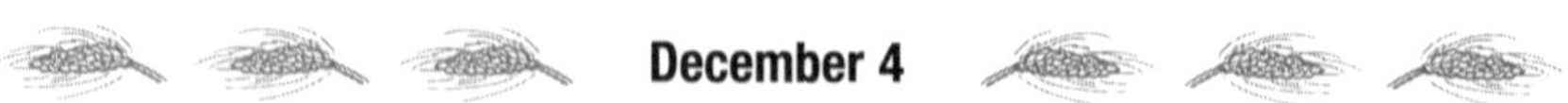

December 4

John 15:5-17, 26-27

Leaving This Earth

It is a rare and unique experience to be with someone who is dying. To see one pass from this life to the next makes you appreciate life and ponder the life to come. I'll never forget my time as a young pastor and being with a dear saint as she passed into the glorious presence of God. It was my first experience with someone who had gone from this life to the next. She had made her "peace" and said her "good-byes" and no one doubted her security and trust in the One who was to receive her. It was a profound experience.

Jesus' words to His disciples in the book of John, have impacted me in a similarly profound way. Jesus, about to die, was saying his 'peace' and final 'good-byes.' It wasn't so clear to the disciples at that moment, but it became clear to all, He was leaving them with some of His most important lessons about how His disciples were to carry on His mission.

In this one chapter of John, Jesus laid out three important instructions or priorities for carrying on the mission He would entrust His followers to complete after He was gone – Abiding, loving, and bearing witness. It is a recipe for living the Christian life. A life of service in the kingdom of God involves the idea of being connected to the Vine of Life. In fact, nothing of eternal significance can come without it (v. 5). Then He challenges us to love as He loved, by laying down our lives for each other. And to close out this chapter, as an "Oh, by the way," the Spirit will come to empower you to bear witness to the world.

These three simple ideas have impacted me in a unique way. They have become a framework for life and ministry. They are profoundly simple; loving God, loving others, bearing witness, but impossible apart from grace, the life-giving substance of the Vine. I hope you will take these words to heart as you live in preparation for the life to come.

Prayer: Thank you God for revealing the way for us to live here so we can later live with You in Heaven. Watch over us and help us always to love, share, and be a witness to Your Word. Amen.

Brian Steenhoek
Former Pastor of Central Reformed Church

Brian and Geselle served Central very well. They were the youngest to serve our parish and it was a great experience. They were called to a Des Moines and have since moved on and now are serving a church in Michigan. Both are NWC grads.

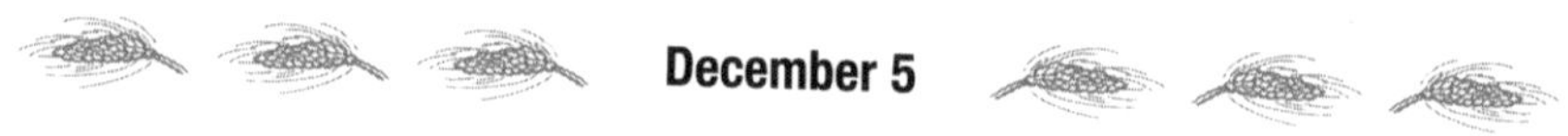

December 5

Psalm 126

My Version of This Psalm

God is a God of second chances, redemption and setting things right ... Hallelujah! The following is my own rendition of Psalm 126.

When the Lord set us free from the tyranny of bondage, His goodness was almost too good to be true. Our hearts and lives were restored and we had so much to celebrate. Others celebrated with us and recounted God's faithfulness.

Even now, Oh Lord, do your work again and again. We are so glad to be free from past strongholds, but our need for You to continue your work is great – even doing a new thing in us daily. I cry to you Lord to fill our lives and marriage, home and ministry, with your joy. Water, renew, grant life to the full.

We claim your promises that no tears are ever wasted in your ultimate harvest. Lord, I want my heart to be good soil, ready to receive the seed of your Word and having it grow deep roots into my reality. May the fruits of your Spirit and Word be a practical, real part of my life. When tears, disappointment or pain are present, keep my heart tender. I long for your ultimate harvest. I want to be there, bringing in the crops, dancing and singing your praises.

I invite you to reflect on Psalm 126 against the back drop of your own life. Bring your whole story before him honestly, and seek Him for His mercy. Praise Him for His redemptive work.

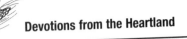

Prayer: Dear Lord, examine our hearts and keep them pure. Protect our lives, our marriages, our families, and our hearts. Amen.

Geselle Steenhoek

Geselle is married to Brian and they have a great ministry together, as well as a great family. They served Central Reformed well and we miss them. We wish them every success, joy, and happiness.

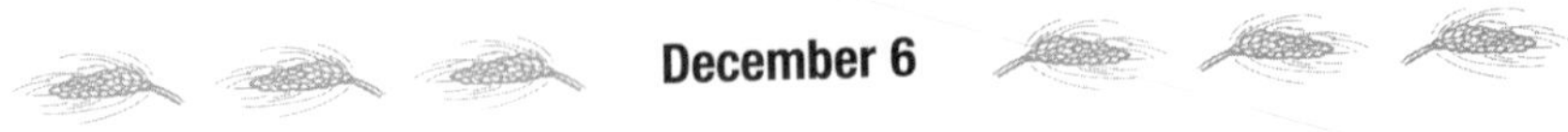

December 6

1 Peter 4:10; Philippians 2:15

Teamwork

As I write this, "March Madness" is in full swing and the Northwestern College women's basketball team just won their third NAIA Division II National Championship. This was a great team and one of the things that made it special was how well each member of the team understood and appreciated the role of each person on the team. The stars on the team recognized the importance of the bench warmers that pushed them in practice, and encouraged them in the games. Everyone on the team had an important role and contributed to the team's success – from the head coach to the manager and trainer.

I love being part of a team – whether it's an athletic team or a team at work or church. A group working together toward a common goal, each member with a role, pushing each other farther then we could go alone, putting the team's interests ahead of our own. As Christians, we're part of the all-time best team – God's Team!

We each have an important role on His team and God has given each of us gifts to use to serve each other. When we work together as a team, God will do great things through us. So whatever gifts God has given you, and the role to which He has called you, "shine like stars" as you serve. Go Team!

Prayer: Heavenly Father, thanks for making us part of Your team. Thank you for the gifts You have blessed us with. Help us to use those gifts to honor You and serve one another. Amen.

Amy and Bruce Schutt
All-American, Hall of Fame NWC Volleyball Player
Amy presently is a CPA employed in Orange City.
She is also an Assistant Coach for NWC Volleyball.

Amy was an All-Stater in High School at Unity Christian and then won every honor possible as a Red Raider. She and her husband Bruce are great parents, church workers, and contributors to the local community, and friends.

December 7

Matthew 6:19-24

Stamps

What's your hobby or avocation? Everyone should have one I think. As I get older I see the importance even more. I started collecting stamps when I was only 8. I have a bunch of 'em after over 60 years of systematic collecting.

How important are they in my life? They have given me a lot of satisfaction and enjoyment over the years. I've learned a lot about history, geography, and organization. I suppose (know) they have quite a dollar value by now, but I'll never find out. Collectors are just that – collectors. The fun is in the collecting, not in accumulating money-value.

Just for a little example of how stamps keep one aware of things think about this. Why is December 7 (that's why I chose this date for this devotional) significant in American History? Of course, it's because it is on this date back in 1941 that Pearl Harbor was attacked and we were drawn into WW II. There are stamps commemorating this historic event. Some people just collect these "Commemoratives" and that can be fulfilling as well.

Are my stamps the first thing I'd think about if the house was on fire? Nope! First – People, Second – Our Kitties, Third – Picture Albums, and then we'd see what else could be salvaged. How do you value your stuff?

Prayer: Thank you Lord for fun. Thank you too for diversity, friends, and family. You can make life so good and filled with joy. We need that but we need You more. Amen.

Dave

 December 8 

1 Peter 5:7

The Lord Can Handle It

One more night and then open heart surgery in the morning. Yet, peace ruled over my body. Normally, I am not laid back, no-worry, no-anxiety type of person. But a serene peace came over me before the surgery. I slept like a log that night, woke up ready to go, and felt good about the procedures that would happen in just a few hours.

On the way to the hospital in Sioux Falls, and even before the nurses wheeled me into the surgery room, perfect calm was still with me. Even as I was wheeled to the operating room, and as my family said good-bye and tears were abundant, I was at peace.

The peace I experienced is almost impossible to describe. It is a perfect peace with no doubts in the mind. It feels like everything will be alright regardless of the outcome of the surgery. I had this feeling many years earlier when my sister was not expected to live through the night after a car accident. I had longed to have that wonderful peace again, and God was again giving that to me before this surgery.

I still have a long way to go, but I have learned to remember that scripture which says, "*Cast all your cares on the Lord, for He cares for you.*" How true; God is faithful! God is good!

Prayer: Thank you God for the peace that passes all understanding. Thank you too for skilled surgeons, nurses, and all those who minister to us at times of need. Amen.

Dick and Ruth Van Holland
Retired Educators

Dick taught with me in the Business/Economics Dept. at NWC for all the years I was there. Ruth was an Elementary Teacher in Orange City. They are both dear and caring friends.

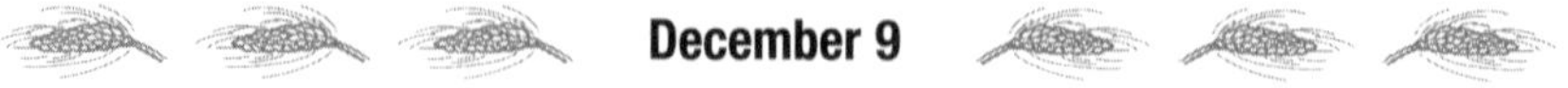

December 9

Romans 3:24-28; Hebrews 10:14; Matthew 5:16; 2 Corinthians 9:6-8; Galatians 5:6; James 2:17

Good Works

Lest there be misunderstanding, let this be said at the outset about good works. Good works are not necessary for justification and salvation. No person is declared just before God simply on the basis of good works he may have done. When God justifies a person, He does not in any sense take into consideration the good a person may present, but He looks solely at the merits of Christ. Be sure to read the above verses!

In parenthesis, let this be a warning to the person sometimes met who when asked whether he plans to go to heaven when he dies, says "Yes, I do." When asked on what basis, he replies: "Well, because I am a decent person. I am honest and law abiding. I obey the Ten Commandments and live by the Golden Rule. I'm a good family man. I contribute generously to charitable causes, etc., etc. That ought to be good enough, shouldn't it?" The answer of Scripture is that it is not.

Too, think of the repented criminal on a cross near the cross of Jesus. He had no good deeds to present. He simply turned to Jesus and said, "*Jesus, remember me when you come into your kingdom.*" Jesus answered him, "*Today you will be with me in paradise.*"

But good works do have a value, and they are important in the life of the Christian. Why? Because God expects them from His children. They are the fruits, the evidences of faith. Without them faith is dead. They demonstrate our faith.

Prayer: I know that you see our efforts as "filthy rags" and that's hard to understand. But help us to do the things that are good because of all the good You have done for us. Amen.

Rev. Henry Eggink

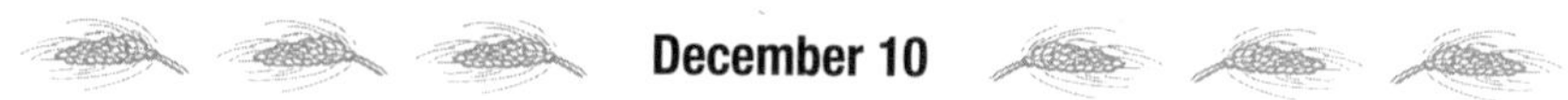

December 10

Ephesians 6:10

Getting HIS Power Behind You

Often times we take the power of God for granted until we need Him. I know that there have been times when I have taken Him for granted. Usually there is a life changing moment when we come to this realization. My situation is no different. Mine came when my wife was diagnosed with breast cancer in December, 2007. Shortly afterward someone gave her a card with this verse from Ephesians on it. Also added were the words, "Nothing AHEAD of you is bigger or stronger than the POWER of God BEHIND you."

She placed this card on her mirror in our bathroom and every day since then as I stand and brush my teeth, I read this message and contemplate its meaning. When you are staring a diagnosis of cancer in the face like my wife is, and our family as we support her, it is reassuring to know that through the physical, spiritual, and emotional struggles, there is the POWER of God BEHIND you.

We do not know what His plans may be, but we do know that even in the darkest moments, He is there with us just like He is in the brightest moments. I know that my wife and our family are fortunate to have the POWER of God BEHIND us.

This devotional is dedicated to my loving wife, Joan.

Prayer: Heavenly Father, we thank You for answered prayer and for healing. Please continue that healing process and use each of us in Your magnificent plan. Thank you for families. Amen.

Barry Whitsell
CEO of Village Northwest Unlimited in Sheldon.

Barry is a former student of mine at NWC and is doing an excellent job at the Village. It is a pleasure to serve on the Board with him and the others. Please pray fervently for Joan and Barry and the entire family. Cancer is such a scary thing but God is the "Great Healer."

December 11

Matthew 28:20

Steadfastness

Sometimes the thought comes to us: How much easier it would be to live consistent, steady Christian lives if Jesus were with us as He was with the disciples. If only we could see Him, His steadiness in purpose, and His great strength of character.

"Jesus Christ is the same yesterday and today, yes, and forever" (Hebrews 13:8), and He has promised to be with us always, "even unto the end of the world!"

Through all the changes, storms, and conflicts of life, we may confidently cling to the changeless Christ.

Prayer: Lord, give us a changeless faith in You. Amen.

Caroline and Bob Vermeer
Retired Homemaker and Optometrist, Members of Central Reformed

Bob and Caroline are also part of our Saturday Night Group. I had both of their kids in school and it is a joy to have them as longtime and close friends. Always remember to pray for them.

December 12

Habakkuk 3:16-19

Habakkuk Is My Friend

For the past 15 years, I have learned more from him than anyone else. And, it is the most important things I have learned! Some might even say that our relationship is that of "soul mates."

I think of Habakkuk every day when watching the news. I see the evil in the world, the injustice, destruction, violence, and the wrong. I respond just like Habakkuk did to the evils he witnessed in Judah. We both cry: "Lord, why don't you listen when I call on you about this? Why must perversion and strife increase? Why don't you do something about this?" How can God see wickedness in the world and appear to do nothing?

Then the Lord answers us, "Watch and be amazed! I will do something that even if told, you would not believe it!" He explains how He will raise up a ruthless and impetuous people who will ravage the whole earth. They will be feared and dreaded, a law to themselves, promoting themselves, bent on violence. In my friend's day, it was Babylon.

The second question we ask God is: "Why do you deal with it in THAT way?"

The answer is: "I am God. Think about who I am! (Don't worry, the evil doers will receive their harsh reward). Then God schooled us on who He is – again! He is the saving Lord of history who has come as the only salvation from our misery and desperation. We ought to stand in awe of Him and what He has done, and be amazed at what He will yet do.

All He wants is for us to recognize Him as God, as everything we in our humanity, in our fallen condition, are not. That is, God is holy – humans are sinful. He is infinite and internal; we are finite and subject to decay and death. God is omniscient; we have limited knowledge. He is omnipresent; we can only be in one place at a time. He is omnipotent; we are weak and dependent. He is immutable (unchanging); we are often fickle. He is righteous, we are unrighteous. God is love; we are prone to choose self over others. He is alive; we are dead in our sins.

Unique to the Christian is the confession that Jesus is Lord. As both God and man, He bridges the gap between God and man. Through Him, and only through Him, can we return to the heart and home of the Father.

After considering my friend Habakkuk, I remember "Peace, Reassurance, Patience, Rejoicing in the Lord, Strength, and Salvation." Read all that Habakkuk has to say.

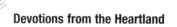

If you haven't met my friend lately, or don't know him well, spend the time to get to know him. It will help you know our BFF (Best Friend Forever – Jesus). You will have a much better time watching the national and world news ... I am sure of it!

Prayer: Thank you Lord for introducing us to Habakkuk. Thank you too for always being there for us. Help us to better understand Your ways. Amen.

Lynette Nystrom
Social Worker

Of course Lynette is Dale's spouse (you will read his devotional tomorrow) and is a very supportive and loving companion. We always have a good time when we are with the Nystroms.

December 13

Proverbs 3:5-6

Life's Path

It was my desire to be a doctor since I was ten years old. I was a patient with a broken leg following a farm accident. The goal was set, right along with my leg.

During the application process, I told God that if He wanted me to do this, He would have to orchestrate my acceptance. Along the way there were many doubts and discouragements. I feared the interviews. I asked myself why I was pursuing this. Sometimes the studying was overwhelming. Demands of time without much sleep were a major adjustment. I saw others drop out of school and was tempted to go back home to farm. Then I talked to the same God who orchestrated my acceptance. I told Him that since He got me in, I was going to stay until He made it clear that I should leave. Instead, He gave me peace to stay.

Residency brought more doubts. I did not get my first choice for my program. After one year and much soul searching, I was able to change programs. God seemed to be saying that He just wanted me to trust Him, wherever I was. Whatever I did, I was to do it to honor Him.

Through all of this, my life's passage became this one in Proverbs 3. I now see that my path was made straight, in spite of all the potholes!

Prayer: Dear Lord, thanks for having a plan for my life just as You do for everyone. Please continue to bolster our trust and faith in You. Thanks too for the love You share with us. Amen.

Dale Nystrom
Medical Doctor (mine and Dot's)

Isn't it great when your doctor is also one of your best friends? Dale and Lynette use to live in our neighborhood and that was nice. He even made some house calls! What a fine fella – his birthday is close to Dot's so they take us out for supper in August. Lynette shares the same date with me so we take them out in February. I wish we could see them more often. I like doctors that pray for their patients.

December 14

Genesis 1:9-13

"And It Was Good!"

Everything in nature shows GOD. Mountain scenes take your breath away and show His majesty. It's very humbling. The oceans and the Gulf – so vast, yet serene enough to calm your soul, watching the waves. We get the sense of timelessness.

Thunder and lightning are exciting! My Dad and I would sit on the front porch and watch the "show" that God provided. I was never afraid of storms. Didn't we all lie on our backs in the grass, watching clouds changing and changing? Is there any BLUE as beautiful as the color of the clear sky?

Mom loved flowers and I felt so close to God in her flower garden, and now in mine. The diversity, the riot of colors! Plants all have a will to live too, and what joy to watch them grow. Even digging in the dirt makes me feel part of the Earth and therefore closer to God.

"God's in His Heaven. All's right with the world." Isn't it wonderful to know God is in charge of all?

Prayer: Creator God, thank you for Your generous, glorious gift of nature that shows us You, and teaches us so much. Thank you for always being there, in charge of this magnificent world. Amen.

Karen and Casey Stengel
Retired and living in LeMars, Casey was the Chief of Police

Karen is my first cousin and we enjoy being together. They love motorcycles and the beach. Kay can make anything grow! – And she does.

December 15

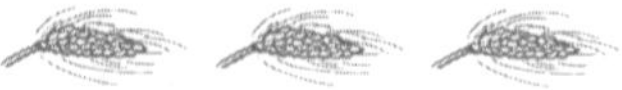

Genesis 29:13,33:4, 48:10

Do You Need A Hug?

Are you a hugger? You can always tell in the initial second of contact if the "other" is or isn't. It's okay either way. One doesn't have to be a hugger. But for those of us who are it creates a good feeling. I don't know if I could stand not getting hugs from my grandchildren.

Often times when I pray, I ask God/Jesus to give a hug to the person I'm praying for. If you are a hugger, let others know when you need one. I can tell you as a husband, dad, and grandpa, I need their hugs. If your loved ones are still living, today is the day. If they live too far away grab your phone, NOW.

We really do need each other.

Prayer: Thank you for loving us Lord and giving us ways to express it. As I think about people I love today, please give hugs to … . Amen.

Dave

December 16

Isaiah 11:1-3

My Dad And His Legacy

As a young girl, I thought my dad was the smartest man on the earth. He always had the best answers and solutions to problems. He was always calm and had a quiet manner about him. Even when I backed our old station wagon into the garage and knocked the garage off the foundation (couldn't find the brake), he was unbelievably calm and went about pushing it back on the foundation. I think I cried harder because he didn't punish me.

Even as I matured, I still looked to him for answers to life's questions. As he lay in his bed in the nursing home, unable to communicate very well, it hit me that those days were coming to an end ... my counselor, my friend, my dad. Dad passed away (on this date in 2009) and I miss him, but I realize how important my relationship was to him and how that relationship is like our relationship to Jesus.

Jesus is our counselor, our friend. The spirit of wisdom and of understanding and the spirit of counsel and of power have been given to Him. We do not have to fear that He will ever go away and leave us. All we have to do is believe like a little child, and we will receive the kingdom of God. He will be there to listen to us in our youth or in the winter of our lives, in the hustle and bustle of the day or the quiet of the dark nights. He will be there. We need to look to Him and ask for guidance in our lives as the world around us seems to be getting more complicated. We can always look to Him for wisdom and understanding.

Prayer: Dear Lord, thank you for being our counselor. Help us to ask for your guidance and reassure us with your calm presence and wisdom. May You be our guide and example, and may we follow in Your footsteps. Amen.

Marilyn (Den Herder) Van Demark
Registered Nurse in Sioux Falls

Marilyn was one of my students in high school and a great statistician for our basketball team. She's also a great nurse. I can testify to that because I married one and later Marilyn provided excellent care after one of my shoulder surgeries. She's the sister of Gene, Vern, and Dan, and her mom is Catherine.

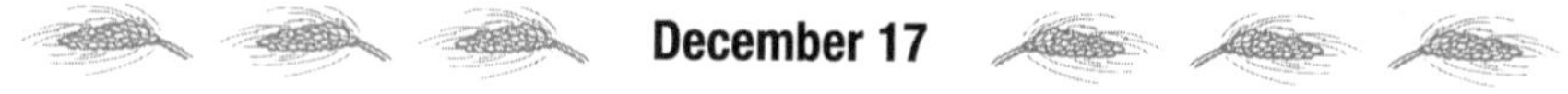

December 17

1 Corinthians 13

The Love Chapter

For me, this passage represents a major theme of the New Testament. Reading many of the books of the Old Testament causes me to worry about violence, sacrifices, and the "eye for an eye" themes.

Then when I read the "Love Chapter," I am comforted by the thought of a loving God, and a Savior who loved humans so much that he gave His life for them.

Coming to the end of the chapter, it is comforting that though no one on earth is perfect, I can work on having faith and hope and also realize that even greater than these two, is the need to love unconditionally. As with many areas in my life, this is a process rather than a completed task.

Prayer: Lord, continue to be with me as I strive to make the love I have for others more nearly like that described in this great chapter of Your Word. Amen.

Peg Juffer
Retired Librarian

Peg and Ron are two of our closest friends. We regularly plan get-togethers for food, much talk, cards, and just lots of laughs. Peg is a great volunteer and service worker. We couldn't have two better friends.

December 18

Matthew 22:37-39

The Greatest Commandment

Faith and Love – The two most important and beautiful words in the Bible. They are the basis for all of Jesus teaching and preaching. "*Thou shalt love the Lord thy God with all thy heart, and with all thy soul, with all thy strength, and with all thy mind; and the neighbor as thyself.*"

Wouldn't it be wonderful if all of the world, universally, practiced this principle? No more wars, no more crime and violence, no more divorce, no more domestic violence, no more hatred. This would be heaven on earth, and sometimes I wonder if that is why God doesn't let it happen. We can't have two heavens.

Marie and I have been married for 65 years, and I love her more today than the day we were married. Sure, it is a little different kind of love – not quite as passionate, but a deeper, stronger, more spiritual love that is the basis for a wonderful life together. Sure, we have our little "spats," but they are soon over and forgotten and love prevails. It is a wonderful life in Christ.

Jesus said, "*A new command I give you: Love one another, as I have loved you. By this all men will know that you are my disciples, if you love one another.*" My study Bible says, "Being loved is the most powerful motivation in the world. Our ability to love is often shaped by our experience of love. We usually love others as we have been loved."

This devotional is sent with our love.

Prayer: Again, we say thank you for loving us first. This has enabled us to love others, and especially our spouses and family. Help us to reach out more and more in Christian love. Amen.

Vern and Marie Mouw
Retired Banker and Housewife

Vern and Marie have been at Central Reformed as long as most people can remember. They are both in my Sunday School Class and Vern subs for me when I have another obligation. Pray for this great couple because **today** is their anniversary! Give them a call!

December 19

1 Corinthians 13

Love Endures

"Love bears all things, believes all things, hopes all things, endures all things."

This verse from 1 Cor. 13 became my mantra one winter when my folks stayed with us for three months while waiting for a new apartment to be open. Mom was in the beginning stages of Alzheimer's, which caused Dad to be very depressed.

When trying situations arose, I wanted to scream or go hide. At those times, I repeated these verses over and over, stressing ENDURES all things. Although my love for my parents, or anyone for that matter, isn't perfect, I can strive to become better. As with other areas in my life, it is a process rather than a completed task. God isn't through with me yet.

Prayer: Lord, help me as I try to make my love encompass more of the characteristics of this great chapter. Amen.

Peg Juffer

This chapter means so much to Peg that she wrote two devotionals about it. I like the way she thinks so both of them are included. Enjoy!

December 20

Hebrews 10:23

The Twists of Life

In one of those twists of life – after my divorce, my children and their mother moved in to a home across the street from my apartment house. Our first Christmas apart I watched the lights on in their house that night. I knew what and how they were celebrating – our Christmas routines had become cherished traditions. Even my trip home to spend Christmas with my parents was not going to happen – my mom called, she and dad were sick – Christmas had been cancelled. I sat alone in my apartment – it was too dark – too quiet and it all hurt too much.

My hurt that night was not any larger or smaller than any you might be experiencing. God's focus is not on whose heartache is bigger, His focus is only on you. My healing came because of this promise, "He took our suffering on Him and felt our pain" (Isaiah 53:4). And when I look back to see what good could possibly have come from all that pain, it was that I had become more like Him. He will take your suffering – become like you –and heal your broken heart. He is faithful, I promise you.

Prayer: Heavenly Father, help us always to trust Your faithfulness, caring, and love. Amen.

Kevin Schmidt

Kevin is the Sunday School Supt. at Central Reformed, a good friend, and someone that has a story to share. Always keep Kevin in your prayers.

December 21

Psalm 51:7b

White as Snow

This morning as I look out over our backyard the view is breathtaking. The snow is sparkling white. The evergreen trees are heavy with snow. The sun is shining, casting blue shadows from the leafless maple trees.

The backyard view is not always so beautiful. Some of the evergreens have bare spots and some have dead spots inside. Sometimes there are brown spots in the grass or worse, weeds. But now with the heavy snow covering it up, it looks beautiful.

It reminds me of our lives. Sometimes they have bare spots and sometimes they have dead spots too, caused by the sin in our lives. As Christians, we are blessed to have God's love and forgiveness to cover and blanket the bad parts of our lives and make us look beautiful. He takes the sin in our lives and covers it. 1 Peter 4:8b says, "love covers a multitude of sins." But because of His great love for us, God, who is rich in mercy, made us alive with Christ, even when we were dead in transgressions – "it is by grace you have been saved." (Ephesians 2:4)

Prayer: "Whiter than snow, yes, whiter than snow. Now wash me and I shall be whiter than snow." Amen. (From the hymn "Whiter Than Snow")

Noreen and Ted DeHoogh

December 22

Revelation 5:12

Bethlehem

When I was on my trip to Israel recently, our group was instructed on many aspects of the Hebrew culture that were most enlightening. One such place we visited was at a ruin in Bethlehem where our guide showed us how the houses of that era usually had the animal stables attached to the homes. The family would sleep above the stable area so the heat from the animals would keep them warm. In the stables were kept the goats and sheep, cattle, even pigeons and chickens, many of which were used as sacrifices at the Temple. The families would raise special animals that were perfect for the sacrifice, particularly at Passover.

When Mary and Joseph arrived in Bethlehem there were probably no inns in this small village. They probably walked through the village looking for a family that would take them in for the night. And as we know, someone was kind enough to provide them with a place to stay -and it was in the stable area of the property.

The amazing thing about this is that just as the sacrificial animals were born and kept in this safe and warm environment, so too, was Jesus, the sacrificial Lamb of God born and kept here!! Only a loving and sovereign God would lay His Word out this way in order for us to understand the significance of Jesus' humble birth.

Worthy is the Lamb, who was slain,
To receive power and wealth and wisdom,
And strength and honor and praise!

Prayer: Thank you Lord for opportunities to learn more about You and Your people. Bless those who work for You and help each of us to represent well the love You have for us. Amen.

Lynn and R.G. Boeyink
Both are retired now, Central Church members

Lynn and R.G. were both high school students of mine and R.G. played basketball and baseball on teams I coached. They are tireless church workers and love the Lord.

December 23

Matthew 7:7

Ask and It Will Be Given

In the winter of 1984, my wife Terry and I were driving to Michigan from our home in Oklahoma City to attend a wedding. It was cold and getting dark. We were somewhere near the Oklahoma/Missouri border when our car, a 1979 Honda, began to make a very annoying noise. I'm no mechanic. Our church in Oklahoma City had taught us much about the power of prayer. By faith, just outside of Rolla, Missouri, we laid hands on our dashboard and prayed for God to heal our car. Moments later, the noise was gone, never to return!

I became better at checking oil levels and doing routine car maintenance after that trip, but I also learned what pleading prayer is like. Give it a try!

Prayer: Dear Lord, we thank you for listening when we pray for whatever concerns us at the time. Thank you even more for answering them. Amen.

Pastor Van Rathbun

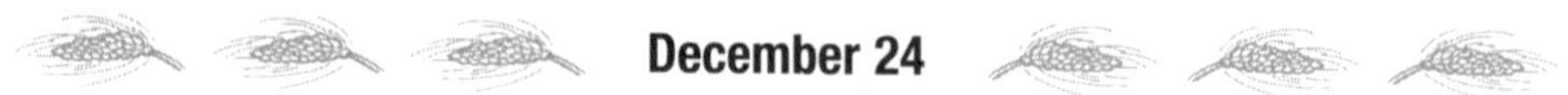

December 24

Revelation 21:1-5

My Hopes For Heaven (Beyond God's Presence)

I know this is the eve of when we Christians celebrate the first coming of our Savior. As I think about His second coming I know it can be imminent. He may "come on the clouds" as the Bible says, at any time – or my "second coming experience" may have already happened as my heart makes its last beat. I hope that doesn't happen any time soon because I really enjoy life here on this earth the Lord has created. But Heaven has to be even better! "Streets of gold and lots of jewels" doesn't excite me much, but here are some thoughts that do.

Of course, no one can actually say what it will be like but here are some hopes:

1. Loved ones healthy and close.
2. Pets.
3. Play sports (baseball and golf in particular) for fun, but still competitively.
4. Great music (Live!) with the stars I like.

5. Eat Anything! (Steak, Potatoes, Candy, Ice Cream, Whole Milk) Anytime – (No Calories to worry about!)
6. Actual and Factual T.V. reruns of the World from the Garden of Eden on (On Command)
7. Personal visits (Lunch) with whomever we or they want.
8. Not to "miss" anybody. This is a toughie!

All of this happening with God close by because He is omnipresent.

What would you add or delete to make Heaven – Heavenly? Have some fun, because it's going to happen.

Prayer: Heavenly Father, it's exciting to think about coming to join You in this great realm. Continue to guide us along the path. Jesus, I know you are delaying Your second coming so that even more can join us. Thank you and Amen.

Dave

December 25

Psalm 51:7

A White Christmas

Christmas, 2009 – a year that will be remembered by the young and the old. Some families enjoyed days together instead of just an evening celebrating, while other families were not able to get together with loved ones at all. They spent that great day alone. While the snow was an inconvenience for many, we were all safe in our warm homes with more than enough food to eat.

As we looked over the untouched fields of snow we saw a beauty that only our Creator could control. Fields that looked like they were covered with sparkling diamonds, evergreen branches bowing down heavy laden with snow. The large drifts were a thing of beauty.

In all of this we're reminded again that Jesus, the tiny baby born so long ago in Bethlehem, came into this world and shed His blood on the cross so that we could be made whiter than snow. Yes, if we repent of our sins and ask Jesus to be Lord of our life, we can be washed clean and be made whiter than snow. That gives a little different perspective on a "White Christmas."

Prayer: Thank you Father for the warm and comfortable homes we live in and the modern equipment we have to remove the snow and make the storms more tolerable.

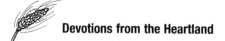

But most of all thank you for Jesus who died on the cross to make us clean and pure and whiter than all the snow. Amen

Norma & Jack Stander
Farmers and School Bus Driver

Jack is part of the DutchMart Coffee Group and one of the good guys.

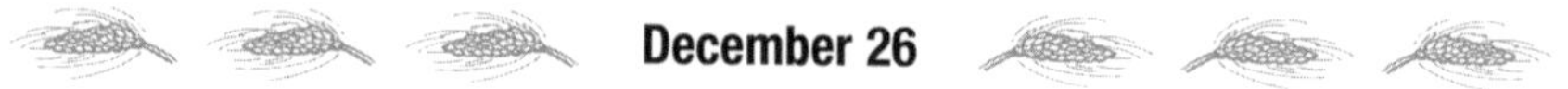

December 26

Luke 2:8-14

What A Night!

The above passage is one of my favorites. It is a little out of place right now, since Christmas has already come and gone. Nevertheless, I love to fantasize about this miracle all year long. I encourage you to do the same.

How I wish I could have been there with the shepherds on that miraculous night. They had probably brought their flocks together to enjoy some fellowship during the long, dark night and to help each other protect the sheep. Suddenly there appeared an intense white light and in the center – miracle of miracles – an angel! They were terrified. They probably fell to the ground or grabbed a friend for protection. Everyone was wondering what he had done wrong, for which he was about to be punished by the Angel of the Lord.

And then the wonderful comforting words, "Fear Not," and the heavens were filled with many angels praising God. What a fantastic night! The sky filled with angels singing "Glory to God in the highest, and on earth peace, good will toward men."

This makes me wonder, where is that peace on earth and good will toward men now? We certainly don't see much of it today do we? When did it all go wrong and why? What shall we do about it?

Prayer: Dear Lord, thank you for coming to us so many years ago. That great miracle of birth continues to live in each of us today. Guide and guard us again this day. Amen.

Vern and Marie Mouw

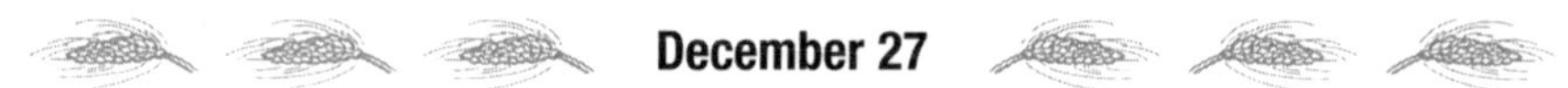

December 27

Hebrews 13:4

Fifty-Plus Years of Marriage

Things we have learned in our 50+ years.

Keep the communication lines open at all times. No matter what the situation, it is better for everyone if you talk about it as a couple/family.

Treat each other and family members with kindness, love and respect. Don't stay mad at each other for a length of time. It's not worth it!!!! My mother said, "Never go to bed mad at each other:"

Always say good night and goodbye with a kiss and an "I love you."

Keep humor in your everyday life.

Pray for each other and your children, and as time goes on, your grandchildren. If you are blessed with great grandchildren continue your praying. Teach them that God loves them and is our comfort and peace in this world.

Material gifts are not that important. When our children were young, for Christmas we were going to buy Marv a small television set for his office at home. This was supposed to be a surprise. About a week before Christmas he bought one himself. Maybe that was a good thing, because it was better than the one we were going to get him. Lesson learned, if he wants something, let him buy it himself, it's usually better quality than I would get him!!!!

Prayer: Thank you Lord for marriage and families. You have taught and showed us how to live for others. Please bless our families. Amen.

Donna and Marv Boone

Donna and Marv are faithful members of Central Reformed and are both semi-retired. Donna continues to do a lot of volunteer work and Marv works part-time for Ver Hoef Chevy in obtaining those special drivers to go to Omaha or Shakopee to pick up cars. I just happen to be one of those special drivers! I love it! By the way, today is Marv and Donna's anniversary – let them know you care!

December 28

Matthew 28:19-20

Here Is The Test To Find Whether Your Mission On Earth Is Finished. If You're Alive – It Isn't!

God has a purpose and a plan for each of us. I think He may have more than one purpose for many. Are you looking and thinking about what yours may be? So have I. At least twice in my life this test has been brought home to me. The first was when I was 15 and wrecked a car. (That's right, I said 15) Everything about that accident was wrong on my part. I could easily have been killed when the car rolled over – but obviously, I wasn't. It's what my Mom said to me at that point that made me think. "DaVID, (she always emphasized the second syllable when she was upset) the Lord must have a real plan for you since He lets you survive so much!"

She was right (as usual). Are you still looking for things God wants you to do? So am I. He's not finished with us yet. I suppose you're wondering about the other time(s). These involved the severe reactions I had to my wheat allergy. That also keeps me on my toes each day.

Prayer: Thanks for giving us purpose. Thanks too, for showing us the way when so many times we struggle finding that purpose. The people and situations You have put in our lives are so precious. We thank You for all of them. Amen.

Dave

December 29

Isaiah 52:12

As Another Year Passes

Security from Yesterday

God requires an account of our past. This brings sadness for my times of blunders and missed opportunities. It brings Joy for my times of obedience seeing God's grace and love at work. God uses those past experiences for my spiritual growth. It is never a standstill deal.

Security for Tomorrow

God's angels can provide a hedge of protection – rear guard. He wants me to follow His plan daily. He is waiting to direct me. How? Through Bible reading and personal devotions. A closer relationship with Him takes time and effort. It's worth it!

Prayer: Heavenly Father, thank you for Your patience and persistence with Your loved ones. Amen.

Dot

December 30

John 3:16

Love Never Dies

Our dear, dear Mother, Sadie Ver Steeg, passed away December 30, 2009 at the age of 99. We miss her so much. But what a peace it is to know that she will live forever in Heaven with Jesus. She loved the Lord so much, and shared that love with each of her 9 children. They shared that love with their spouses.

That same love was shared with their children (46 of Mom's Grandchildren and their spouses), who shared it with their children (116 of Mom's Great Grandchildren and their spouses on top of that) who shared it with their children (39 of Mom's Great, Great Grandchildren).

Someone sent me a poem "Loss of Mother." It ended with "Love does not die, people do. So, when all that's left of me is love, give me away as best you can."

Just imagine how much love was shared from just one person.

SHARE GOD'S LOVE!

Prayer: Dear Lord, thanks for loving us so much and help us today to show and share that love with others. Thanks too Lord, for faithful moms. Amen.

Shirley and Marty Wierda
Semi-retired Radio Station Worker and Farmer

Mart and Shirley are two very close friends. Mart and I taught and coached together at SCHS and we officiated a lot of basketball and baseball games as well. Each year we take about a 3-day trip to watch major league baseball. He likes the Red Sox and of course I'm for the Cards (I continually remind him of the 1967 Series!). Our wives like the games but rapidly choose whoever is ahead as the 9th inning approaches. They don't like free baseball (extra innings)! Suffice it to say – these are dear friends that we cherish.

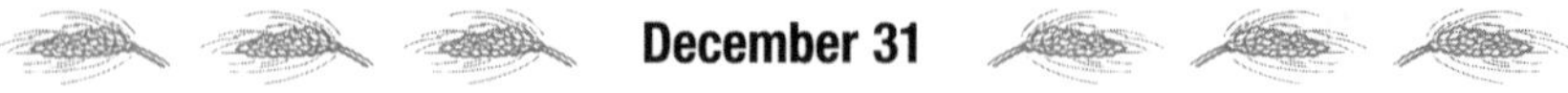

December 31

Genesis 1:26-27

Ode To Harold

I bet you've met some unique/eccentric people during your lifetime. The fella that wrote the prayer that closes this book falls into that category.

He had a very keen inventive mind. He could be somewhat of a recluse. He did beautiful work with wood and stained glass. He was a historian. He was very interesting to visit with, and Dot did that many times.

Harold Wandscheer has gone on to his eternal reward. But among many other things, he left us this prayer. Use it often. God Bless You.

Harold Wandscheer's Evening Prayer:

At this hour we wish to give thanks for keeping us from harm and danger throughout the perils and events of the day. We ask You to extend unto us health, wisdom, strength, and happiness. We acknowledge that we have sinned, be it inadvertently, upon impulse, or otherwise. We ask for the forgiveness of ALL our sins and ask that You remember them no more. As we await Judgment Day we take great comfort in Your promises when You shall say that the gates of heaven shall be opened unto thee, and the wrath of the gates of hell shall follow you no more. As we now stand before our Lord, Savior, and Judge, we attest and accept Thy saving, loving, grace, and into Thy hands we give and commit our souls forever. We now wish to pay deep tribute to Jesus for His sacrifice on Calvary for our sins, thus opening the way for all of those who believe and follow Him into the glory of heaven. We stand in deep gratitude and in awe, with great joy! All this in the name of Jesus Christ. Amen (2-1-2002)

Dave